MW01516483

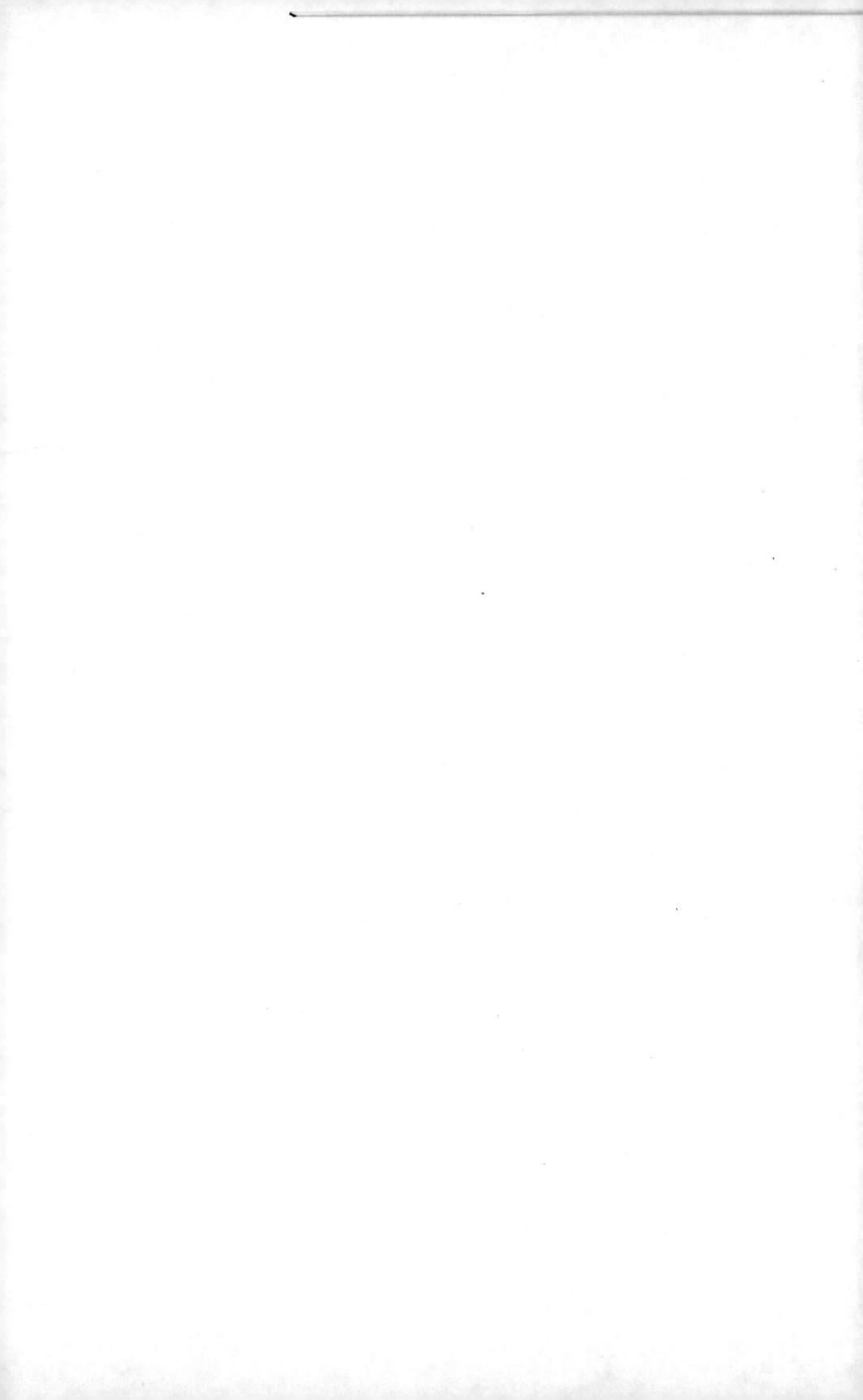

The Fate of
Democracy

Volume 16 of *Humanism Today*

The Fate of
Democracy

edited by
Robert B. Tapp

*in cooperation with the North American
Committee for Humanism*

Prometheus Books

59 John Glenn Drive
Amherst, New York 14228-2197

Published 2006 by Prometheus Books

The Fate of Democracy. Copyright © 2006 by the North American Committee for Humanism (NACH). All rights reserved. No part of this publication may be reproduced, stored in a retrieval system, or transmitted in any form or by any means, digital, electronic, mechanical, photocopying, recording, or otherwise, or conveyed via the Internet or a Web site without prior written permission of the publisher, except in the case of brief quotations embodied in critical articles and reviews.

Inquiries should be addressed to
Prometheus Books
59 John Glenn Drive
Amherst, New York 14228–2197
VOICE: 716–691–0133, ext. 207
FAX: 716–564–2711
WWW.PROMETHEUSBOOKS.COM

10 09 08 07 06   5 4 3 2 1

Library of Congress Cataloging-in-Publication Data

ISSN 1058–5966
ISBN 1–59102–328–9

Printed in the United States of America on acid-free paper

For Information on Leadership Training and Other Programs, please contact:

THE HUMANIST INSTITUTE
2 West 64th Street
New York, NY 10023

Contents

Acknowledgments

Grateful acknowledgment goes to the authors for their willingness to revise their essays on a tight schedule. This editor has allowed some capitalizations of democracy and humanism where it seemed necessary to convey authors' intentions. Canadian/British spellings have also been preserved when appropriate. Thanks also to Paul Kurtz for facilitating the publication by Prometheus Books of this series; to Editor-in-Chief Steven L. Mitchell for his wise suggestions; and to my wife, Ana Martinez, precision proofreader, continuing pillar, and *manantial de paciencia*.

Volumes of *Humanism Today* are published by The Humanist Institute, which was founded in 1982 by the North American Committee for Humanism (NACH) as an educational venture to train professional and lay leaders for existing humanist organizations. The guiding principle has been that studying together would enhance all forms of nontheistic humanism, whether they described themselves as religious or secular; Ethical Culturist, Unitarian Universalist, Humanistic Jew; rationalist or freethinker; agnostic or atheist.

More than ninety students have completed a three-year graduate-level curriculum. The Institute's adjunct faculty has gathered annually to consider pressing topics, and this book grows out of the 2004 colloquium. The adjunct faculty will be reassembling in 2005 to re-assess viable education undergirdings for endangered democracies, the shaping roles of traditional humanisms.

Robert B. Tapp

Preface

Democracy, however defined, is clearly an historical and contingent structuring of human relationships. When Lincoln adapted Theodore Parker's 1850 phrase "of all, for all, by all" into his Gettysburg address as "of the people, for the people, by the people," he was clearly bringing the Enlightenment vision of the Declaration of Independence into the more-restricted constitutionalism of the new republic. An original insistence that slaves were persons had set the stage for continuing extension of that concept. Women, children, illegal immigrants, foreign visitors, and in our own time, persons taking up arms against the country—all were declared subject to the same rule of law.

Contingent and historical? Assuredly. Dependent upon the shared definitions of a particular time and place. Historical in the sense of changing over time, with no guarantee that the changes would extend/improve the concept. The current "war on terrorism" has led many to support sharp restrictions on freedom of speech and movement that were only recently intolerable.

Historical also in the sense that better analyses of the past call into question many settled understandings. Did democracy come from the Greeks, or just from those Greeks in Athens? And even in that case, the Pericles depicted by Thucydides defines his own political structure quite differently after the first year of war.

Contingent in the sense that philosophico-religious understandings affect people's political horizons. If this world is about to end, social orders become unimportant. Such apocalypticism was not only a view of the earliest Christians. It has re-appeared again and again when life became difficult. And in the United States today, this eschatological and apocalyptic view has not only revived but has spread beyond the have-nots to the haves, and even into the Congress and White House. Some newer religious groups as different as Bahai's and Jehovah's Witnesses have chosen not to participate in current political life. Whatever a group's involvement with societal maintenance and change, it will be deeply embedded in ideological factors.

The recent resurgence of evangelical and fundamentalist Christian trends within US life should remind us of the tenuous linkages between Christianity and democracy. The founding fathers clearly viewed religion as suspect in supporting the kind of new society that they envisaged. They viewed European histories as underscoring the non-democratic roles played by religion. The secularity of both their Declaration and Constitution bear this out. And the more problematic revolution that followed in France underscores this distrust of establishments of religion.

When we move from the definitional to the historical, the radical changes of the eighteenth century become clearer. And in the US case, the preconditions of democracy become more apparent. First, the shared heritage of English history—steadily restricting the arbitrary power of the monarch. When laws stem from a parliament rather than the arbitrary whims of the monarch, new assumptions about regularity and progress emerge.

Add to this the Protestant stress on literacy and education. Then count in the moderations to this Puritan heritage that time wrought, plus the beginnings of Enlightenment reflection on science and reason. The American frontier, while not uninhabited (Native Americans, French, Spaniards, Russians were there too), was available for conquest. This provided new spaces for dissenters, as well as openings to societal experiments of all kinds—communal, religious, economic.

Current literature speaks of "failed" democracies and "flawed" democracies. The risk with such terminology is that it can too easily be based on some single historical model and make its judgments by that standard. Many modern democratic societies have differently structured Freedom and Equality, for instance—and both are values that almost all historians and political scientists would see as necessary for a society to be deemed democratic. There is more equality in Sweden than in the US, for instance. But there is surely more equality in any tribal society than in either developed country if we mean equality of material possessions.

If equality means One Person, One Vote, yet another historical mapping would occur. Not only slaves but women have been historically deprived of such power. And the "representative" structurings of democracy that have emerged have used different schemes in balancing equality with the politically expedient recognitions of prior privileges. Those privileges may pertain to social class as in the British House of Lords or to political entities (states) as in the US Senate. In the 2000 election dubious classifications of voters as felons served to distort the franchise. Whatever historical compromising has been involved, we ought not too glibly refer to equalities of power.

Other historical qualifiers on the implementation of Equality have been imperialism and hegemony. Strong societies have dominated weaker ones by exercising economic as well as military power. Whatever the actual mix of powers, the result has been lessened equality for the dominated and inevitable uprisings against colonialism both by the colonized and by democratizing forces within the colonizing countries.

This book is the sixteenth in a series titled *Humanism Today*. These are the results of annual colloquia of The Humanist Institute. The adjunct faculty members of the Institute held its 2004 meeting around papers on democracy, and that discussion has produced this volume. In 2003 when we chose this topic we were already alarmed at the problematic state of US democracy. Things are far worse at this time. Irrational forms, within almost each of the world's religions, have strengthened. Conservative forces, here and abroad, support theocracy. Liberal forces have been weakened by many forms of post-modernism and multiculturalism—topics of previous colloquia.

The humanism embodied in the Institute and in the several organizations where its students and faculty are involved is naturalistic and nontheistic. Interested readers can get a fuller idea of our activities from our Web site—http://www.humanistinstitute.org/.

For naturalistic humanists, the democracy created as a result of Enlightenment emphasis upon the powers of reason in free individuals is a very central value—situated in history and contingent upon a rule of law that is in turn contingent upon an educated citizenry. And education *can* be a supporter of freedom when it widens individuals' perspectives on human possibilities. The development, maintenance, and expansion of these principles is a central value—and threats to the democratic structures must be recognized and combated.

The now-concluded struggle over the charter of the European Union points up this problem. The Vatican, Poland, Portugal, and Spain (at least before its latest election) all wanted reference to a Christian or Judeo-Christian heritage. The chief drafter, Jacques Chirac, and those from many other countries opposed this, arguing that to credit religion for the development of democracy would be to distort history. As one put it, Christianity "came late" into the struggles for democracy.

Many polemicists in the US, however, try to argue that this is a "Christian" country, that its founders were "Christian," and that the basis for morality is "Christian." While such claims reflect inadequate knowledge of US history, they must nonetheless be met. And the risks to democracy in pursuing such assumptions need continually to be exposed. A secular state can co-exist with many religions so long as they remain private. When one or a coalition attempts to become public, the threats to democracy become evident.

Contributions to this book could be grouped under three headings—academic and detailed, personal and reflective, and theoretical. Joseph Chuman reviews the recent development in church/state demarcations, arguing against Integralists and Accommodationists. Carmela Epright discusses rights and liberties as a philosopher concerned with the corrosions associated with the concept of "terror." Sarah Oelberg details the corporatization of the media and the effects this has upon citizen awareness and action. Michael Werner describes some recent critics and defenders of democratic values.

Vern Bullough brings his historian's perspective to the actual hurdles that have beset democratic development in US society such as race, religion, and ruralism—noting the persisting issues related to federalism. Kurt Johnson focuses on religions that are behavior-based and some recent re-assessments of wisdom traditions, arguing that Gandhi, Mandela, and Annan can best be understood from these perspectives—and that such an understanding is important for humanists.

The third group of contributors move in more theoretical directions. Robert Tapp suggests that more stress on excellences could reduce the risks of populism. Andreas Rosenberg argues that the US has not yet moved from oligarchy to democracy, and wants to find a scientific foundation for it rather than a mythological one. For him, the Athenian model deserves re-appropriation.

Philip Regal takes a neurobiological approach that takes seriously the non-cultural side of human existence where the universal undergirdings of democracy reside and resonate, and then explores reasons that hierarchies came to dominate so much of the historical experience of our species. Regal's lengthy chapter seems justified in view of his critique of some aspects of sociobiology that may not be so widely known. Harvey Sarles emphasizes the slow processes of cultural change that made democratic societies possible. In many ways, one needs to read both Sarles and Regal to sense the wide range of science relevance—from biological to social.

Howard Radest describes many of the ways that democracy is fragile and may be debilitated by terror attacks. He suggests elements in the humanist vision that need to be center-staged. Paul Kurtz focuses on four of the main threats to the democratic structures in US society—plutocracy, mega-corporations, media-ocracy, and theocracy. Some of these forces are new, some undergoing revivals.

No book on democracy could be complete. But the preservation/extension need has never been greater in the US, and the contributions of these humanists deserve serious attention. Some non-humanists accuse this tradition of being too anthropomorphic; and a vocal minority among humanists decry an over-emphasis on the sciences. These essays both illustrate the wide-ranging concerns of humanist leaders and the values that they share and defend. They also illustrate the many ways in which humanists have long since abandoned polarized nature/nurture discussions. We offer them not as a "last word" but as an urgent call for shared concern regarding this "last, best hope" of earth—now a highly endangered species.

1.

From Separation
to Accommodation—
And Back Again

Joseph Chuman

At times the most innocuous happenstance is suggestive of torrents which rage beneath. In mid-May of this year, my wife and I journeyed to rural Orange County, New York, to participate in "Grandparents' Day" hosted by our grandson's public elementary school. Members of the first generation were invited into the second grade classrooms to discuss their own childhoods and present artifacts from their younger days. Some displayed war memorabilia, and a few brought with them and explained photos taken at the time of their holy communions. With regard to the latter, though religion was invoked in the public school, there was certainly no line crossed. Indeed, an attempt to quiet such discussion would not only have been violative of free expression about religion, it would have displayed an inappropriate and discriminatory animus toward religion.

This year's event contrasted notably with an occurrence at the same event last spring when we were invited to the class of our older grandchild. At that moment, no doubt motivated by good will and an impulse to share the "good news," another invitee held forth on the benefits of a life lived by the lights of Christian faith and the love of Jesus. This moment of sharing caused the teacher, recognizing the impropriety of such discourse, to hurry the presentation along, but without much success.

15

As a humanist, whose formative years coincided with the Warren Court and the heyday of strict separation of church and state, I could only recoil at the transformation of a second grade public school classroom into an arena ripe for evangelism. In the 1960s, and until twenty years ago, I could feel confident that my repulsion would have been shared by a solid majority of Americans, and my intuitive understanding of the place of religion in the public square, and not least the public schools, would have been affirmed as normative. Today, I am not so sure.

THE CHALLENGES WE CONFRONT

The conflict over the proper relations of church to state lies at the focus of our contemporary cultural wars. Since the emergence of the evangelical subculture into the political life of the nation, in the late 1970s, we have witnessed an ongoing series of religiously grounded public issues, which have divided religious conservatives from liberals. Included among them have been continuing efforts to return prayer to the public schools and the public square; the move to support private, including parochial schools with public funds; the teaching of "creation science" in parallel with evolution; "abstinence only" curricula as the core of sex education; the "charitable choice" initiative, which gives public funds directly to churches to support social service activities; and struggles over the legalization of gay marriage. The abortion debate, perhaps the most divisive of the culture wars, is framed and fueled primarily within a religious context. Behind the abortion imbroglio is the wider religio-cultural conflict regarding the empowerment of women in the light of enduring patriarchal interests issuing from conservative religious values.

The culture wars most basically pit Northeastern secular and religious liberals, together with West Coast progressives, against the residents of the South, Midwest and Mountain States, who have long considered themselves in the shadow of the Washington-Boston axis. Though Christian evangelicals comprise the religious right's strongest base, it would be incorrect to define its apologists as exclusively fundamentalists or anti-modern. Those poised against the perceived liberal establishment comprise an intriguing reconfiguration of religious conservatives, many of whom were traditional adversaries before the contemporary phase of the culture wars. The new religious right links conservative Protestants with conservative Catholics and some orthodox Jewish factions. Furthermore, not all apologists for the religious right's agenda are themselves religious. Many secular neo-conservatives see a common cause in the infusion of politics with religious values. Others such as Yale law professor and Episcopalian, Stephen Carter, who is uncomfortable with the excesses of the fundamentalist wing of the movement, would define themselves as religious moderates.

The current strife manifests itself in shifting legal doctrine as it pertains to church-state separation and the intent of the religion clauses of the First Amendment. But lying beneath these judicial struggles and propelling them are broader philosophical assumptions about the role of religion in sustaining the moral fabric of American society.

The intent of this paper is to sketch these contrasting judicial doctrines. I will also discuss at greater length the philosophical and moral arguments of those defending greater accommodation of the religion by the state, and then point to fallacies and dangers for American freedom resulting from the accommodationist position.

My thesis assumes as given that humanism in the United States has long been identified exclusively with a strong position of church-state separation, exemplified by the Jeffersonian metaphor invoking a "wall of separation." Making reference to the political views of free-thinkers in the late nineteenth century, the precursors of contemporary humanists, historian Susan Jacoby noted the following: "Unlike eighteenth-century deists, nearly all of whom identified with Jeffersonian democracy, American freethinkers of the late nineteenth century were anything but unified in their political views. . . . The one political concern which did unite all freethinkers was their support for absolute separation of church and state. . . ."[1]

Because freethought was poised against ecclesiastical authority, its adherents as well as contemporary humanists, gravitated more readily to a defense of the Establishment Clause rather than the Free Exercise Clause. But the latter has also been upheld by humanists, issuing from support for freedom of conscience, their status as a minority within a pervasively religious society, and because of commitment to the values of tolerance and diversity.

In the 1947 Everson case, Supreme Court Justice gave powerful, if not apodictic, expression to the religion clauses of the First Amendment, rendering what has ever since been the normative position of humanists on the matter.

> The "establishment of religion" clause of the First Amendment means at least this: Neither a state nor the Federal Government can set up a church. Neither can pass laws which aid one religion, aid all religions, or prefer one religion over another. Neither can force a person to go to or remain away from church against his will or force him to profess belief or disbelief in any religion. No person can be punished for entertaining or professing religious beliefs or disbeliefs, for church attendance or non-attendance. No tax in any amount, large or small, can be levied to support any religious activities or institutions, whatever they may be called, or whatever form they may adopt to teach or practice religion. Neither a state nor the Federal Government can, openly or secretly, participate in the affairs of any religious organizations or groups and vice verse. In the words of Jefferson, the clause against establishment of religion by law was intended to erect "a wall of separation between Church and State."[2]

Everson confirms a stance of state neutrality vis-à-vis religion and non-religion.

Yet neutrality is an ideal position, recognizing the inherently conflictual nature of non-establishment and free expression. This conflict, if not paradox, in the relationship of the religion clauses to each other ensures that the boundary separating them be a wavering one, which eludes the imposition of a flawless principle to resolve disputes. Indeed, free exercise presupposes at least a minimum of accommodation in some circumstances if government is not to be hostile toward religion. Everson itself deemed permissible the use of tax money to pay for student transportation to private, including Catholic parochial, schools. Even the majority, including Black, recognized that the prevailing decision aided religious education, though in the majority's opinion, the safety of schoolchildren prevailed over the separation principle as found in the First Amendment.[3] As Leo Pfeffer points out, government-supported chaplaincies in the armed forces are deemed permissible on parallel grounds and with reference to the notion that the free exercise clause is no less weighty than the establishment clause.[4] Organized prayer in the public schools is prohibited on non-establishment grounds, but school authorities may not forbid teachers from wearing non-intrusive symbols of their religious faith in the classroom, clearly exemplifying the notion that the line divided free exercise from the accommodation of religion vanishes to an unde-tectable narrowness. In circumstances that bear upon contemporary polemics over "charitable choice" it should be noted that as early as 1899 in *Bradfield vs. Roberts*, the Supreme Court validated the con-stitutionality of tax dollars used to support sectarian hospitals, and by extension religiously derived social service agencies, provided they sustained a mandate to assist the public at large with services not dis-tinctively religious. Noteworthy was that the Bradford case involved public aid to Catholic hospitals at a time in American life when nativist anti-Catholic sentiment was especially strong.[5]

The resurgence of the political right, in great measure fueled by the conservative churches, has pushed the accommodationist argument into new territory. Foremost is the assertion that the neutralist position of the state, as confirmed by Justice Black among others, is both chimerical and per se hostile to religion. By identifying the state with a position of neu-trality between religion and non-religion, government is de facto identi-fying with the latter at the expense of religious values and practice.

Contemporary expression was given to discontent with the tradi-tional separationist position by Senator Joseph Lieberman when he served as Connecticut's attorney general. Lieberman noted:

> The Court has been alternatively weighing and using two different tests to determine the constitutionality of Establishment Clause cases. Which test they use usually determines whether or not they find a government program involving religion to be constitutional.
>
> The first is called the *Lemon* test and usually results in a finding of unconstitutionality. In *Lemon v. Kurtzman*, the United States Supreme Court said that if a law or program involving religion is to be upheld, it must meet each of these standards: 1) it must have a secular legislative purpose, 2) its primary effect must not be to inhibit or benefit religion, 3) it must not produce an entanglement of government and religion.

On a few occasions, when the Court has wanted to avoid the logical conclusion of the Lemon test, it has abandoned it and applied another test.

That one is called the rule of accommodation, and its advocates are known as accommodationists. Accommodationists believe that the Lemon test is too restrictive and, if applied arbitrarily, will strike down every governmental program which remotely involved religion because it can be argued that every such program benefits religion to some extent and entangles government and religion, even if it has a secular purpose. Accommodationists feel strongly that that is not the result the Constitution's authors intended, nor is it what we should want today. Accommodationists believe that it is reasonable for government to accommodate itself to religious observance and practice so long as no one religion is established as the official national faith and no individual's right to exercise his own religion is limited in any way.[6]

The consequences of Lieberman's analysis and those like it have been far reaching. In the hands of the Moral Majority and the Christian Coalition, state neutrality inherent in church-state separation is reified into an officially sponsored "religion of secular humanism." For less doctrinaire commentators such as Michael McConnell, the primacy of the secular state, and its stance of neutrality ". . . is actually a deeply embedded ideological preference for some modes of reasoning and ways of life over others—rationalism and choice over tradition and conscience." If the government has not established a new religion, it at least privileges one worldview, that issuing from the Enlightenment, over other worldviews, specifically those based in religion.

The payoff of this privilege is to allegedly reduce believers to the status of second-class citizens. To enter into the realm of public discourse, as Stephen Carter asserts, a believer needs to check his or her religion at the door. "In our sensible zeal to keep religion from dominating our politics, we have created a political and legal culture that presses the religiously faithful to be other than themselves, to act publicly, and sometimes privately as well. As though their faith does not matter to them."

Behind the doctrine of separation, and propelling the believer into the shadows of public discourse, is the dynamic articulated by the founders that sought not only to separate religion from the state, but to relegate religion to the private sphere. Following Locke, Jefferson concurred that while the affairs of state were of public and common concern, matters of salvation were exclusively between a man and his God. As he famously wrote in Notes on Virginia, "It does me no injury for my neighbor to say that there are twenty gods, or no God. It neither picks my pocket nor breaks my leg." By privatizing religion, religious belief and practice were protected from the corruption by secular concerns, while the state remained free of religious control, thus preserving the integrity of religious conscience for all. Despite the various religious views of the founders, the separation principle merged the diverse historical currents reflected in the American experience of which Roger Williams and Jefferson were contrasting epigones. For Williams, separation protected the garden of religion from encroachment by the wilderness of the secular realm. For Jefferson, mindful of the European experience of religious warfare, and ever contemptuous of ecclesiastical power, the state needed protection from the tyranny of religious absolutism.

Critics of the hard separation principle find fault with the assumptions behind privatization, which reinforce their call for greater accommodation. Locke's and Jefferson's prescription, as McConnell would have it, "is not with its desirability, but with its congruence with reality." The relegation of religion to the private sphere, as Jefferson's reasoning implies, is to render religion completely otiose with regard to human conduct. As McConnell notes,

> With all respect to Locke and Jefferson, it would be naïve to assume that civil society is unaffected by the moral and theological teachings of the major religions. . . . Today feminists have no doubt that the patriarchal character of many major religions (in their eyes) has earthly consequences. . . . Environmentalists are not oblivious to the earthly consequences of the "stewardship" and "dominion" models of man's relation to Creation.

Locke's own rejection of Catholics and atheists from the commonwealth, on grounds that their loyalties were situated elsewhere or they could not be trusted, itself speaks to the belief that thought informs character, and character informs behavior.

McConnell's observation, as far as it goes is compelling. If the religious and civil spheres are indeed separable, then no conflict arises. But as noted, this often is not the case. If civic action is religiously motivated, then a conflict emerges that seeks adjudication. For Locke, when religious conscience collides with civil authority acting on behalf of the common good, then the former must defer to the latter. The contention of religious conservatives and accommodationists in the light of our secular government (as evinced in Lemon, for example) is that the dominion and mandates of secular governance prevail, again reducing the religiously motivated actor to the margins and banishing him or her to the realm of second-class citizenship.

Church-state separation imposes not only a putatively second-class status on the serious believer; it also forces him or her to live a divided existence. One can recall the invocation of Moses Mendelssohn, both an exponent of the Enlightenment and an orthodox Jew, to the effect of "Be a man in the streets, and a Jew at home." The response to this alienation and the problem of the problem of the divided self is what political scientist, Nancy Rosenblum calls "integralism." "Integralists want to be able to conduct themselves according to the injunctions of religious law and authority in every sphere of everyday life, and to see their faith mirrored in public life."

The strongest and most comprehensive variant of integralism, defined by Rosenblum, is "foundationalist" integralism. It "demands public acknowledgement of the sacred foundation of secular values, law and political authority." Not only does such religious foundationalism eschew the premises of separation, it downplays the autonomous claims of Enlightenment rationalism, while seeking the anchor for socially cohesive values deeply lodged in ancestral religion.

Integralism, so understood, has been given expression in the thought of Judaic scholar David Novak. In his essay "Religious Human Rights in Judaic Texts" Novak affirms the importance of religious freedom but then makes the following point:

> . . . without the emphasis of religious liberty in a society that is secular by definition, those who see a religious foundation for the human rights that are affirmed by a secular society such as ours have no entry into the moral discourse of the public square. The task of religious believers who wish to enter into this moral discourse . . . is to persuade others that a religious foundation for human rights can respect the realm of the

secular where these rights are exercised much easier than "secularism" can respect the realm of the religious. In other words, the task of the religious believer—Jewish, Christian, or Muslim—is to provide a better foundation for the moral claims of the secular realm in which the vast majority of its citizens profess religious belief and, indeed, see their very allegiance to that secular realm as itself being religious.[7]

The implications of Novak's position could hardly be more far-reaching. Implicit in his argument is the notion that religion serves the function (by definition) of grounding all other values which are to be subsumed under the religious and not vice versa. Under the construct of modern secular government, the state can be understood to "grant" religious freedom along with the panoply of other "rights," e.g., freedom of the press, association, and so inverts the appropriate order. Religion becomes merely one among a permissible roster of rights. The state, thereby, not only divests religion of its primacy, it also engages in an act of condescension with regard to religious believers. In other words, it may be argued, it is not in the power of the state to "grant" what is foundational and primary, namely, religious values that themselves inform the state, and on which it is itself ultimately based. Religious values are asserted as the basis of all rights and freedoms.

A more common position is what Rosenblum calls "moral integralism." In this form "Believers do not always insist that morality is impossible without religion, but they do insist that religious belief of and association strengthen moral conduct and compensate for the failures of secular values, institutions and authorities."[8] The morally salutary, indeed essential, function of religion in supporting a benevolent and morally cohesive social order justifies government extending its support to "faith-based" institutions. As Rosenblum notes, ". . . integralists commend public support qua religious groups. The moral effectiveness of religious associations is said to depend on their uninhibited religious identity, precisely because they offer prayer along with job training, drug rehabilitation, schooling and counseling."[9]

The most influential advocate in intellectual circles of a strong moral integralist position has been Richard John Neuhaus. Following Alasdair MacIntyre, Neuhaus asserts that ". . . a public ethic cannot be reestablished unless it is informed by religiously grounded values . . .

and . . . the values of the American people are deeply rooted in religion."[10] Neuhaus takes it for granted that religion has been banished from the public square, which has consequently been rendered naked of those values necessary for the maintenance of democracy. Though Neuhaus is skeptical of the anti-intellectualism of his fundamentalist allies, he nevertheless concurs in the arguments that a new "religion of secular humanism" has been born out of a commitment to church-state separation, and out of the vacuum thereby created:

> The notion that this is a secular society is relatively new. It might be proposed that, while society is incorrigibly religious, the state is secular. But such a disjunction between society and state is a formula for governmental delegitimation. In a democratic society, state and society must draw from the same moral well. In addition, because transcendence abhors a vacuum, the state that styles itself as secular will almost certainly succumb to secularism. Because government cannot help but make moral judgments of an ultimate nature, it must, if it has in principle excluded identifiable religion, make those judgments by "secular" reasoning that is given the force of religion. Because this process is already advanced in the spheres of law and public education, there is a measure of justice in the complaints about secular humanism. "Secular humanism," in this case, is simply the term unhappily chosen for ersatz religion.[11]

Neuhaus' integralism goes far beyond the oft-proclaimed assertion that the morality of the civic culture, as taught primarily in public school is "thin" morality, in contrast to the transcendent, and thereby "thick" morality of the traditional faiths. For Neuhaus the public square rendered naked by the displacement of religion is a transitional phenomenon. As with nature, the public square abhors a vacuum, a vacuum which the state will necessarily fill. From the standpoint of traditional separationists, and especially for rationalists and secularists, this is not a bad thing. For Neuhaus it is demonic. Speaking of those skeptical of religion's hegemonic tendencies, Neuhaus proclaims, "They would cast out the devil of particularist religion and thus put the public square in proper secular order. Having cast out one devil, they unavoidably invite the entrance of seven devils worse than the first."[12] "[B]ecause the naked square cannot remain naked, the direction is toward state-as-church, toward totalitarianism. And again, the available form of totalitarianism—an aggressively available form, so to speak—is Marxist Leninist."[13]

The accommodationist position has virtually become normative in American public consciousness and has placed separationists on the defensive. Its compelling character on the eyes of its supporters is deeply embedded in and propelled by the tectonic cultural and political shifts in American sensibilities. It is apiece with the aforementioned entrée of the evangelical churches as full-blown and well-organized players on the political landscape. As previously apolitical churches have attained worldly power, they have demanded "equal treatment" for religion, interpreting separation as derogating from equality, rather than providing protection, as separationists aver.

The historicist and multicultural character of changing church-state paradigms was given articulate expression by legal scholar Jeffrey Rosen in a broadly discussed article written for the *New York Times Magazine*. Rosen contends that the separationists' position as it has come to be accepted in the post-war period was exceptional, and reflected a judicial enthusiasm of limited duration. "One thing is clear," Rosen avers, "the era of strict separation is over. For a surprisingly brief period, from the early 1970s to the late 1980s, strict separationism commanded the support of a majority of Supreme Court justices."[14]

The causes for the acceptance of strict separationism and the changes in that paradigm are rooted in the dynamics of multiculturalism. In Rosen's analysis, separationism reached its pinnacle as a result of Protestant dominance and its long-standing fear of the ascendance of Catholic power. With exception of the "Jewish seat," positions on the Supreme Court have been, until recent decades, exclusively held by Protestants. Black, who did more to champion and articulate the separationist doctrine than his colleagues on the Supreme Court, as Rosen reminds us, was "a former Alabama Senator, Ku Klux Klan member and enthusiastic anti-Papist."[15] The separationist doctrine was invoked consequentially to check the drive of Catholic advocates to gain aid for parochial schools, but it was also strongly incorporated into the political stance of the established Jewish community, who viewed separation as the best way to protect the Jewish minority within a Christian-dominant environment.

But, as Rosen notes, the contours of religious alliances have dramatically shifted since the late 1970s. The centuries-long Protestant-Catholic enmities for the most part have been quelled in contemporary America. The emergence of Jewish neo-conservative spokespersons has signaled Jewish success and mainstreaming allowing, (it is argued) for the dismantling of the defensive posture reflected in separationism. Quite unthinkable, even thirty years ago, religious alignments have been recast, defined by an alliance of evangelical Protestants, conservative Catholics and orthodox and neo-conservative Jews poised against secularists, liberals and mainline religionists. It is an inevitable shift on which Rosen bestows his blessing.

> The Supreme Court is on the verge of replacing the principle of strict separation with a very different constitutional principle that demands equal treatment for religion. And far from threatening public life, or for that matter religious liberty, the revived cooperation between church and state may be an inevitable and perhaps even healthy result of treating religion as just another aspect of identity politics in a multicultural age.[16]

ACCOMMODATION, ITS FALLACIES AND DISCONTENTS

But is it? Separationists foresee a more ominous scenario materializing on the political horizon. They note that despite deeply rooted racism coursing through American history, unlike the historical European experience and the current paroxysms of violence spurred by religious nationalism across the globe, American society has been relatively free of inter-religious violence. This, combined with flourishing of religion in America, is owed in no small measure to the brilliant, and at the time unique, formulation of church-state separation laid down by the Founders. Separationists also note the irony inherent in the ascendance of accommodationist doctrine and practice at a time when the United States, though remaining overwhelmingly Christian dominant, is experiencing an explosion of religious pluralism and experimentation.

Stephen Carter defends accommodationism as a victimized outsider, and Jeffrey Rosen asserts its historical inevitability. Both positions, as articulated, cannot be true, and from my perspective neither is.

But beyond the veracity of viewpoints, the question must be asked as to whether accommodation is feasible. Are there weaknesses and fallacies that go unexplored by its apologists?

The pervasively implied, but seldom analytically explored, presumption of religious accommodationists is that religion is predominantly a force for good. The view of religion held by such thinkers is of a sunny religion—a view that remains comfortably unmindful that the establishment clause articulated by the Founders was built in no unsubstantial manner on the deeply held fear of the fusion of ecclesiastical power with the arms of state. Commenting on the Act Establishing Religious Freedom in Virginia, Jefferson wrote to Madison in 1786,

> In fact, it is comfortable to see the standard of reason at length erected, after so many ages, during which the human mind has been held in vassalage by kings, priests and nobles; and it is honorable for us, to have produced the first legislature who had the courage to declare, that the reason of man may be trusted with the formation of his own opinions.[17]

Often invoked by religious apologists are the universalizing and ethicizing dimensions of religion, those aspects of religion that promote regard for the stranger, concern for the poor and disenfranchised, and respect for the dignity of man as "created in God's image" thus also validating the unity of humankind. The fact that religion endows these moral precepts with a transcendent, absolute, timeless and unchanging character putatively protects them from the contingencies of human history and the vicissitudes of political fashion ultimately rooted in power struggles. It is this transcendent ground that conservatives like Neuhaus long for, and nourishes their deep skepticism about secularism, which in their eyes remains too contingent, too relative to do the work of sustaining a moral social order.

As compelling as the logic of this position may seem, it falters on at least two points. While one cannot doubt the benign influence of religion as an inspirational source and conveyer of benign moral values, the long reach of history reveals that this universalizing and "prophetic" stream of religion has comprised religion's minor tradition. Dostoevsky reminds us that if Jesus were to return preaching his prophetic gospel, he would go unrecognized. Novak's assertion that "a religious foundation for human rights can respect the realm of the secular where these rights are exercised much easier than 'secularism' can respect the realm of the religious" is merely predicated. It's an assertion that requires massive defense.

Far more powerful and pervasive has been religion's sectarian side, its ability to serve as a focus for absolutes, drawing in stark relief the boundaries between insiders and outsiders, the saved from the damned, those favored in the eyes of God from those who are lost. History tragically too often reveals that when religion's absolutizing qualities are joined to its claims of ultimacy and harnessed to political power religion can metastasize into xenophobia.

Despite the claims of apologists who invoke the need for religion as the ground for democratic values and the maintenance of a democratic polity, religion in practice seems to show no overarching capacity or willingness to do so. Even within the American context religious ecumenism, where it exists, is often tenuous and hard won. When it comes to intergroup tolerance and the defense of universal rights, the religions have shown a stronger propensity for defense of their respective freedom, and correspondingly little interest in defending freedom in general. For while duty is intrinsic to the religions, liberty, on which democracy is based, is not a powerfully instantiated or expressed value for the traditional faiths.

The persistence into our era of religion's penchant for solidifying parochial loyalties at the expense of its loftier values remains the strongest rationale for the separationist position, and conversely exposes accommodationism most consequential weakness. The defense of accommodationism must squarely come to terms with religion's underside.

The claim that religion overcomes the relativism of secularism, and thereby serves to ground in a cosmic, transcendental reality the values necessary for a democratic order is often heard in academic and popular circles. Yet seldom articulated are the countervailing dangers of appeal to the transcendent. The absolute ground on which I wish to preserve democratic values may prove to be the same ground used to justify their violation. Michael Ignatieff tersely makes this point in its application to grounding human rights. In noting the moral intuition not to beat, torture or coerce other human beings, he makes the following observation:

Believing that humans are sacred does not strengthen these injunctions.

The reverse is often true: acts of torture are frequently justified in terms of some sacred purpose. Indeed, the strength of a purely secular ethics is its insistence that there are no "sacred" purposes that can ever justify the inhuman use of human beings. An antifoundational humanism seems insecure, but it does have the advantage that it cannot justify inhumanity on foundational grounds.[18]

Appeals to religious transcendentalism as a necessary ground for democratic (and anti-democratic!) values reveals a second fallacy inherent in the accommodationist position. The universally over-looked assumption is that "religion" is not a unitary phenomenon. In the strictest sense there is no entity such as "religion." There are only religions. In the words of rights theorist Louis Henkin,

> Theologians, philosophers, other academics, properly distinguish "religion" from "religions." But in that distinction, "religion" is abstracted, and the claims that are made about it are made about an abstraction. In the public mind, "religion" does not exist; there are only "religions." Surely in the political universe in which human rights is played out and matter "religion," cannot avoid identification with "religions," with every—any—particular religion. And unhappy as this is to say, every religion at some time, in some respect, has had to answer to the human rights idea for human rights violations, many of them unspeakable.[19]

In short, Christianity is not Judaism, is not Islam, is not Rastafarianism, is not Scientology, and their collapse into a single entity "religion" is the construction of a chimera. Accommodationism presupposes governmental support of all faiths, yet avoids the practical and legal conundrums of arbitrating between the multitudes of religions with their competing sancta, theologies and truths—a function which secular government is incompetent to fulfill. Here Rosenblum's observation is fretfully being played out in George W. Bush's "charitable choice" initiative, as well as in lesser forms of religious accommodationism:

> Advocates of a publicly endorsed moralizing role for religion assume a felicitous congruence between religious and democratic values. They also assume that government recognition and support for reli-

gious pluralism will increase political harmony. This is doubtful. When religious associations shift from the classic self-protective, separationist aim of exemption from burdensome public obligations and aim instead at public subsidy, ecumenical cooperation is likely to be replaced by sectarian division. Groups allied in support of a generous interpretation of religious free exercise and autonomy are more likely to collide when it comes to carving up public funds. After all, government support is ultimately inseparable from endorsement of the value, if not the truth, of religious tenets and practices. Citizens, believers and non-believers, are not likely to approve public subsidy for schools and social missions sponsored by the Nation of Islam, the Church of Scientology, or a just-formed charismatic "cult."[20]

Not only does accommodationism force government to overreach its limits conditioned by its secular character in order to pass judgment on matters of religious integrity and theological character, it also invites the state to provide preferential treatment to "acceptable" religions at the expense of minority or unpopular faiths—in direct violation of function the religion clauses were intended to perform. Despite the alleged discomforts placed on the traditional believers by the maintenance of government neutrality with regard to religion, it is impossible to conclude that the fundamental injury caused to religious minorities is not far greater. Religious accommodationism ultimately leads to the tyranny of the majority, in direct contradiction to the purport and spirit of the Bill of Rights.

CONCLUSION

The principle of the separation of church and state lies at the very heart of American democracy. The rapid destruction of the "wall of separation," which has been underway for the past two decades, and has accelerated at an alarming rate in the current administration of George W. Bush, bears far-reaching consequences legally, socially, and politically. As demonstrated, the replacement of separationist doctrine with religious accommodationism has moved along apace with the triumphalist assertion of conservative religious power on the political and social scene.

Among other effects, it has ensured the entrée of a religiously motivated political agenda into the highest echelons of state power. Jefferson and Madison would have been aghast at daily Bible sessions in the White House, Congress, and the administrative offices of the federal government. But they would have been no less concerned, if not bewildered, by a domestic and foreign policy fueled by the conservative churches in America, and the consequent routing of rational, secular, and Enlightened discourse in the public square.

Humanists eschew determinisms and hold as axiomatic that the future is always open and subject to human agency. Those who cherish democracy, the open society, and freedom, including religious freedom, stand at a dangerous moment. If cultural alignments have changed prefiguring a shift in church-state relations, as Jeffrey Rosen contends, then humanists might look to what has not changed.

Despite being lamentably unschooled in constitutional principles, Americans remain reflexively uncomfortable with the imposition of ideologies not our own. When pushed to the last trumps we remain restless individualists whose resistance to having beliefs dictated to us still engenders a spirit of tolerance for difference.

As we enter a more repressive period, such may seem like a thin reed, and left to itself it is not enough to push back the night. What's needed is for all those who understand what is at stake in the destruction of the "wall of separation"—humanists, secularists, liberal and moderate religionists, even libertarian conservatives—to join forces in order to win back the ground we have lost. The legacy of American freedom and the practical wisdom of the separationist arrangement should give us hope.

NOTES

1. Susan Jacoby, *Freethinkers* (New York: Henry Holt and Company, 2004), p. 153.

2. From Joseph L. Blau, "The Wall of Separation," *Union Seminary Quarterly Review* 38, nos. 3&4 (1984): pp. 281–2.

3. Leo Pfeffer, *Church, State and Freedom* (Boston: Beacon Press, 1953), p. 476.

4. Ibid., p. 477.

5. Holy Name Hospital, on whose medical ethics committee this writer serves, receives government funds but forbids the performance of abortions, tubal ligations, and other procedures in violation of Catholic doctrine. Nevertheless, Holy Name must serve the public-at-large and heed federal non-discrimination statutes in its hiring practices. This instance serves as a common example of the long-standing but wavering application of the separation principle when applied to agencies operated under religious auspices.

6. Remarks given before the Rabbinical College of America, Sheraton Meadowlands Hotel, Secaucus, New Jersey, December 13, 1987.

7. Michael McConnell, "Believers As Equal Citizens," in Nancy Rosenblum, ed., *Obligations of Citizenship and Demands of Faith* (Princeton, NJ: Princeton University Press, 2000), p. 103.

8. Stephen Carter, *The Culture of Disbelief* (HarperCollins: 1993), p. 3.

9. McConnell, "Believers As Equal Citizens," p. 94.

10. Ibid., p. 96.

11. Nancy Rosenblum, "Pluralism, Integralism, and Political Theories of Religious Accommodation," *Obligations of Citizenship and Demands of Faith*, p. 15.

12. Ibid.

13. Ibid., p. 20.

14. David Novak, "Religious Human Rights in Judaic Texts," in M. Broyde and John Witte Jr., eds., *Human Rights in Judaism*, p. 33.

15. Ibid., p. 16.

16. Ibid., p. 17.

17. Richard John Neuhaus, *The Naked Public Square* (Grand Rapids, MI: William B. Eerdmans Publishing Company, 1984), p. 13.

18. Ibid., p. 82.

19. Ibid., p. 86.

20. Ibid., p. 89.

21. Jeffrey Rosen, "Is Nothing Secular," *New York Times Magazine*, January 30, 2000.

22. Ibid.

23. Ibid.

24. Cited in Blau, p. 278.

25. Michael Ignatieff, *Human Rights As Politics and Idolatry* (Princeton, NJ, and Oxford: Princeton University Press, 2001), p. 88.

26. Louis Henkin, "Religion, Religions, and Human Rights," *Journal of Religious Ethics* 26, no. 2 (1998): 229–30.

27. Rosenblum, "Pluralism, Integralism, and Political Theories," pp. 17–18.

2.

Rights, Liberties, and the Response to Terrorism

Carmela Epright

I feel privileged to be invited to write on such an important and timely issue. How the US has and will respond to the incidents that took place on 9/11, as well as to the continuing threat of terrorism in our country and throughout the world, is not a continuing source of discussion and debate merely among academics.

Concern about how to strike a balance between protection from the seemingly random and certainly unpredictable violence of terrorism and our personal liberty currently fills the editorial pages of our newspapers, and finds its way into the discussions that we have with our friends and neighbors. Furthermore, I strongly suspect that our exposure to and interest in this topic will only expand as the 2004 presidential election heats up.

There is much to say about the conflict between rights and security—one could, for example, begin with a discussion of the Patriot Act—a piece of sweeping legislation that greatly expanded governmental power and limited individual rights. The Patriot Act was passed by both Houses of Congress on October 25, 2001—just six weeks after the 9/11 terrorist attacks. But as a philosopher, I believe that to begin our discussion here is to ignore the larger, more universal concerns inherent in this controversy—namely, where rights come from, what they mean in the context of civil life, and why they are a continuing source of controversy and conflict. Indeed, I believe any responsible discussion of the relationship and the tension between rights and security must start with a discussion of rights theory.

I'm sure that I am merely stating the obvious, but the term "right" tends to be employed fairly loosely. Nearly every day I hear some new declarations of rights. We speak of a "right to our opinions;" a right to happiness and self-fulfillment; property rights, animal rights; parental rights (grandparent rights); religious rights; the right to bear arms; a right to privacy. Here is my favorite example: one of my students recently informed me that I was infringing on his "rights" by assigning a take-home quiz over the weekend of homecoming.

So pervasive are rights claims that I suspect that the average person can't get through the average day without running into the rights language in one or another form.

Yet I would hold that our use of the language hides tremendous ignorance. If one were to ask my students—and I frequently do—to define "rights," one would likely receive a list of examples of rights, but no understanding of the larger concept.

What exactly are rights? Were do they come from? How do we determine which declarations of rights are legitimate, and which are wholly fantastic? Must I respect that student's right to a homework-free weekend? My Islamic neighbor's right to religious freedom? My cat's right to a can of tuna each week and the opportunity to sleep on my freshly ironed clothing?

For our purposes here I will limit my discussion to legal and civil rights—and I will try to steer clear of the more complex and ambiguous ground occupied by moral rights. I also want to avoid lists—it means little to provide a laundry list of legal and civil rights, without grounding these rights in their theoretical and philosophical context. My goal here is to briefly outline rights theory—to explain the part that rights play in civil society in general, and American society in particular.

In the discussion that follows I will make four main points about the nature and role of rights in American law and society.

1. First, I will show that our common understanding of rights—that rights are privileges controlled by and extended to citizens at the

discretion of the governing body—is entirely backwards. Instead I will show that citizens hold rights in reserve. This is to say that the government does not grant rights. Rights emanate from our status as rational beings, not from the state's desire to grant them. Rights are, as the Declaration of Independence states, self-evident and inalienable. Your and my status as rights holders must in fact be protected against governmental interference (this is the primary role of the courts with respect to the free exercise of rights). Our rights are not (or at least should not be) dependent upon the will or whim of governmental bodies or agents.

2. I contend that rights cannot exist without their logical corollary: duties. For example, my right to physical security means nothing if you are permitted to strike me at will. In order for security to be a meaningful right, someone must, at the very least, have a duty to not deprive me of my security. This, I think, is where much of the confusion lies with respect to our understanding of the connection between individual rights and the role of the government. If citizens have rights, then governments have corresponding duties to ensure that citizens are not deprived of those rights. Needless to say, governments frequently fail to ensure such protection. Failures of this sort often have the practical consequence of truncating or compromising individual rights. But the fact that governments can and often do act to infringe upon individual rights does not mean that the government should be granted the power to curtail or abolish rights at will.

3. Next, I will discuss some situations in which the majority of citizens come to believe that rights can be, and perhaps should be, forfeited for the sake of other, more pressing concerns. The threat of terrorism is perhaps the most dramatic example of this sort of situation. Yet if I am correct about points 1 and 2, that governments do not grant or provide rights, that government's role is to instead to protect rights—that rights themselves are intrinsic and inalienable—then it is not up to the majority to decide when and whether rights should be forfeited. The majority, like the government, might as a matter of pragmatic reality, possess the power to effect and even trample upon individual rights—however, in principle, rights should not be dependent upon or subject to the will majority. The "tyranny of the majority" that John Stuart Mill so passionately feared ought never be powerful

enough to override individual rights—even if eliminating rights could potentially result in tremendous utility to society.

The pervasive idea that majority rule can or should supercede individual rights is, I believe, what was at issue in the Alabama case concerning the monument to the Ten Commandments. Chief Justice Roy S. Moore has consistently defended placing the monument in the capital building by pointing out that a majority of citizens of the state of Alabama support the monument. This, however, is not the point. If there is a right to the free expression of religion (and the US Constitution says that there is), then the will of the majority is irrelevant. As John Stuart Mill claims: "If all of mankind minus one were of one opinion, mankind would be no more justified in silencing that one person than he, if he had the power would be justified in silencing all of mankind."

Similarly, in a case in my hometown of Greenville, the city has suggested placing video surveillance monitors on public streets. One line of defense for this action is that the majority of Greenville residents do not mind. The prevailing opinion seems to be: if you're not breaking any law, why would you mind if you are being monitored? However, whether or not the majority of citizens want to preserve their right to X is irrelevant if this is determined not to be a right. Moreover, my reasons for wanting to protect my rights are also not at issue. In other words, "only the guilty would want to have that right" is not a compelling reason to overturn the right in question.

4. My final claim is less theoretical and more pragmatic. I will argue that because it is impossible to limit the rights of one group without threatening the rights of all other citizens, and because placing limitations on individual rights has historically resulted in negligible gains with respect to the safety and security of the citizenry, policies that threaten or limit individual rights ought to be studiously avoided. Or to use the words of Thomas Jefferson, each of us should be eternally vigilant against the forfeiture of our liberties. This, I acknowledge, might appear to be a rather radical position to take in the wake of 9/11, but I believe that it is a position that can be justified by a close reading of rights theory and a study of history. Perhaps more important, it is a position that is only as radical as the position embodied by our governing document, the United States Constitution.

THE ORIGIN OF SOCIETY: HUMANS, NATURE, AND THE STATE

Let me warn you, what follows in this section is an utterly "quick and dirty" overview of political theory—I cut lots of corners—if you want the whole story I can't give it to you in thirty minutes—you have to take my social political philosophy course!

In brief I will contend that the rights embodied in the constitution have their origin in a very particular understanding of human nature, a view that is most cleanly and clearly articulated by Enlightenment thinkers. Such thinkers posit individual rights as a means of recognizing that adult human beings, with few exceptions, are rational agents. This is to say rights stem from our status as rational autonomous beings. Because we are capable of making our own decisions about what constitutes a good and satisfying life, we should be entitled to do so. In short, our status as rational, self-determining beings does not depend upon the government.

To understand this concept and how it underpins the relationship between individuals and the state, let me start by explaining the Social Contract theory offered by Thomas Hobbes.

Hobbes begins his analysis of the relationship between the individual and the state with a thought experiment. He asks us to imagine a world where all persons are roughly equal in their ability to destroy one another—some are smarter, some meaner, some sneakier . . . but each person has one or another capacity that if used judiciously would permit him or her to slaughter everyone else.

Hobbes refers to this as the state of nature—it is not too far-fetched to imagine that such a state of human existence would be possible. However, day-to-day life in such a world would be far from pleasant. It is not hard to imagine that I must constantly worry about Harry's sneakiness, and Ryan's treachery; they and I would constantly be in a state of war. Hobbes states that in this hypothetical state of nature, "every person is enemy to every person." As a result, there would be little industry, no art, no literature, no community—no one would build hospitals to nurse the sick, sidewalks so that we could visit one another, or fire stations to protect our homes. Indeed, each of us would be so consumed with protecting our life and property that there would be no time or energy left for much else. Hobbes describes life in the state of nature as one lived in "continual fear . . . [of a] violent death. . . ." Such a life, he says, "would be solitary, poor, nasty, brutish—and short."

How do we escape the state of nature? By banding together to create a society with laws. This is not an act that we do easily or without trepidation because we are, by our very nature, egoistic individuals who want nothing more than to maintain our freedom. But in the state of nature our freedom is vastly limited. We can't really get anything done because we live in constant fear. If we want to have children; build homes, schools, roads, hospitals; create art; or produce objects for mercantile exchange—we must endow a governing body with just enough power to protect us from the unrestrained freedom of everyone else. Thus, we give the government power for the purpose of insuring our liberty. Let me be clear: such a view shows that the government does not create or distribute rights—on the contrary—individuals grant the government precisely enough power so that it can take on the duties that are a necessary corollary to our rights.

Remember, rights mean little if no one has a corresponding obligation to see that our rights do not meet interference.

It should be clear that this is risky business—living in a society is a constant balancing act: if we create a government that is too powerful—if, for example, the government is endowed with the power to dictate every aspect of our existence or to dictate what rights we will and will not have—the very idea and purpose of government falls apart.

Why on earth would we consent to be governed by a dictatorial body? After all, we entered into this agreement to have more freedom, not less. Why trade the tyranny of the state of nature for the tyranny of a government?

This is to say that we—individuals, rights holders, if you will—both create and grant power to the ruling body. Our rights—to self-determination, to pursue our own conception of a good and satisfying life—these we hold in reserve. *These are what we do not give to the government.*

My point here is a simple one: the governing body comes from us, from the rational agreement of the governed, which is to say that it does not endow us with rights—any power that the government has comes from our will, from the consent of rational beings.

In this respect our rights are not a political creation, they are a natural extension of our dignity as human beings.

What does all of this have to do with terrorism? Since the attacks on 9/11 I think that it is fair to say that there has been a willingness on the part of both the government and the citizenry to overturn individual rights.

Most of us, myself included, are eager to forfeit some of our personal liberties for the sake of greater security—For example, I am willing to get to the airport two hours early, to consent to being searched, to remove my shoes. But would I be willing to undergo a strip search? Or is this too much of an imposition on my liberty?

Interesting, because there is no right to fly, because flying is a privilege, like driving, they can in fact require a strip search—provided they do not single me out for being a woman or an ethnic minority.

There is no right to fly, but there is indeed a right to equal treatment. And this is a question that I can answer definitively: I will not consent to an overturning of the equal protection clause—I do not wish to live in a country that permits the strip searching of all Middle Eastern–looking men. I could not in principle consent to such an infringement on rights—even if I believed that strip searching Middle Eastern–looking men would actually make us all safer and less prone to terrorist attack.

Let me return briefly to a discussion of the Patriot Act, as this piece of legislation more than any other has raised red flags for rights advocates. The act provides the government with greatly enhanced powers to search—our homes, our records, our phone lines—without warrants, without probable cause, and often without notifying us.

There will be court challenges to the Patriot Act in the near future, as there are several ways in which its provisions could be in violation of the Constitution.

According to the ACLU Web site, section 215:

Violates the **Fourth Amendment**, which says the government cannot conduct a search without obtaining a warrant and showing probable cause to believe that the person has committed or will commit a crime.

Violates the **First Amendment's** guarantee of free speech by prohibiting the recipients of search orders from telling others about those orders, even where there is no real need for secrecy.

Violates the **Fourth Amendment** by failing to provide notice—even after the fact—to persons whose privacy has been compromised. Notice is also a key element of due process, which is guaranteed by the **Fifth Amendment**.

If the ACLU is correct—and most legal scholars agree with their analysis—such violations would clearly not be acceptable, according to the arguments that I outlined above. Furthermore, such an infringement on rights would be illegitimate, even if the majority of citizens consented to these restrictions. Even if we would actually be safer if we tolerated such violations.

Our rights are not the property of the government—they are an extension of our humanity, our dignity, our rationality. They are not intended to serve societal utility; they are intrinsically valuable, even if they fail on all counts to serve the interests of the majority.

What I have offered above is a moral and philosophical argument for the preservation of rights, even in the face of foreign threat.

I will leave you with a different sort of argument—one based not upon a conception of human nature, but upon pragmatic considerations.

In short I will contend that limiting rights hardly ever results in the sort of rosy consequences promised by those who advocate such limitations. And the long-term consequences of imposing such limitations are often deeply deleterious to principles upon which constitutional democracies are based.

Take the following argument:

1. That the threat of terrorism not only permits but *requires* the restriction or suspension of rights in order to insure security.
2. Terrorism constitutes a sort of emergency whereby every citizen's continued freedom—indeed, continued existence—is so seriously jeopardized that restricting individual liberty is the

only way to protect human life, much less any notion of personal freedom.

Desperate times, one might argue, call for desperate measures, and terrorism is desperate—it does not resemble conventional warfare; it is far more akin to a natural disaster. If governmental power is intended to protect individuals, this sort of terrorism clearly requires the government to step in to stop the madness in any way possible.

Even if this means squashing some rights.

The argument goes that in such a situation absolutely anyone, except perhaps the most irrational ACLU activist, would be willing to suspend rights in order to provide some opportunity for the continued existence of the citizenry.

Of course, one must ask such questions as:

Whose rights?
Which rights?
How far do we extend our restrictions? And for how long?

But if one restricts one's attention to what is literally thought necessary for an effective response to the threatened terrorism (considered as the sort of emergency situation that I have described), then the answer is apparently easy:

We must act to restrict or suspend every right whose existence somehow prevents you from putting up the best and most effective fight against the terrorist threat.

Many would claim that this is precisely that sort of situation we are in following the 9/11 attacks.

We are vulnerable and defenseless against the unpredictable nature of terrorism and the openness and freedom permitted within our borders acts as a form of assistance and comfort to the enemy.

Herein lies one of the problems with this argument: because we cannot know in advance what specific rights to restrict to stop the terrorist threat, we must restrict or curtail many, many rights.

Only in hindsight will we know which restrictions were necessary and which ultimately had no discernible effect on the incidence of terrorism.

The British government found itself in exactly this sort of frenzy in the 1980s while attempting to contend with the unpredictable violence wrought by the IRA.

In response, the British government forbade the airing of any opinions voiced by Sinn Fein or any other Irish nationalist organization that could be in any way associated with the IRA.

Of course, these actions horrified and alienated civil rights groups, and with good reason. Most of the restrictions proved to be unnecessary, and many people who were completely uninvolved in terrorist activities were jailed, searched, or surveiled. What is most important about this example is that these actions had almost no discernible effect on either the number or the effectiveness of the IRA's attacks.

During this ban the IRA bombed the London Stock Exchange and sent a mortar shell into the backyard of 10 Downing Street, among other attacks.

Eventually, the measure was quietly dropped, although many lives and livelihoods were ruined in the process.

The lesson that we ought to glean from this debacle is this: the reason such approaches are so deeply problematic is that they infringe not only the rights of the terrorists, but of individuals who have nothing to do with terrorism, and who cannot be written off as either sympathizers or potential sympathizers.

In a democracy such as ours, restricting anyone's rights inevitably means restricting everyone's rights.

I will end by leaving you on the horns of a dilemma. If what I have said above is true or at least defensible, the following problem must be reckoned with: it seems that any constitutional democracy that respects its history, philosophical underpinnings, and principles is unable to effectively respond to the sort of emergency situation outlined above—although it is the very society most prone to such emergencies.

And, if such a society *does* effectively respond by issuing a wholesale restriction of rights—the success comes at the expense of its principles—which would, of course, make it something other than a constitutional democracy.

Therefore, even if one accepts the claim that restricting democratic rights is a necessary part of the response a terrorist emergency, striking this balance—and maintaining a country that is worth fighting and dying for—is, to say the least, extremely difficult.

3.

Free Press and Democracy in Times of Terror

Sarah Oelberg

... if it were left to me to decide whether we should have a government without newspapers or newspapers without a government, I should not hesitate to prefer the latter.

Thomas Jefferson

Democracy and Humanism share many basic ideals and tenets. Indeed, it is possible that neither could exist without the other. Both believe in the inherent worth and dignity of humans, and trust in human ability to influence life and events, that we are not mere slaves to destiny. This basic belief assumes that we are dependent upon increased knowledge, which, in turn, assumes we have true and accurate information on which to base rational decisions. Democracy requires truth that is really true, and that falsehood can be vanquished through true discussion and debate and sharing of discoveries. This, in turn, requires free minds—unfettered by doctrinaire ideologies that cannot be questioned because they are preordained or absolute. It also

---

This was written in the fourth year of the administration of President George W. Bush. Many of the references are in the present tense, referring to that time. It is to be hoped that by the time this is published, many, if not most, of them will be able to be put in the past tense. It is doubtful, however, that the overall critique of the press and media will change much. Many of the problems are too embedded in our culture to respond to easy answers.

requires that we consult our consciences and reflect upon right and wrong and knowledge and events in the light of reason, being ever ready to change our views as new information dictates. Both humanism and democracy also depend upon trust and faith in others, an acceptance of differences, and a belief that people can arrive at good decisions if given good information.

Just as democracy and humanism are dependent on each other, both are also dependent upon a free press as a source for information. Fundamental to both is easy access to the truth and differing opinions. This is the reason for the first amendment to the Constitution, making the right to seek truth inviolate. The Bill of Rights states that "Government shall make no law . . . abridging the freedom of speech or the press. . . ." Protection of free speech and press is at the top of the obligations of a democratic government. Having them is a basic right. But this right has a corollary obligation which is that citizens of a democracy are expected to keep themselves informed and use their minds and judgment to make the best decisions they can. As John Adams said, "Liberty cannot be preserved without general knowledge among people."

Today, however, the press is under pressures and attacks which render it, in the words of Bill Moyers, "neither free nor independent." At a time when we have access to more technology and global information than ever, Americans are less informed than they need to be to participate responsibly in our democracy. There are several reasons for this. Among them are:

1. an incestuous relationship between news and entertainment;
2. attempts by the government, accelerated considerably during the Bush administration, to control the sources and output of information;
3. deregulation, mergers, and corporate control of the media;
4. media as business, which leads to a lack of investigative journalism, presenting what pleases audiences and financial backers rather than hard truths.

There are many problems with today's media, such as the elitism and lack of connection with the grassroots of most reporters; the manufacturing of non-news into news; announcing and copycatting and repeating things before they are verified; accepting bogus stories and reporting them as fact, or at least as speculation designed to influence or justify a point of view; taking government press releases at face value and simply repeating them in the name of reporting; reporters being so "embedded" in situations that they cannot see the larger picture; and not questioning or challenging statements made by partisan interviewees. For the purposes of this paper, however, I will address only the four major problems listed above.

1. AN INCESTUOUS RELATIONSHIP BETWEEN NEWS AND ENTERTAINMENT

> All media exist to invest our lives with artificial perceptions and arbitrary values.
>
> —Marshall McLuhan

On the day that Justin Timberlake ripped open Janet Jackson's blouse during the Super Bowl half-time show, American soldiers numbers 523 and 524 died in Iraq and fourteen were wounded, and two suicide bombers killed over 100 Kurds and wounded over 200 more, yet these important events were not reported in the mainstream press, except in very few instances and then only in Section B on back pages. The media focused on Jackson's bared breast 24/7 for over a week, while unemployment rose to its highest level (5.6 percent, or 8.3 million, not counting those who have given up or have very part-time or non-sustainable jobs) mostly due to outsourcing and globalization; over 40 million Americans had no health insurance; the huge government deficit threatened the future of SSI; per pupil spending in public schools declined by over 4 percent in the last two years, and Bush's proposed education budget was $30 billion less than one year's support for Iraq; the 2004 budget lopped 7 percent off from the Environmental Protection Agency and slashed $1.4 billion from human services, including money for alcohol-use reduction, arts in education, and programs for low-income youth. But the media hardly noticed these things, or gave them only scant coverage. Because of the very limited reportage, there was almost no public outrage over these events, but in the first two days after the Super Bowl, the FCC received more than 250,000 complaints about Janet Jackson.

This illustrates one of the problems of the relationship between news and entertainment. It is an example of the media choosing to ignore hard news in favor of reporting things which are more sensational. It is taking something which is not really news and turning it into a major "news" event, and continuing to cover the manufactured news event as long as there is any interest or payoff in doing so. It is taking a "backstory" and putting it on the front page, in order to get people's attention. So the media cover Martha Stewart like her trial and tribulations are as important as the war and subsequent problems in Iraq.

On the day that Michael Jackson surrendered in California, after being accused of abusing a child at his Neverland ranch, there were two terrorist bombings in Turkey, protests in Miami over the Free Trade Area of the Americas, and a coalition-building trip to London by President Bush. Yet the event that dominated the news that day was the pop star's legal battle. Michael Jackson's legal fate and indiscretions have little to no bearing on most Americans' safety, their pocketbooks, or their children's future. Even the simultaneous story of the abuse of hundreds of young people by Catholic priests over many years did not rate nearly as much press coverage. As a result of such selective reporting, more people know the name of Jackson's defense attorney than that of the Attorney General. Perhaps if the media did a better job of covering the more serious issues, more people would be interested in and knowledgeable about them.

Another problem is the conflation of facts with fantasy, turning news stories into entertainment. A good example of the crossover between news, entertainment, and advertising was the Jessica Lynch story. Here was a real story—a wounded soldier captured by the enemy. The *Washington Post*, which used "unnamed sources," first reported it to exaggerate the details and turn it into a saga of suffering and heroism that would have been remarkable, had it been true. It was soon turned into a sensational rescue operation from her fiendish Iraqi captors by the derring-do of the night-raiding US Army Rangers who braved death to snatch this young woman to safety. Thanks to the foresight of the military, an Army cameraman was brought along lest these heroic doings go unrecorded. For several days afterward, Jessica and her friends dominated all the US news channels, who repeated and embellished it without questioning its veracity.

It was a Canadian newspaper, the *Toronto Star*, that discovered and reported that not only were there no guards preventing her from leaving the hospital, the Iraqi medics had tried to heal her wounds and turn her over to the US. The paper wrote that the so-called daring rescue was essentially a "Hollywood-style stunt."[1] A few weeks later the BBC did a full exposé on the whole episode, but apart from a quick mention on CNN, a story in the *Washington Post* and an indignant column in the *Los Angeles Times*, the business was ignored by the mass media. In fact, even when the facts were known, the media continued to pursue and sensationalize the story. CBS News tried to get exclusive rights, writing a letter to the Army that blurred the distinction between news and entertainment, "we believe this is a unique combination of projects that will do justice to Jessica's inspiring story."[1,2]

This made it difficult for any of CBS's "distinguished" journalists to question Lynch dispassionately, or report the true story. Yet it was ABC that landed the exclusive interview with her, which was followed in quick order by interviews on other major networks, and NBC that won the right to run a two-hour fictionalized "docudrama" about her ordeal. In the ABC interview, Jessica said the lies by the media had caused her hurt, and she could not believe they would make up stories that had no truth. She praised others who had died in the crash and had fought, one who would eventually receive a Silver Star for heroism, and received almost no media coverage. The blonde girl fighting off tormentors and surviving torture made a better story, so it was the one that was told—and sold.

The relationship between the TV networks, both the news and entertainment divisions, and the nation's publicists is incestuous. Guests on "news" shows are often entertainment and sports personalities pushing their latest releases or accomplishments or spreading gossip. Many are editors and writers for mass-market magazines. According to L. Brent Bozel, president of the Media Research Center, "News media is becoming more and more indistinguishable from tabloid outlets like the National Enquirer." Circulation of the *National Enquirer*, in fact, far outpaces that of the *New York Times*, the *Los Angeles Times*, and the *Washington Post*.[3] Is it any wonder that many news organizations and programs have blurred the line between entertainment and real news events? Is it any wonder that many Americans confuse the stories in the tabloids and the monologues on late-night TV shows with real news? In this new day, younger people especially are not getting their political educations on the front pages and in the editorials of newspapers. A recent Pew poll reported that more than 20 percent of eighteen- to twenty-nine-year-olds say they get most of their political education from late-night television. About the same proportion looks to the Internet.[4]

Another example of the merging of news and entertainment was the reporting of the "embedded" journalists in the Iraq war. As Christiane Amanpour said,

> here were the on-camera personalities, their American flag lapel pins glittering, who whooped and hollered as they and the military went a-romping through the Iraqi desert. Day in and day out, hour after hour, they tingled with happy excitement as they strained to infect their viewers with their enthusiasm for this strange adventure on the sands of Araby. These were not the people to so much as whisper that it was all a charade. . . . War packaged as a reality show played around the clock on the news channels as the journalistic war profiteers promoted themselves and their careers.[5]

Again, the conflation of news and entertainment not only confuses the public, who see the same kinds of images on their TV screens when they are watching the news as when they view many shows, which glamorize violence and play on people's fears. The story is to "get the bad guy and make him pay for his sins," whether it be a fictional character or a real one. Portraying real villains as monsters contributes to public support of wars and executions. The line between reality and entertainment becomes blurred, and some people can no longer make a distinction.

A somewhat similar distraction from what is real and important is the media's use of and devotion to religion in reporting. We have come to expect people like Pat Robertson to claim that the 9/11 attacks were God's vengeance for America's sexual sins, or that God personally assured him that President Bush will win in a landslide. The scary thing about this is that another substantial percentage of the American public gets their news almost exclusively from such sources.

More frightening is the extent to which mainstream media play the religion card. The mass media did all they could to help Mel Gibson promote his provocative film, *The Passion of the Christ*, making everything about it into "news." It also assisted San Francisco mayor Gavin Newsom in turning thousands of legally questionable gay marriages into a made-for-TV spectacle. And it gave national notoriety to Alabama Judge Moore when he set the altar of the Ten Commandments in a courthouse and defied a federal injunction to remove it. In all these cases, the "religious (read Christian)" view was offered over and over without challenge, as though it is inappropriate to question anything which is based on sincere religious beliefs.

In fact, the media encourage and solicit religious views as news. *Newsweek* asked Howard Dean, whose wife is a Jew, if he accepted Jesus as his savior. Not to be outdone, Dan Rather did his best to turn a Democratic presidential candidate debate into a Sunday school class by demanding that the four participants complete "in terms of your own spirituality, or if you prefer religiosity . . . the sentence, 'This I believe . . .'" And *New York Times* reporter Elisabeth Bumiller closed the debate by asserting that President Bush has claimed that "God is not neutral" in the nation's wars, adding: "He's made quite clear in . . . speeches that he feels God is on America's side." Then she asked each candidate to respond "really quick: Is God on America's side?"[6] The big, important issues that should figure prominently in the campaign were never raised. Apparently even the most respected media representatives are now willing to present faith as more important than facts in choosing our leaders.

2. ATTEMPTS BY THE GOVERNMENT TO CONTROL SOURCES AND OUTPUT OF INFORMATION

> They [the press] don't represent the public any more than other people do. In our democracy, the people who represent the public stood for election.
>
> Andrew Card, Bush's chief of staff

The best way to get the news is from objective sources. And the most
objective sources I have are people on my staff who tell me what's
happening in the world.

President G. W. Bush

Access to information about government actions, the ability to share
that information with others, and the right to protest policies are all
basic to a representative democracy. Open government and open
records and a free and unfettered press are all essential if the citizens
are to participate meaningfully in the government. Yet the Bush
administration has been more effective at throttling the mainstream
news media and managing the message than any administration in
memory. It seems to be "obsessed with secrecy, and is spending billions of our tax dollars in an anti-democratic lockdown to keep public
information from . . . the public."[7]

There are several ways in which this administration is keeping
journalists at bay and managing the news. One is its basic attitude
toward journalists, seeing them not as representatives or servers of the
public, but as lobbyists, pleaders, liars, and protectors of the liberal
interests! So the Bush administration has been especially successful in
stonewalling and throttling the media, keeping the White House team
"on message" and all but abandoning the traditional presidential news
conference. Through February 10, 2004, President Bush had conducted only eleven solo news conferences. Other presidents had far
more by the same point in their first term—when there was much less
to talk about! Eisenhower had 78; Lyndon Johnson, 79; Nixon, 23;
Carter, 53; Reagan, 21; George H. W. Bush, 72; and Bill Clinton, 40.[8]

When he does hold news conferences, Bush is apt to spend much
of the allotted time in giving a prepared and scripted speech, and then
calling on only pre-selected reporters who are told what they can and
cannot ask. His scornful attitude toward journalists has made the traditional media more compliant and enabled the Bushites to ride
roughshod over them. White House correspondents have been reduced
to being stenographers taking dictation from the press office. Only
after the evidence of so many lies and deceptions have the media been
somewhat emboldened and begun to challenge him more aggressively.

Another technique for managing the news is to stifle the flow of information in the name of national security. Using this excuse, crucial government Web sites have been shut down, access to presidential records has been dramatically limited, proper congressional committees have been refused vital information they have requested, information which might redound negatively on administration policy is banned, like the directive that there would be no arrival ceremonies for, or media coverage of the arrival of coffins of deceased military personnel. Similarly, news outlets not liked are snuffed out—especially the views coming from Arab sources, as when the al-Arabiya TV network was raided to stop the broadcast of an audiotape from Saddam Hussein. The Bush administration also shut down the newspaper *al Hawza*, which often criticized US conduct in Iraq, even though it did not print any calls for attacks. Apparently, in spite of Donald Rumsfield's bragging to the Press Club that there is now a free press in Iraq, the press is only free to report what the occupiers accept. It is ironic that, while the US tries to bring democracy to Iraq, it attempts to manage the news and control the press. Shutting down a newspaper that is critical of US policy sends a message of fear that the truthful presentation of facts will not persuade the Iraqi public of what really happened. It is a message of weakness that we do not believe our ideas will prevail. Worst of all, it is a message of inconsistency that for all our talk of freedom we do not really mean it when we are the ones criticized.[9]

In the first Gulf War, daily "briefings" were held showing our smart bombs and the success in killing the enemy we were having. The media were mostly kept out of any other venues, to their great frustration. The media were told other information might be useful to the enemy and couldn't be given out. For the second war in Iraq, a new technique was used—"embedding" reporters with actual military units. The first reports were very positive—the media were actually in the thick of things. But reporters had to stay with their units, even sometimes becoming engaged in the actual fighting. They developed a strong loyalty to the unit, and had to stay with it. Because they couldn't go beyond to look at the whole picture, we got a very narrow view of the war. At the same time, reporters stationed at headquarters were spoon-fed canned information, and "independent" reporters were harassed and discouraged in various ways. The war in Iraq became a cable TV extravaganza, run by "embeds" and armchair generals. The question of why we were in the war was not asked or answered. Yet, as Bill Moyers said, "the greatest moments in the history of the press came not when journalists made common cause with the state but when they stood fearlessly independent of it."

Even before the September 11 terrorist attacks gave them a political excuse, the Bush administration removed more than 33 million public documents from public scrutiny—nearly a 50 percent increase over the previous year. Since 9/11, they "classified" many more documents, stamping as secret things that might prove embarrassing. Attorney General John Ashcroft, with the blessing of the administration, has limited access to information about government actions, restricted the ability to share information with other citizens, and trampled on the right to protest government policies—all rights fundamental to a representative democracy. Peaceful demonstrators have been forced into so-called Free Speech Zones—out of sight and sound of the president and the press covering him. Other less benign techniques are also used to discourage free speech, including arresting, videotaping, harassing, and even beating protestors, and checking on people's reading and Internet records.

Another favorite technique is information through "leaks." The Bush administration is expert at this. Over and over, it has leaked to the media or inserted into speeches intelligence nuggets of questionable value—aluminum tubes, Nigerian uranium, mobile weapon-manufacturing trucks, the undocumented Prague meeting, etc.—and then retreats when pressed, but sees that it gets repeated and kept alive through the friendly press. When the mainstream press finally is able to debunk it, simply replace that leak with a new one. This technique, which depends upon the lack of attention and perseverance and knowledge of the American people, is very successful. It may not be outright lying, but it is deception, and it has the results desired. For example, as we face the 2004 presidential election, the majority of Americans still believe there is a connection between Saddam Hussein and al Qaeda, and that Iraq is still a threat to the US and probably does have weapons of mass destruction. That is because, even as the evidence comes in to the contrary, and even government officials deny them, these ideas continue to be implanted in speeches and "news" reports. The administration is able to do this repeatedly through unfiltered media access, speeches and appearances on talk shows, and "photo-ops." The lengthy effort it takes to discredit these planted ideas is not nearly as accessible to the citizenry.

Finally, when the news becomes embarrassing, the administration uses tactics like creating diversions, or even rewriting history. The president and his staff are experts at "reading" the news, and when it is saying something they don't want to have known, coming up with some other "news" story to overshadow the negative reporting. This has given us things like the brouhaha about gay marriage, flag burning, steroid use in sports, questioning John Kerry's military record, timely terror alerts, and many more. If a new diversion is not available, it is useful to drag out an ongoing one—like Martha Stewart or Kobe Bryant or Michael Jackson's legal difficulties.

More serious, however, is that on both the foreign and domestic fronts, the Bush administration is trying to rewrite history, to explain away its current embarrassments. One way is by making excuses and blaming everyone and everything else. Thus, the budget deficit is in no way the result of Bush's fiscal policies—it is the result of the stock market collapse that began in early 2000, an economy recovering from a recession the present administration inherited, 9/11 and other serious security threats, etc. Similarly the history of the Iraq war is being altered as it unfolds—the reasons for going to war have changed remarkably from those first presented. We are bombarded with misinformation, misremembering and misstatement.

We would like to think that the American people can see through such tactics and that they will backfire. But it is difficult to discern the truth when powerful forces control the media, and most people don't take the trouble, or even have access to alternative trustworthy sources. This leads us to the third problem. All of this allows the administration to play on the public's fears. Terrorism is the topic that underlies much of the media's reporting in one way or another, and terrorism is a valuable tool in setting an agenda which otherwise would be unpalatable to the public.

3. DEREGULATION, MERGERS, AND CORPORATE CONTROL OF THE MEDIA

> If the state has an interest—which it does in preserving democracy, then there has to be a limitation on how deeply the media companies can penetrate every community. To the extent of even having two or three or four outlets in a single community, that kind of information control is not compatible with democracy.
>
> Howard Dean, radio speech

The line that separates truth from fiction has never been easy to draw, and the advent of the Internet, talk radio, and tabloid news has blurred it still further. As mainstream media are increasingly owned by large corporations which pay off or are fed by political parties and candidates, their objectivity becomes less reliable. There are many "alternative" sources, but these, too, are mostly commercial ventures with noticeable agendas and viewpoints. The Internet is touted as an objective source, and perhaps if one were able to access everything on it, the Internet might provide the whole range of views. But remember that all the largest Web sites are also owned by the same giants. In our modern free-enterprise system, media outlets are the best that money can buy.

The result is that much of what is presented on the media is slanted. Any organization can call what it presents "news" and sufficient numbers will accept it as such. The proof, for example, that Fox news is "fair and balanced" is that it says it is. Yet it is more a large propaganda machine. Recently, the National Rifle Association said it would purchase a TV or radio station and declare itself a news organization to be exempted from limits in the McCain-Feingold campaign finance law. This would seem to be outrageous, and illegal, until we remember that Pat Robertson's Christian Broadcasting Network has a "news bureau" and nightly "news report." Ideological spin portrayed as news has no trouble finding listeners, many of whom get all their "news" from one source. There is a conflict of interest between the media and the public interest due to corporate control.

Indeed, it becomes more and more difficult to get news from more than one reliable source. Each year, TV and radio become less local and provide less local news. The number of newspapers declines annually, and the ownership of those that remain becomes more concentrated in the hands of a few large corporations. Eleven companies in this country control 90 percent of what ordinary people are able to read and watch on television. More than a thousand radio stations are owned by the Clear Channel conglomerate.

This concentration means that, across the nation, the programming quality is more predictable and less palatable. Across the nation, a plethora of talk-show hosts can be depended upon to run the gamut from the mushy center to the far right. Only National Public Radio even pretends to be objective, which results in it being labeled "liberal." A couple of new efforts to provide actual liberally slanted programs are having a difficult go of it. And, although there is a cable channel for virtually every niche market, the major networks have a sense of sameness. There is too much penetration by single corporations in media markets all over the country, and too much reliance on one or two sources, like AP, for most of the news. There is a frightening lack of media diversity for the conduct of a democracy.

What we are seeing is the result of deregulation in the US broadcasting system. Formerly the Communication Act required stations to determine the local community's needs and interests and target programming to meet them. Now stations are allowed to provide programs that meet the economic and ideological needs of the owners, resulting in news bias and distortions. The FCC also used to require stations to provide equal time—even free time—to air all sides of public issues of importance. Now a small group of companies can control all the sources of news and information coming into a given community.

Ronald Reagan began deregulation in 1980, and for two decades power steadily moved to the owners at the expense of the public. In 2004, FCC chairman Michael Powell, son of Secretary of State Colin Powell, proposed to further loosen restrictions. In June of 2003 the FCC ruled that a single company could increase its ownership of TV stations covering US households from 35 to 45 percent. So far, it has not gone into effect because a bipartisan group of senators twice pushed through a vote to roll back the FCC's new rules. The House leadership has suppressed a vote, fearing it would embarrass President Bush, who supports the new rules.

The lopsidedness of coverage might be solved by starting new stations providing different views, but there are a very limited number of frequencies available, and they will probably go to the highest bidder—who will be one of the giants. In June 2004, a federal appeals court rejected the FCC rules. The issue is not likely to go away, however. Look for new attempts to consolidate media outlets.

This causes great concern that a very few, or even just one or two, huge corporations could control both the production and dissemination of most of our news and entertainment. While this seems both scary and improbable, consider that the media giant known as Viacom-CBS-MTV controlled both content and communication of the Super Bowl. The other five big corporations that control the media are 1) Murdoch-FoxTV-HarperCollins-*Weekly Standard-New York Post-London Times*-DirecTV; 2) GE-NBC-Universal-Vivendi; 3) Time-Warner-AOL-CNN; 4) Disney-ABC-ESPN; and 5) the biggest cable company, Comcast.[8,10] And Comcast has bid to take over Disney. If the $50 billion deal is successful, the six giants would shrink to five, with Disney Comcast becoming the biggest. Rupert Murdoch would not stand for being number two, so he would take over a competitor, perhaps the CNN-AOL Time Warner group, making him the biggest again. Meanwhile, cash-rich Microsoft, which already owns 7 percent of Comcast and is a partner of GE's MSNBC, would swallow both Disney-ABC and GE-NBC. Then there would be three, on the way to one.

Given the current climate of merger mania and the personnel involved who apparently never see a merger they don't like, this is not unrealistic. And it is not just media outlets. In Philadelphia, Comcast owns the hometown basketball team, its stadium, and the cable sports channel televising the games as well as the line that brings the signal into Philadelphians' houses. This attempt at absolute top-to-bottom information and entertainment control is called "vertical integration," and it contributes to the fuzziness of the lines between news and entertainment. The media giants are getting fewer as they get bigger, and even alternatives like the World Wide Web are also part of their mediaopoly. Soon they may be able to dominate, if not completely control, what we see and hear and write and say. As technology changes and corporate power grows, how do we protect the competition that keeps us free and different, independent and a democracy?

As the mega-mergers continue, the media giants blithely reassure the public that they are committed to making sure there is still local news coverage. What they don't say is that without competition, all news can be presented with a certain agenda and slant. That the media can influence opinion by the way they present supposedly objective "news" is shown dramatically by several recent studies. The findings reveal a disturbing gap between the facts and the public's beliefs.

One comprehensive study involving seven different polls by the Center on International Policy Attitudes and the Center for International and Security Studies at the University of Maryland asked whether average Americans are "misperceiving" information about Iraq and the war. The answer was yes.

> A substantial portion of the public had a number of misperceptions that were demonstrably false, or were at odds with the dominant view in the intelligence community . . . (which) have played a key role in generating and maintaining approval for the decision to go to war.[11]

Early in 2003, for example, 68 percent believed that Iraq played an important part in the terrorist attack on the World Trade Center, and 13 percent claimed they had seen "conclusive evidence" of such involvement. By August a *Washington Post* poll reported that 69 percent of Americans still believed that Saddam Hussein was "personally involved" in the attack. And as late as September, approximately half of respondents said the US had actually found evidence that Saddam was working closely with al Qaeda, and 35 percent believed that weapons of mass destruction had been found in Iraq; 22 percent believed Iraq used such weapons during the war! Finally, the researchers asked, "How do all the people in the world feel about the US going to war with Iraq?" Thirty-one percent expressed the mistaken view that attitudes overseas were evenly divided on the issue, and another 31 percent believed that a majority of people in the rest of the world favored US action.

One would wonder how the American public could be so mistaken about such important issues. The answer is that their misperceptions are closely related to their news sources. When asked where they get most of their news, 19 percent said newspapers and 80 percent said radio and TV. The primary source of radio and TV news was two or more networks, 30 percent; Fox, 18 percent; CNN, 16 percent; ABC, 11 percent; CBS, 9 percent; PBS-NPR, 3 percent. The degree of misperception is related to the source of news. Those who receive most of their news from Fox were most apt to have misperceptions; those who receive most of their news from PBS-NPR were least likely to. It has become patently obvious that Fox News Channel's host Bill O'Reilly is most of all a Bush apologist.[12]

Actually, Fox news watchers were three times as likely to believe the Saddam–al Qaeda connection, the existence and use of WMDs and the world supporting US action in Iraq than those watching the next most watched network. In the PBS-NPR audience, an overwhelming majority held none of these misperceptions. In all three issues, the misperception percentages decreased when moving from Fox to CBS to NBC to CNN to ABC, to print media, to PBS-NPR. Even PBS-NPR's relative accuracy and objectivity is eroding. Although the Corporation for Public Broadcasting was set up to distribute federal dollars to public radio and TV and shield public programming from political influence, it is under attack. One way is by decreasing funding. More serious, however, is that President Bush has been packing the CPB board with Republican ideologues—his two latest being major GOP donors and activists—and the CPB agenda is now tilting to the right.

The study concluded that citizens are significantly affected by the news media, that the media are fostering a considerable amount of misperceptions about issues of great public importance, and that these misperceptions tend to follow the ideological lines of the media sources they use. The connection between the public's misperceptions and the administration's support of further media deregulation and the interests of the broadcasting industry is an unholy alliance. The problem would be serious enough if we were talking about an ordinary industry, but we are dealing with information—the lifeblood of how citizens form and exchange opinions which provide the basis for how they vote. Democracy cannot survive for long if the citizenry, with state approval, is systematically misinformed.[13]

Adding to the problem is evidence, confirmed by a recent Pew survey, that people are increasingly picking their media on the basis of partisanship. This causes the media to increasingly cater to their customers' (partisan) tastes. News slowly becomes even more selective and slanted. This sorting of audiences by politics poses dangers for both the media and the country.

> All news organizations must satisfy their audiences. If they don't, they go out of business. If liberals and conservatives migrate to rival media camps, both camps may ultimately submit to the same narrow logic: like-minded editors and reporters increasingly feed like-minded customers stories that reinforce their world view. Economic interests and editorial biases will converge . . . ideals of fairness and objectivity will silently erode.[14]

4. MEDIA AS BUSINESS

> [T]he vast majority of Americans will not watch or read news, unless it's local news, sports or gossip. Anyone who thinks otherwise will go broke trying. . . . In peacetime the functions of mass media are advertising, entertainment and inculcating the norms and opinions that a nation, terrified of disunity, wants in its people.
>
> Christiane Amanpour

There was a time when the American public could, for the most part, assume that the "news" was just that—an objective reporting of facts. Commentary on those facts was reserved for the editorial page, and was labeled as opinion, analysis, or interpretation. This is no longer the case. As CNN journalist Christiane Amanpour said:

> A minority of Americans, doubtless influenced by too much study of eighteenth-century political philosophy, believe in a press whose responsibilities do not include helping the government to win a war. These are the people who talk of objectivity, telling it like it is, etc. Such opinions would have long since been relegated to Unitarian Church seminars were it not for the news industry using these slogans as the basis of a never-ceasing advertising campaign for itself, one similar to automobile advertisements in being a mishmash of truths, lies, and in-betweenies.
>
> If people believe that the media are supposed to be free, nonpartisan, fearless, objective and independent, it is in no small mea-

sure because the industry never stops telling the populace that is what they are. The mass media's description of the role they play is a haphazard reflection of the actualities.[15]

In today's capitalistic society, where profits are king, journalism has lost any claim to objectivity, or even responsibility. Journalistic integrity has disappeared in the quest for circulation, ratings, and higher profits. One result is that most American mass media most of the time contains little or no foreign news, except as it affects the United States. All but a couple of hundred of the nation's thousands of radio stations broadcast no news at all, literally not a word. In peacetime, television stations and newspapers, with perhaps twenty-five exceptions, skip coverage of events abroad. Partly this is due to the conservatism of the few corporations that own virtually all of the mass media. But mostly it is because their market analysis shows that most Americans are not interested in what is happening outside their own lives, communities, or country. There is a negative correlation between the amount of international news and the ratings.

Since all media outlets receive the same ratings results, they all aim their programming to the same audience. This is why so much of what we see and hear looks and sounds the same. It basically is. It is what pays the best. So most guests on the morning "news" shows and the late-night talk shows are actors and musicians plugging their latest releases. Some are writers for mass-market magazines. NBC's "Today Show" broadcasts stories that first appeared in *People* magazine. At some affiliates, it is possible to buy interview time. In Tampa, Florida, the NBC affiliate has a show that follows the *Today Show* which will allow almost anyone hawking almost anything to be interviewed for four to six minutes in a journalistic-like format. The station claims this is OK because it is the entertainment division rather than the news division that produces the show. But the "News Channel 8" logo remains at the bottom of the screen.[16]

A frightening example was the broadcast by NBC of a version of the ever-popular "reality" and "survivor" shows, in which five families competed, on air, for the right to adopt the child of a sixteen-year-old girl. The mother, along with Barbara Walters, interviewed the candidates and during the hour decided who got the prize. This was on

20/20, which is still advertised as a news program, although it has long since morphed into entertainment. One has to wonder—if a respected journalist like Walters can engage in such a farce, who in the industry can be trusted to present truth?

Newspapers are hardly better. Many now accept ads—sometimes full-pagers—that are formatted to look like news articles but are really propaganda. For example, a new religious right group, Save America Now, ran full-page ads in the *New York Times*, the *Washington Post*, *USA Today*, the *Chicago Tribune*, the *Boston Globe*, the *Seattle Times*, the *San Francisco Chronicle* and several other publications. The ads, headlined, "America is in Trouble," assert that the nation faces dire consequences because of efforts to remove the Ten Commandments from courthouses, the failure of public schools to inculcate Christianity and activity by gay-rights groups. The ads looked like news, and the small print identifying it as an advertisement was barely noticeable.[17] Many Americans, who believe what they want to hear, accepted it as fact, and the ads have been referenced in other articles and "news" stories which claim the information was "reported" in such-and-such newspaper. Again, when supposedly respectable and responsible news venues become involved in such questionable practices, who can be trusted?

The American audience is fickle. They think their own feelings should matter and be reflected in the media. The media are also fickle. They want to be liked, and they want to make money. So they react to the ratings and the writing and the ranting of the public and give the public what it wants. To do otherwise in today's market is foolhardy, because if you don't keep your audience and your profitability, you lose your voice. Reporters are also scared—if they go too far in exposing some unpopular truth, they might lose their jobs, or at least their "access" and privileges. If they ask the hard questions, they are apt to get "cut off" by either the networks or the government. To a good reporter, access is everything, so caution becomes necessary. The result is the lack of skeptical journalism.

Ironically, it is when we are most vulnerable, when we most need journalistic integrity, that it becomes most problematic. In time of war and love of Bush, anyone who questioned the government's wisdom was attacked. When investigative journalism did raise some basic questions, it was labeled "liberal" and its ratings went down. Listeners switched to the sources that were biased their way. In the wake of 9/11, journalistic skepticism went out of fashion. Even during the campaign of lies leading up to the Iraq war, reporters routinely praised Bush's "steely resolve" and kingly bearing.

(These attributes were still being touted by the media in coverage leading up to the 2004 presidential election!)

Only when some of the propaganda became apparent did the nation's allegedly liberal press begin to fact-check and report inconsistencies. Until then, according to Michael Massing, former editor of the *Columbia Journalism Review*, some of the truest believers in Iraq's WMDs were the editors and reporters of the *New York Times*, the *Washington Post*, and other beacons of the establishment press. Only the newspapers of the Knight-Ridder chain appear to have been properly skeptical of what one analyst called the Bush administration's "faith-based intelligence."[18] The rest mostly ignored or buried what reporters and editors ought to have known. Some journalists admit muzzling themselves to protect their own careers.

Every year, various independent or academic groups identify stories which should have been reported, which would have been very important, which were ignored by the mainstream press. Some of them, had they been put into the American public's knowledge bank, might have made significant differences or impacts on how things evolved. For example, Sonoma University, under a program called "Project Censored," compiles a list of the twenty-five most important, yet underplayed, news stories. Number one for this year was the Project for a New American Century. This was a think tank that years ago drew up the blueprint for the "pre-emptive" war launched against Iraq. The group was funded by neoconservatives who envisioned extending America's military power around the globe, and who saw an invasion of oil-rich Iraq as the most obvious first step. Key players were Dick Cheney, Donald Rumsfeld, and Paul Wolfowitz. Though it wanted to invade Iraq, the group acknowledged in a 2000 report that the idea would be a hard sell without a catastrophe, "a new Pearl Harbor." That event came on September 11, 2001. The other twenty-four are equally sobering, including titles like: "Homeland Security Threatens Civil Liberty," "US Illegally Removes Pages from Iraq UN Report," "The Pentagon's Plan to Provoke Terrorists," "The Effort to Make Unions Disappear," etc.[19] Where was the investigative press when we most needed it?

The answer, unfortunately, is that the media, being owned by giant corporations which are involved in many areas, are no longer free to tell the truth. The American ideal of a free press has gone. It is now press for pay—the bigger the payoff, the bigger the story, whether it has much to do with reality or affects people's lives or not. The media are in bed with the moneymakers, and the public is being whored. Incest is running rampant—between the government, the media, the corporations, the military and the public. We are all in this together. Democracy is at stake.

REFERENCES

1. Christiane Amanpour, "Playing Piano in the war whorehouse," *Index*, Nov. 10, 2003.

2. Walter Brasch, "Dissolving Journalistic Integrity: Entertainment and Profits in America," *Liberal Opinion Week*, Dec. 22, 2003.

3. Lou Dobbs, "All the news that's fit," *US News and World Report*, Feb. 23, 2004.

4. Richard Reeves, "Comedy is King—Or Kingmaker," *Liberal Opinion Week*, March 29, 2004.

5. Amanpour, "Playing Piano in the war whorehouse."

6. Gene Lyons, "Will God Pick Our Next President?" *Liberal Opinion Week*, March 29, 2004.

7. Jim Hightower, *Liberal Opinion Week*, March 1, 2004.

8. David Shaw, "Administration Is Adept at Keeping Journalists at Bay," *Los Angeles Times*, February 18, 2004.

9. Floyd Abrams, "Democracy Means a Free Press—Even in Iraq," *Liberal Opinion Week*, May 3, 2004.

10. William Safire, *New York Times*, Feb. 17, 2004.

11. William F. Fore, "Truth, Lies and the Media," *Christian Century*, Nov. 29, 2003.

12. Peter Hart, "Fox's O'Reilly—A Bush Apologist," in *Liberal Opinion Week*, March 22, 2004.

13. Fore, "Truth, Lies, and the Media."

14. Robert J. Samuelson, "Picking Sides for the News," *Newsweek*, June 28, 2004.

15. Amanpour, "Playing Piano in the war whorehouse."

16. Brasch, "Dissolving Journalistic Integrity: Entertainment and Profits in America."

17. *Church and State*, March 2004.

18. Gene Lyons, "Welcome the Return of Skeptical Journalism," *Liberal Opinion Week*, Feb. 23, 2004.

19. Peter Phillips, "The Most Censored News Stories of 2003," *Liberal Opinion Week*, October 27, 2003.

4.

The Dangers and Promises of Democracy

Michael Werner

D emocracy as both an institution and an ideal has been pummeled by historic forces in recent years and its future is predicted on one hand as an historic inevitability and on the other as a broken, dangerous and idealistic naïveté. Recently the renewed interest in the meaning and future of democracy has spawned much intellectual debate after a lull in the subject in the second half of the twentieth century.

The minimal definition of democracy is "having free, fair, meaningful and competitive elections."[1] But Tocqueville wisely perceived that liberal democracy is far richer than the theory that's used to justify it.[2] The richness extends into the foundations of Humanism, the whole debate around the various concepts of freedom and the ideal of the ethical society. One of the perennial debates that has been around since the Greeks has to do with whether trust in governance can be placed in the uneducated and easily manipulated masses or should reside in some sort of educated mericratic elites. Plato saw a philosopher king in charge, and even our founding fathers clearly wanted a republic of elected elite officials. The debate over egalitarian versus elitist control continues in unspoken ways today as we will see later.

Colonialism in the eighteenth and nineteenth centuries gained much of its moral credibility based on the idea that some societies were too primitive and did not possess the required cultural base in liberty, human rights, law and civilized behavior to make democracy work. These societies, it was argued, should be brought along slowly until democracy and other Enlightenment values were ingrained in their culture. England's one-hundred-year tutoring of India is an example. Even Locke saw value in building the Enlightenment foundations in a culture before casting it into liberal democracy. Also, we have modern examples of this cultural mentoring tactic used in the postwar Japan and our more current attempts in Iraq.

At the beginning of the twentieth century T. H. Green's influence was very formative and brought about a shift in thinking, seeing idealistic virtues at the center for the justification for democracy. He believed that progress and democracy have "constituted largely just in the widening of the number of persons among whom there is conceived to be a common good and between whom there is a common duty."[3] This new idealism of democracy shaped John Dewey's thought and the new burgeoning movement of modern Humanism. His view rejected the notion that democracy was simply the rule of the many. He saw democracy as only one part of an organic society where our ethical ideals are embodied not just in the political outcomes, but the process of empowerment and communication. Democracy is an emergent process of an advanced culture and civilization.

This idealistic view of democracy clashed immediately from birth with the harsh reality of both Fascism and Communism in the thirties. Democracy worldwide was under attack by authoritarian regimes. The experience of prewar Germany led several who escaped the horrors to have their faith shaken in democracy and liberalism in particular. Liberalism had failed to curb or even slow down the onslaught of authoritarian regimes of any stripe. Liberal idealism and reason, tolerance and freedom were proven impotent in the thirties in the face of evil. It was argued that idealism led to ideology, which led to absolute, totalistic thinking, which led to oppression. Leo Straus, Isaiah Berlin, James Luther Adams, the whole Frankfurt School of thought, and later Sidney Hook, Irving Kristol and other intellectuals sought causes for these failures and then worked to reformulate remedies.

Isaiah Berlin saw the liberal project flawed as it placed too much emphasis on idealism and the notion that there were single rational solutions for life's problems. He saw that ideology of any sort was wrong because in fact there were many rational paths and most high values were in deep conflict. Still, we must choose and the "tragedy" of liberalism is to constantly be trading off and compromising our high values with no overarching correct way to decide between them.

James Luther Adams criticized as too tolerant, too relativistic those Humanist Unitarians who lacked the emotional power to combat evil. He saw emotional commitments as crucial and more important than a cold intellectualism. This changed viewpoint signaled the rejection of his former Humanist stance.

Leo Strauss moved more toward a Machiavellian posture, harking back to the ideas of Plato. He led those who followed him to see that the masses of people must be pragmatically controlled by elites who use democracy as both a goal and a manipulative tool. His heirs became the neoconservatives who pushed for war in Iraq.

The Frankfort School of thought that resulted in Postmodernism saw Enlightenment values as a part of the problem. Reason, it is argued, turns back on itself and is used as a rationalization for those seeking power and control. Notions of freedom and democracy are illusions where in fact we are actually socially derived agents of a manipulative culture seeking power and control.

All these thoughts led to a recent spate of articles denouncing democracy in one way or another. Let's look at some of these.

RECENT CRITICISMS OF DEMOCRACY

In many ways most of the new criticisms are reformulations or restatements of the old arguments. Patrick Kennon in his book *The Twilight of Democracy*[4] argues that "those societies that continue to allow themselves to be administered by individuals whose only qualification is that they were able to win a popularity contest will go from failure to failure and eventually from the scene." He argues that democracy as practiced is an illusion from the idealization as people fight to have it, but once they do have it they stop voting. History shows that voting worldwide drops off once countries achieve it. Then, as Noam

Chomsky says, power and money elites can "manufacture consent." We get the best government that money can buy. Kennon argues that the world is too complex now, that it requires specialized technocrats, and that democracy must wither. Kennon argues this side while Francis Fukuyama argues just the opposite—that democracy is a historic inevitability.

Amy Chua argues that democracy leads to violence as markets concentrate power in so few hands that eventually an embittered and vengeful majority has enough and disposes of the sham democratic process.[5] Generally ethnic violence ensues.

Some have argued that the modern state is coming to an end. The European Union in particular is seen as moving toward a democratic non-state where there is governance without government, and where bureaucrats run the affairs of government in diffuse relationships. Mark Plattner sees this as dangerous in that "for democracy to work, there must be an overarching political order to which people feel they owe their primary political loyalty. In short, a state with clear boundaries and clear distinctions as to who does or does not enjoy the rights and obligations of citizenship."[6]

One of the more important critics is the respected Fareed Zakaria, who says that "Democracy has its dark side." He sees many governments who have democracy flourishing, but not liberty. Where in the West, "Capitalism and the rule of law [came] first, and then democracy," and this is the ideal pattern, in many other countries (in Africa, for instance) people had liberty first with no rule of law—and both democracy and freedom were lost due to instability, chaos, lawlessness and corruption. As Mr. Zakaria says, "What Africa needs more than democracy is good governance." Last, he finds the war against elitism a very dangerous affair because "we then produce a hidden elite that is unaccountable and unresponsive to the public interest."[7]

Andrew J. Bacevich fears that many of today's leaders say and actually believe that they are acting toward building democracy in the world, but in fact their motivations may be more attributable towards an agenda of global hegemony.[8] This imperial overstretch is actually undermining many democratic governments—especially the United States. The neoconservatives of the present era are prime exponents of such a policy.

Judge Richard Posner, the legal jurist, in his book *Law, Pragmatism and the Democracy*, argues for pragmatism over idealism and democracy.[9] He finds looking at the pragmatic consequences of decisions is more important than adhering to an idealistic goal of democratic perfections that is unattainable in any event. This is one reason that we have representative democracy. This is also why the law and principles should be bent and controlled by responsive elites. The over-idealization of democracy by Dewey is a stumbling block for effective government. Again we hear echoes of Plato.

I don't intend in this paper to critique these specific positions, but let me say that while there is much that is wrong in their arguments, there is also a persistent ring of truth in much of what they say. Their arguments must not be easily dismissed. What is certain, it seems, is that there is enough evidence at this point to say that the Deweyan legacy of viewing democracy as a high and maybe highest social value has been severely undermined. I have read articles on Humanism that have stated that democracy is the first foundation for Humanism. I am quite certain at this point that this is a misguided faith.

If we look at the simplest definition of democracy as the open election process for government, it certainly appears that power of mass media has changed our faith in "free choice." Money is the universal oil seeping into all the nooks and crannies of government and the election process. Mass media now have the ability to manipulate images and words with armies of "spin doctors" whose powers of persuasion change the nature of the election game.

On the level that Dewey proposes, where democracy is not just a process for electing officials but a furthering of the civil society and an ethical process that engages all of us in the common welfare, we have seen the corruption of that ideal, the backfiring from unintended consequences. The practical historical reality that does not jell with the vision of the ideal. Voter apathy is a reality that has punctured much of the bubble of communication-building idealism. Let's now look at some responses that offer a positive outlook for democracy.

LARRY DIAMOND AND
AMARTYA SEN'S POSITIVE RESPONSE

Larry Diamond takes the critiques seriously but challenges much of the scientific data and assumptions.[10] He argues that optimism for democracy stems from these facts:

- The preponderance of power is held by liberal democracies.
- The majority of states, 121 out of 193, are liberal democracies.
- There is broad normative appeal for democracy.
- The historical trends are toward recognition of democracy as a basic human right.
- Sovereignty of states has given way to freedom and democracy.

He takes on the argument that developing countries cannot be democratic by pointing out the example of Mali, a poor, illiterate, Muslim country where the life expectancy is forty-four years old. Benin, Mali, Malawi, Mozambique, and Nepal, despite their third world status, have established resilient democracies. The argument that some countries are too poor, too illiterate, too religious, too backward for democracy does not hold up in the light of these increasing global examples. He contends that an electoral process, the rule of law with an independent judicial system, civil liberties of freedom of belief, speech, religion, association, etc., must be in place before liberal democracy can be established—and that this may mean the rule of law should be emphasized rather than democracy. Still, this will remain only a transitional strategy since authoritarian regimes have a way of establishing themselves.

But, the historical path is clear. Even in South America we now see that thirty of thirty-three countries are democratic. Only in the Arab countries has democracy not taken hold.

The "clash of civilizations" expounded by Samuel Huntington sees the Arab Islamic culture as intrinsically opposed to liberal democracy. This is true in many respects, but the Afrobarometer survey indicates that "Muslims are as supportive of democracy as non-Muslims." There may be a latent desire for democracy in Arab countries that is masked by totalitarian rulers intent on retaining their power using religious and tribal prejudice.

Amartya Sen has been most eloquent in the defense of democracy.[11] He argues that the world now sees democracy as a universal value—and this is the most important thing to come out of the twentieth century. People anywhere can see it as valuable. Democracy has three virtues in its favor. One, democracy offers political freedom which is of intrinsic value in the lives of people. Two, democracy has, in support of Dewey, instrumental value in that it engages people in political communication. Third, democracy has constructive purpose in that it helps us learn from one another and encourages progress.

The argument for democracy being a universal value is a powerful one. It challenges the notion of democracy being just a Western idea that is not applicable in Eastern and more primitive cultures. Democracy does have crosscultural value and utility, and that is its incredible power as a historical force.

In summary, democracy is one of those cultural institutions that has been relatively uncritically accepted in the West until recently. Some of the critiques have been old ones, such as the Platonic elitist one of the egalitarian model, and some have been substantially new, such as the one that democracy causes national strife. More importantly for humanists, we have seen a questioning of some of the core foundations of humanism as embodied in liberal democracy.

One way I view this problem of the idealistic notion of democracy and the practical needs of good governance is to see it in ethical terms of the classic battle of the good and the right. The high principle of democracy has been almost deified in some cases as the highest principle. One naturalistic theologian, Neil Shadle, sees democracy as a full and complete theology. As usual, our greatest loves seem to betray us since we are blind to our love's flaws. In this case the principle of democracy, the "right," is in historical conflict with what may be more elitist governance aiming at the "good." Several African countries have spilt much blood after the end of colonialization when the parent countries threw them into democratic rule without the benefit of civil liberties and the rule of law having been already established. The debate and conflict over elitist vs. egalitarian rule will continue as do most ethical and practical dilemmas; there is no "right" answer, and in this case having the opposing viewpoints in a healthy dynamic serves as a kind of check and balance. The danger comes when either the pragmatic or the principled point of view is served up as the only and best way. Even within Richard Posner's spirited defense of pragmatic rule is an undercurrent of principled behavior. Even in the principled idealism of Dewey we hear his pragmatic strain urging us to do what is best in the end. It seems to me we should always strive for the ideal of an inclusive democracy and push it as far as we can, but realize that sometimes the ideal does not work to the good and we must do the pragmatic thing. Our founding fathers knew this when they set up a balanced government with limited democracy in the form of a republic.

To me, any linking the foundations of humanism with democracy is based on a misunderstanding. Humanism indeed has a moral foundation of seeing each person as having inherent worth and dignity. This is a prescriptive injunction though, not a descriptive one. Treating each person as valued is different than saying each person is the same in ability. Our civil liberties, our morality, our daily interactions are based on this prescriptive egalitarianism because it works, not because it is true. Democracy is only a tool as well, not some metaphysical reality. We use it because it works as the best tool for organizing society. Most of the time it works but sometimes it doesn't. The romantic appeal and the general pragmatic appeal for democracy still does not erase the fact that sometimes it is not the right system for governance at a specific time and place—and a slavish adherence in the face of other cultural problems can lead to great harm. Sometimes, as in 1930s Germany, Nigeria today, and some would say even the USA today, we see examples where democracy was/is deadly wrong. The democratic principle may need to be compromised and other pragmatic solutions may need to be employed as democracy fails at times, and badly. Of course, most of us would say that despite the problems with democracy, we have to stick through the tough times because like science, it is ultimately self-correcting. Even African nations, it is argued, will learn through their mistakes, and will eventually correct themselves. While I agree this is probably true, it is still a matter of faith. And the reality is that many people can die in the process. Forty million died in World War II as a result of decisions made in the thirties by the majority of people. The mass of people were wrong then yet history seems to place much of the blame on one man.

The dangers for democracy are very real today. Control of the mass media by the rich and powerful is increasing. So is voter apathy, worldwide. The diffusing and destroying of state identities in Europe and elsewhere is increasingly leading to an unresponsive, unaccountable, bureaucratic government. Anarchy is a real possibility in case of major disasters or social breakdown. The desire for more effective, elitist-led government always will challenge elective democracy. Still, it seems to me we need to always push the borders for where democracy can be used. Many countries heretofore thought to be unprepared for democracy have shown that ability—resoundingly so. We need to hold democracy as both a very high pragmatic tool and as a high ethical principle for which we stand ready to make compromise. Still, it is not an infallible tool and we must be ready to bend democracy towards pragmatic effectiveness. But only when not doing so jeopardizes society in very significant ways.

Humanism still stands as a philosophy of life devoted to enhancing the welfare of all and to mitigating suffering. Democracy has been one of our greatest tools both for effective governance and toward building that more humane society. Democracy's future is not entirely certain, nor will it be without occasional accommodations. How democracy will play out in the end may parallel the future for any humanism.

NOTES

1. Larry Diamond, "Universal Democracy," *Policy Review*, June 3, 2003.
2. Mahoney, "Review of Skepticism and Freedom: A Modern Case for Classical Liberalism," *First Things* 139 (January 2004).
3. Robert Westbrook, *Dewey and American Democracy* (Ithaca, NY: Cornell University Press, 1991).
4. Patrick E. Kennon, *The Twilight of Democracy* (New York: Doubleday Books, 1995).
5. Amy Chua, "Vengeful Majorities," *New Prospect Magazine,* December 2003.

6. Mark Plattner, "Sovereignty and Democracy," *Policy Review* December 2003.

7. Fareed Zakaria, *The Future of Freedom* (New York: W. W. Norton, 2003).

8. Andrew Bacevich, *World on Fire: How Exporting Free Market Democracy Breeds Ethnic Hatred and Global Instability* (New York: Doubleday, 2003).

9. Richard A. Posner, *Law, Pragmatism and Democracy* (Cambridge, MA: Harvard University Press, 2003).

10. Diamond, "Universal Democracy."

11. Amartya Sen, "Democracy as a Human Value," *Journal of Democracy* 10.3 (University Press, 1999), 3–17.

5.

The Problems with
American Democracy

Vern L. Bullough

N early forty years ago, when I was disillusioned with the seeming inability of the government to act on what I regarded as significant issues, I wrote an article arguing that our Constitution set up a government that was more or less designed to fail. It established three different units—the executive, the legislative, and the judicial—and only if all three agreed could anything be accomplished. I held that a parliamentary system, such as that in the UK as well as most of the rest of the democratic world, would be far more effective. I still think so, but recognizing the near impossibility of such a radical change, the problem is how to make what we have work effectively. The problem in doing so is recognizing that our founding fathers for the most part were suspicious of both strong central government and popular democracy. This has often handicapped us severely because the history of American government, at least over the last hundred years, has been the growth in power of the central government and of popular democracy without its citizens really thinking about what effect this would have on our ability to govern ourselves. I think a strong central government dedicated to the enforcement of civil liberties and civil rights is all-important in charting our future. Let me explain.

SOME GENERALIZATIONS

It must be remembered that there were disagreements among the founding fathers. We originally started with a confederacy which proved so ineffective it was replaced by a new "federal government" after the ratification of the Constitution. Before ratification many of the key issues were discussed in the *Federalist Papers,* written by Alexander Hamilton, James Madison, and John Jay. The essays are still regarded as a major contribution to political theory, and the disagreements expressed in them still remain important. In the papers, Hamilton (Jay fell ill and contributed only five of the essays) emphasized the importance of an energetic federal government, while Madison emphasized the need for restraints on the federal government and the importance of the division of powers with the states and the checks and balances of the tripartite government. In Madison's mind the federal government was only to deal with truly national issues such as war and foreign policy. Most issues were to be left to the states. I should add that many of Hamilton's ideas were ones I could not subscribe to, although I agree with the importance of a strong central government. The debate in various forms has continued over the course of American history. It seems clear, at least in retrospect, that a major concern of those emphasizing state power over federal was the fear of the Southern slaveholding states that a strong national government would intervene in their right to hold slaves. To avoid this potential threat, the Southern states as a group effectively, for much of early American history, opposed any federal attempt to regulate interstate commerce or to construct roads or establish a national bank or other elements of a national economic structure. In fact, John Adams was the one and only federalist president, after which the Federalist Party itself went into decline. With the election of Jefferson in 1800 the antifederalists gained control of the government and held it until the Civil War, although certainly John Quincy Adams tried to strengthen the federal government. Intellectually this struggle over the nature of the government has often been described as a struggle between the Jeffersonian interpretations of the constitution versus the Hamiltonians. While Jefferson and the anti-federalists dominated the federal government until the outbreak of the Civil War, it has become increasingly clear in our own time that the dominant voice has been that of Hamilton. These different views of government were not always absolute since, even in the time of Jefferson, taking national actions did not necessarily pose a threat to states' rights. In fact, Jefferson, through his mounting of the Lewis and Clark expedition and his purchase of the Louisiana territory from France, extended the influence of the federal government immeasurably, but it was not until the question of whether the states in the new territories would be free or slave that the South awakened to the potential dangers such an acquisition had. The first major defeat of the anti-federalists was the Civil War. The Southern slaveholding states felt that Lincoln and the Republicans would challenge their right to control slavery, let alone expand it. Though Lincoln tried to assure them this was not the case, they turned to secession. Their right to secede was, at the base, justified by the belief that the rights of the states was threatened by the federal government. Following the Northern victory and the emancipation of slaves, there was an attempt to extend federal governance in the South to see that the anti-slavery laws were enforced, requiring the states to drop slavery and emancipating the slaves, but by 1876, the federal government removed itself from the South. Though slavery was no longer legal, in many ways much of the South continued to do what it had done before the war through strict segregation and severe economic discrimination of African Americans, segregation which was often enforced by terroristic activity. Even when states violated federal policy, as the Southern states did, the federal government was reluctant to intervene. A major reason for not interfering was the power of the Southern legislators, who mostly were Democrats. The Southern Democrats, who were mostly rural, allied with the Northern Democrats in the larger cities, and it was through this odd alliance that the Democrats finally gained political power.

It must also be remembered that the founding fathers were fearful of popular democracy and deliberately called their creation a Republic, following Rome, and not a democracy, following Athens. Athenian failures, then interpreted as due to popular demagogues, had given democracy a bad name for centuries and the term only became rehabilitated in the twentieth century. In fact, Alexis de Tocqueville, offered the Constitution of the United States as an example of how the excesses of majority rule could be tempered. The founding fathers, for example, stipulated that on the national level those eligible to vote could vote only for their congressman but not for the senators, the president, and the federal judges, including those of the Supreme Court. Senators were elected by the legislatures of the state, the federal judges were appointed by the president, and the president was chosen by the electoral college. Only with the Seventeenth Amendment in 1913 were senators directly elected by their constituents.

Who could vote in elections was also mainly left to the state, although slaves could not vote nor, except for a brief time in New Jersey, could women. There was, however, no constitutional prohibition against women having the vote, and in the last part of the nineteenth century several states allowed them to do so. Voters had to be twenty-one, but a state could and often did put all kinds of economic and other conditions on voters, including property ownership or a poll tax or literacy. Only gradually did the barriers fall. The Fifteenth Amendment (1870) gave the right of all "citizens" to vote, regardless of race, color, or previous conditions of servitude, but again left the power to regulate this to Congress, which after 1876 more or less ignored the enforcement. The Wyoming and Utah territories were the first to allow women to vote in 1869 and 1870, respectively. In fact, so engrained was the concept of state rights that the suffrage movement, rather than mounting a national campaign, concentrated their energy on individual states giving women the right to vote. By 1912, however, only ten states had done so, all in the West. It was only after the defeat of suffrage in 1915 by the four large northern and eastern states of New Jersey, New York, Pennsylvania, and Massachusetts that the suffragists adopted as their national policy the need for a constitutional amendment. The result of this switch in strategy was comparatively rapid passage of the Nineteenth Amendment in 1920. The hesitation of the suffragists to do so earlier emphasized the importance given to state rights even by the reformers. Poll taxes and most other restrictions were not eliminated until the 1960s and 1970s, again mostly by federal action.

It is also important to note that during much of the nineteenth century, Washington, DC, while the capitol, was a sleepy town and not considered a particularly desirable place to live. In the beginning, Congressional seasons were so short the federal legislators rarely lived there. Most congressmen and senators lived in boarding houses when Congress was in session and returned home as soon as they could. This meant, however, that there were opportunities for considerable inter-action among elected officials and the voters, much more than is pos-sible on the federal level today. There was also an effort to make sure that Congress was representative of the population since the Constitu-tion stipulated that Congress be reapportioned every ten years fol-lowing a national census. Reapportionment itself was left to the states, which found arbitrary and unique ways of reapportioning. The term *Gerrymander* was coined in 1812 to describe the salamander-like characteristics of a Massachusetts redistricting. Although the size of the membership in the Congress has increased from low two-digit fig-ures in the early nineteenth century to hundreds over the years, the number of constituents grew also. Members of Congress today repre-sent much larger populations and have ten or more times the number of constituents as they did in the nineteenth century. This results in the members of Congress having far less direct contact with the people than they did in the past. The power of an individual member of Con-gress is also largely dependent by the Congressional practice of seniority for committee and other assignments, which meant that those states which could redistrict to favor incumbents had the most power. In practice, this gave the South a disproportionate influence in com-mittees and decisions since there was less turnover in Southern mem-bers of the House of Representatives.

One reason Washington, DC, did not exercise much influence in the nineteenth century is that the central government had very limited power. It was in charge of foreign policy, mail delivery, coining money, col-lecting tariffs, taking a census every ten years, organizing the defense of the country, controlling the Indians, admitting emigrants, patrolling the borders, admitting new states and administering or disposing of vast quantities of land which had not yet been settled. Indian policy was also set by the federal government. Still, states had their own militia and the number of federal troops was limited. Probably most people had little contact outside of mail delivery with the federal government. It was gov-ernment for the most part as Thomas Jefferson had envisioned it.

There were, moreover, some unsavory compromises in the Constitution in favor of states' rights. Southern states got a disproportionately large vote since the slaves were counted as three-fifths of a person in the population but could not vote. It was no accident that most of our early presidents were from the South. Even in 1828, when Andrew Jackson was elected over John Quincy Adams, had not the non-voting slaves been counted under the three-fifths rule, Adams, not Jackson, would have been president. The result was that the rural South got a disproportionate share of government appointments and was the most obstinate in extension of federal power. Even after Reconstruction ended in 1876, the South, in terms of actual voters, remained disproportionately small since so many blacks were discouraged from voting, and it had the most barriers to voting, such as poll taxes, of any other groups of states.

The greatest growth in federal power came during the Civil War when the government was forced to develop federal power to conduct a large-scale military conflict. Though efforts to expand the powers of the federal government in the post–Civil War period were often thwarted by the courts, government was forced to change, if only because the United States itself was rapidly changing. For example, the nature of the population was changed by the vast numbers of immigrants flocking to the United States in the last part of the nineteenth century, large numbers of whom settled in the expanding northern cities. Before the Civil War, Americans had been overwhelmingly rural, primarily descendants of English-speaking peoples. This became less and less true as the century progressed. The Industrial Revolution taking place in the last half of the nineteenth century also encouraged the growth of cities, further challenging traditional ways. Industry based on the rich coal and iron resources (and later oil) expanded and millionaires spouted up all over the country. Since the new commercial and industrial enterprises did business across the borders of various states, it became increasingly clear that the federal government had to intervene. The first attempt to do so was the creation in 1887 of the Interstate Commerce Commission. The powers given to the new commission by Congress, however, were almost immediately curtailed by the federal courts, and it was only by slow incremental legislation that the commission finally in 1940 gained de facto rate-making authority for railroad, pipelines, trucks, and barges. Other federal agencies and policies slowly emerged, including the establishment of a professional civil service, federal regulations of interstate banks, control over interstate corporations, special legislation to protect women and children, establishment of national parks, all marking the growing influence of the federal government in people's lives. Probably the capstone was the establishment of the Federal Income Tax by the Sixteenth Amendment to the Constitution in 1913, which finally gave the federal government a major new source of income which could help finance its interventionist policies.

Interestingly, on some issues, federal regulation appeared early because states-righters who opposed economic and social federal legislation often favored what might be called "moral" legislation. One of the early efforts was to control the reading content acceptable for delivery by the US mails by banning "pornography." The first such federal effort was the Comstock Act enacted in 1873 to control obscenity and prevent dissemination by mails (or through importation into the country) of, among other things, information about birth control or birth control devices. It took nearly a hundred years of agitation before the last portions of it were repealed or declared unconstitutional. The Comstock law was not alone. Would-be reformers attempting to raise the moral level of Americans were successful in their campaign to abolish the manufacture, selling or trading of alcoholic beverages with the passage of the Eighteenth Amendment in 1919. It was perhaps the ultimate federal intervention into the private lives and habits of its citizens, and it was done for "moral" reasons. This intervention on a national scale also sparked a massive rebellion against federal government policy, which ultimately led to the repeal of prohibition by the Twenty-First Amendment in 1933. Interestingly, one result was the establishment of national police force by the revitalization of the moribund Bureau of Investigation (later the FBI) with J. Edgar Hoover at its head in 1924. But Prohibition was not the last attempt to regulate American morals. In recent years there have been proposed constitutional amendments to ban abortion, and the latest effort, to make same-sex marriages unconstitutional, usually advocated by groups opposed to other forms of federal intervention.

World War I again led to expansion of federal power, but as was true in previous periods of federal expansion, there was a reaction, a return to normalcy after it ended. Calvin Coolidge is perhaps symbolic of the comparative lack of federal power since he took a whole summer off from Washington to spend it in Yellowstone Park, from where he governed the country. It was the economic crisis of the Great Depression, however, which again forced a change. The government under the New Deal expanded central influence and power all over the country by a whole alphabet of federal agencies. For a time the courts tried to curtail any such extension but the Roosevelt New Deal still managed to extend federal power into employment conditions, guaranteeing labor the right to organize, into retirement benefits through social security, into subsidy of the arts, and a whole alphabet of agencies.

Federal powers were further expanded by World War II and its immediate aftermath. For example, the return of millions of soldiers home, required federal action. The returning soldier was supported by GI loans for the purchase of housing, by the GI Bill for going to school, and any number of other federal programs. Moreover, the government, following the wartime project to build the atomic bomb, saw a need to establish federal agencies to encourage scientific and technological exploration. A whole alphabet of new agencies from the National Science Foundation to the National Institute of Health provided vast sums of money for new developments. Much of this was developed in cooperation with the various states, but increasingly it was the Hamiltonian vision of a strong central government which seemed to be the dominant political philosophy. The changing nature of the country and the world simply demanded a strong central government. Our role in the United Nations reinforced the need for federal powers. Increasingly it was the Hamiltonian vision of a strong central government which seemed to be dictating our economic and social policies.

One result of this growing intervention by the federal government into new areas was an attempt to force individuals and states to live up to the guarantees of the Bill of Rights. This was mostly done through appeals to the Bill of Rights, the provisions of which had been much ignored by various state and local governments. In my mind, the major force in this attempt to enforce rights guaranteed by the constitution was the American Civil Liberties Union, founded in the aftermath of

World War I, and other groups, such as the NAACP Legal Defense Fund, which soon followed. Roger Baldwin, the founder of the ACLU, felt that the Bill of Rights meant what it said, and gradually the federal courts came to agree with him. This effort to enforce the Bill of Rights has been the most controversial aspect of federalism since the effect was to challenge long time customs, beliefs, and institutions which had continued to exist throughout the country, in spite of the fact that they violated the Bill of Rights. Let me illustrate with examples of changes brought about in religious freedom and in racial restrictions.

RELIGION

The question of religion has been particularly troublesome in American history, in part because it was not always clear what freedom of religion meant. While the Bill of Rights served as an inspirational guide, the rights were, in a sense, paper rights because violations had been generally ignored since the beginning of the Republic. It was clear that there was not one sect or religious group which could directly be supported by the federal government, but it was also clear that the federal government could not deny the churches their rights to exist. Still, many of the traditional institutions in American life were strongly influenced by a concept that the US was a Christian nation, and mainly a Protestant one. Catholics, Jews, and dissenting Protestants in the nineteenth century had great difficulty with what might be called semi-official Protestantism and its view of the Bible. This more or less official Protestantism varied from state to state—from Baptists and Methodists in the South to Unitarians and Congregationalists in New England to Mormons in Utah. One of the few actions the federal government took against any religious group in the nineteenth century was the case of the polygamous Mormons. Almost all of those who identified themselves as Christians condemned them with the result that Utah had to make polygamy unconstitutional in its own constitution to become a state. Discrimination against Catholics was much less severe, but a major reason for the establishment of the Catholic parochial school system was that the developing public schools in the nineteenth century used the Protestant Bible and were strongly influenced by Protestant assumptions.

There were, of course, numerous kinds of Protestantism, with the more liberal denominations more able to adjust and accept the changing world. By the 1920s, however, Protestant fundamentalism had coalesced into an organized movement fighting the spread of religious modernism and cultural secularism. In many areas of the country it dominated the curriculum of the public schools, and Darwinism had become the bête noir of the true believers. The issue came to a head in the Scopes trial in 1925, which found Scopes guilty. The defense theory that the Constitution guaranteed individual freedom and strict separation of church and state, however, was later adopted by the US Supreme Court in a series of decisions, most notably *McCollum v. Board of Education* (1948), barring public school religious instruction; *Abington Township School District v. Schemp* (1963); and *Epperson v. Arkansas* (1968) and other cases eliminating religious requirements.

Until the court decisions began to mount, there had been little questioning about religious indoctrination or about religious discrimination except for the Mormons. Anti-Semitism was rampant, and, though Judaism was tolerated, it was obviously not welcomed by the vast number of Americans, who blithely continued to try to maintain state support of Christian practices, which they assumed to be normal. Most Americans, in fact, thought of themselves as citizens of a Christian nation and did so well into the twentieth century. Woodrow Wilson, for example, was called the "greatest Christian statesman of all time" by Carter Glass, the Democratic Senator from Virginia. The Federal Council of Churches (later reorganized and expanded into the National Council of Churches) called the First World War a conflict "between forces that make for the coming of the kingdom of God and forces that oppose it." George Albert Coe, a professor at Union Theological Seminary, proposed that the phrase "kingdom of God" should be replaced by the ideal "democracy of God" to better describe the success of the United States in showing the true path to Christianity. President Wilson, in fact, said that the major task Americans faced was to make the "United States a mighty Christian nation, and to Christianize the world." When critics of the Supreme Court and the federal government claim that the government is anti-religion, it is because these Wilsonian ideas are not longer accepted as national policy.

Even as late as the 1920s one of the more influential intellectual groupings in the United States centered around the leaders of what might be called liberal Protestantism, those religious leaders who modified Darwinism to apply to the religion of progress in which they believed and advocated. Its theologians saw themselves as living in a universe in which God's moral law reigned inviolable and that the US prospered as the nearest approximation yet to God's kingdom on Earth. Many saw Germany in World War I as the last impediment to that kingdom. By the Second World War the religious rhetoric had begun to decline, but the religious leaders proclaiming United States a bastion of Christianity remained extremely influential. Reinhold Niebuhr was almost a household name, although his interpretation of Christiantiy was no longer that which had existed in the First World War, and Protestantism itself had become less influential in formulating American policy.

RACE

The federal courts and national legislation during the second half of the twentieth century undermined traditional assumptions about race as well. Though the Civil War abolished slavery, it did not much change American attitudes about race. After 1876, racial segregation became a fact of life in the South, and many of the practices were given sanction by the Supreme Court in the concept of separate but equal. In the North, segregation in housing was the norm, especially in the larger cities where ghetto life became an established reality. Blacks were denied rooms in major hotels, refused admission to restaurants, and relegated mostly to venial jobs. Washington, DC, the national capital, was one of the most segregated and discriminatory cities in the country. Interestingly, it had not always been so, since the most drastic restrictions in Washington, DC, were put in place after Woodrow Wilson took office in 1913. Since the District of Columbia was controlled by Congress, the Southern segregationists in Congress, almost all Democrats, were able to impose their will. Blacks quite clearly were second-class citizens, although it was probably somewhat easier to live in the North than in the South. In Chicago, where I once lived, the Free Religious Fellowship was a Unitarian-affiliated congregation composed mostly of middle-class blacks and a few dedicated individuals of European descent who believed both in humanism and in black equality. Some critics of the fellowship said it had been established by the American Unitarian Association to deal with the problem of what to do with a humanist black Unitarian-affiliated minister. Whether or not it was established for this reason, it was the first organized humanist interracial fellowship. While there were a couple of black professionals in the congregation, e.g., physicians and attorneys, a surprising number of the members worked for the federal government, primarily in the US Post Office, mostly as mailmen or clerks, and in fact even the professionals tended to work for government agencies since comparatively high-paying positions in private industry were almost non-existent unless the industry itself catered to the black community. There were, however, limits in how high a black could climb in the government service. In the 1960s when the civil rights movement got underway, federal intervention toward minorities became more positive. My friends who had been relegated to low-level civil service jobs, some for more than twenty years, moved rapidly up the ladder. One becoming assistant postmaster of the city of Chicago, another headed up the postal inspectors, another moved into being head of the City Department of Health, and others assumed executive positions across the country. They had always had the talent and the ability, but their opportunities had been limited.

Again it was the federal government that basically challenged longtime customary discrimination and segregation. Jackie Robinson had broken the color barrier in the segregated national game of baseball in 1947, but even the military had been segregated until President Truman began desegregating it in 1948. This marked the beginning of government intervention into long time discriminatory practices. For the most part it was the federal courts which led the way. *Brown v. Board of Education* in 1954 marked the beginning of the end of official desegregation in the public school system. The federal government itself, after Truman, did little, until in 1964 Lyndon Johnson, cajoled, pressured, and almost blackmailed reluctant congressman to pass the Civil Rights Act. This was followed by the Voting Rights Act of 1965 outlawing legally sanctioned disenfranchisement and voter intimidation.

The result of these and other court decisions was the assertion of the federal government to establish the reality of the Bill of Rights and to supersede local laws and customs which supported such drastic discrimination. This expansion of federal interpretation entered into other areas as in *Roe v. Wade* (1973), which recognized the right of abortion. The effect was to anger and irritate large segments of the population in the United States against what they felt was federal interference in lessening the practices which violated the federal constitution. They claimed that the courts were legislating rather than interpreting the law. The problem was that the Bill of Rights had not been enforced very effectively before and recent court decisions helped remove most of the censorship barriers, end many standardized religious practices from public crèches to prayer in the public school, eliminate most forms of segregation and discrimination, assert the rights of women under equal opportunity regulations and decisions—the list can go on. The result has been a radical change in American life, which many groups and individuals have found difficult to accept. They tend to blame such changes on the federal government and its courts.

THE OPPOSITION

Probably the most hostile section of the country to this government expansion was the block of southern states which had prevented effective civil rights legislation for much of the twentieth century and which also had been most prone to violate the provisions of the Bill of Rights. It was also the most rigidly stratified of any other area of the country and traditionally had been the poorest. As the courts increasingly voted against their segregationist policies as well as traditional symbols such as the confederate flag, declared abortion legal contrary to their religious tradition, extended the rights of women, the South rebelled. Other areas and groups of people were upset, but the South in particular saw itself as a victim of the federal government, a view, which while there since the days of slavery, was exacerbated not only

by the civil rights legislation but other legislation and judicial decisions such as those recognizing the cancerous properties to tobacco,
the source of much of its major industry and farming.

Much of the opposition to change in the South had been focused
on the race issue, but as most Americans gradually accepted integration, the South had to find a more effective way of combating government intervention. They could no longer use the race issue. Instead
they revived the traditional one which had been their battle cry, the
federal government itself. The federal government had ignored traditional rights and customs; in fact, the South argued that state and local
power in many areas of decision had been weakened if not destroyed
by the federal government. Leading this battle, and first showing its
political viability, was George Wallace, the militant segregationist
governor of Alabama, who found a new populist rallying point for the
former segregationists as well as conservatives everywhere who were
increasingly hostile to changes taking place. The real enemy, Wallace
said, was the federal government itself. Government intervention and
programs and court decisions were destroying traditional values. He
became a leader of a populist reactionary movement which for a time
threatened both the Democratic and Republican parties. Though Wallace's career was cut short by an attempted assassination which
severely handicapped him, his basic message was seized upon by
President Richard Nixon, who proceeded to blame the liberal big-
government advocates who had forced change as the enemies. Nixon,
who had risen to power and influence by fighting the "communist conspiracy," which he had seen everywhere in the 1940s and 1950s as the
force which had led America astray, now saw the liberals and big government as the enemy. Though Nixon began the change in the Republican party, it was amplified and developed by his successors. It was
perfected by President Ronald Reagan, who found the easy answer to
curtailing big government, namely, to cut taxes. Since spendthrift liberals then could not carry out their social policies because there was
not enough money to do so, more power would devolve to the states
and Washington interventionism would lessen. The real source of the
troubles, to Reagan and others, was government regulations enacted
by the liberals and a runaway Supreme Court which "legislated rather
than interpreted" the law. Many groups agreed. Family Life groups,

for example, could jump in and say it was the immoral liberal government which was trying to control their lives and destroy the family. Libertarians could buy into it because they wanted free market and little regulation, and de-regulation became a mantra of the new Jeffersonians. Government became an evil and every government policy and institution had to be questioned and discarded if at all possible. As funds were cut, the resultant failures in government programs mounted, and the morale of those working in government agencies decline. The result was an attempt to return to the past where local agencies and local government without meddling by the federal government were held to be the solution. Liberals, who were seen to favor government intervention in economic matters and in social matters about integration and equal opportunity and many other issues, were the new enemy. Once established, the myth grew stronger, and both conservatives and liberals tended to downplay the importance of the federal government.

In the period of a rising stock market, the anti-federalists, now including many of the larger business interests, claimed the government was stealing from its constituents by keeping pensions tied to a set social security income and refusing to let individuals benefit from the ever-rising stock market. Although the fall of the stock market cut out some of the most windblown rhetoric, it was still argued that it was high taxes which were the evil, and they had to be cut. Cutting taxes made it ever more difficult for government to carry out traditional services, and the failure to do so was again blamed on the government. Among the government agencies cut most heavily was the internal revenue department, where taxes could be audited. But who was to carry out the necessary tasks of caring for the poor, the sick, the mentally ill, the homeless, and others? Little was said about this except President Bush said that faith-based organizations should take greater responsibility since the government could no longer do it. There was little recognition that it had been the failure of such organizations in the past that had led to federal intervention.

Business itself had jumped on the anti-federalist bandwagon with the appearance of what some, including Paul Kurtz, have called "evangelical capitalism," which sought unfettered freedom for huge corporations in order to meet the demands of a global market. The new capitalists opposed any governmental interference with corporate actions. They believed that the government should let business be, as well as get out of the social welfare, education, and public health programs the government ran. Though "evangelical capitalism" had its base in libertarianism, it not only emphasized the economic role of government, but almost totally ignored civil liberties and civil rights or social welfare. In their mind the free market was a panacea for all social ills; the inevitable result was a growth of unmet needs from welfare, to environment, to transportation, to national parks, and a growing disparity between the classes in the United States. In the minds of the advocates taxes were an evil not socially useful and the answer to problems of unemployment not welfare in order to get the public to consume more. This, it was argued, could only be possible if taxes were cut, which would leave individuals with more to spend, and the government could no longer "waste it." It is not mentioned, however, that it is the rich who are taxed disproportionately less, while the poor get little benefit at all. It is also not mentioned that the less the government has the more burden is put on others to do what it did, and so far no solution to this problem has been found.

If I paint a rather dismal picture of recent events, it is because I think the problem with democracy, at least in the United States, is coming to terms with the radical changes which have taken place, particularly in the last thirty or so years. Problems of adjustment to change have always been with us, but recent change has been so radical as we shifted from an industrial to a service economy that many have failed to adjust and they react with dismay and even hostility seeking to blame someone for the problems. The convenient source of evil to blame in recent years has been the federal government, which, it was argued, destroyed local mores, beliefs, and institutions, and challenged traditional morality with abortion rights and recognized that homosexuality was not a criminal act.

In a sense this is a kind of nostalgia for a past which never existed and is somewhat like the novel by Thomas Wolfe, who in 1940 wrote *You Can't Go Home Again* in reflecting the dilemma we have to face. The main character, a disillusioned internationally known novelist, made an unsuccessful attempt to return to his roots in his hometown. He found that the morality he believed once existed there had become shoddy, and though he was convinced that a corrupt society destroys each individual in it, he still seemed to retain an enduring faith that the true fulfillment of "our spirit, of our people, and of our mighty and immortal land is yet to come." Wolfe's character found he could not go home again but still retained a faith in a better world yet to come, a belief which has been a mainstay of the American dream. But if it is to come, there has to be a willingness to confront change, to realize that change demands compassion and concern as we seek to find new ways of solving traditional problems. The problem is that we are in denial, both about what has happened in the past, and what is happening now. Jefferson's fears of a strong national government have been reinvigorated as Hamilton's ideas have become the reality and we become even more schizophrenic.

Even the evangelical capitalists demand protection both from and by the federal government although they do so at the expense of the poor, the underpaid, the less skillful, the sick, the handicapped, and others whose federal support has been cut back if not eliminated. While the federal government in the past has often failed to help those most in need, it certainly had attempted to do so in the recent past until the anti-federalists became so strong. Unfortunately, the issues today are ever more critical and are no longer state or regional ones, if they ever were, but national ones. Medical care, unemployment, education, equal opportunity, and an increasing number of other issues can only be dealt with on a national scale. The US government is the main source of funding for scientific and technological research. It regulates food and drugs, sets auto safety standards as well as a variety of other nationally distributed items and products, provides for social security, sets standards for minimum wages and numerous other issues dealing with working conditions and the quality of life. It simply needs to expand to meet the needs of today's world, but the problem is expanding while keeping the basic freedoms listed in the Constitution and many of them only recently established in reality.

The United States today quite simply is radically different from anything our founding fathers could have envisioned. It is a multicultural, ethnically diverse, secular society which requires a continuous and ongoing adjustment in institutions and attitudes to meet changing conditions. The world around us has also changed, with former third world countries like China becoming an industrial juggernaut. Outsourcing and job loss cause severe economic crisis. Our changeover from an industrial to a service economy has lowered the living standards of vast numbers of Americans since service jobs as a general rule pay less than industrial ones, which the unions had been successful in organizing. The current tax policy has led to the creation of a greater social gap between the haves and the have-nots than has existed since the 1930s, and to a major decline in social services. There is an increasingly vicious effort to turn the clock back, to remove the very policies of government which I and others worked so hard to establish. The problem is that large numbers of people really do want to go home again, and unfortunately the home they want to return to never existed in reality, but only in their fantasy. This does not stop them from trying to make their fantasy real.

What can Humanists do? We cannot go home again either. One hopes we can be rational, accept some of the changes, and campaign against the others. Free market economics are good in some ways, but we need to campaign for social justice. We need to emphasize a free market that recognizes the principles of equity and fairness, welfare and justice, and concern for the common good. We also need to point out the contradictions in those who want to eliminate market regulation but at the same time eliminate a woman's right to choose or the right of two people to cohabit or marry if they want. Most of all we need to emphasize that the United States has changed. It is no longer a rural society populated mostly by those of British descent but a very pluralistic society with many groups who have different outlooks on life than the traditional Protestant establishment of the past. I had almost given up hope of getting civil rights legislation passed in the 1950s, but Lyndon Johnson finally got it through Congress. Many of the programs I worked to establish are now threatened, and some might not have turned out the way I envisioned, but what we need to do is organize, campaign, agitate, recognize our own failures. In spite of the inefficiency and contradictions in the Constitution, change can be brought about. We need to support a new kind of federalism which not only guarantees the rights and liberties we so long fought for but also establishes or enlarges programs to care for the poor, the down and out, the aged, the ill, the handicapped, children, the less powerful;

in fact see that all of its varied citizens are not neglected; and do what is necessary to make the US became a more equitable society. In my mind this can only be done by a new kind of federalism—it cannot be left to individual states or communities. States and local governments would still have an important role to play, but meeting the basic economic needs of our citizens requires strong federal programs working either independent of or in collaboration with the states. Federalism is not an evil. Neither for that matter is equitable taxation. Whether or not changes take place, the United States of the future will be different than in the past, but hopefully in my mind it will be one in which the federal government has to play a more prominent role than it has in the recent past.

REFERENCES

Most of the information in this paper is standard American history and can be found in any history of the United States. The interpretation, however, is mine. For those interested, there are many editions of *The Federalist Papers* as well as of the writings of Alexis de Tocqueville readily available. For Woodrow Wilson, whom I quoted, the best source is *The Papers of Woodrow Wilson*, which Arthur S. Link began editing in 1966 and which were published by Princeton University Press.

6.

Democracy, Religion, and the Language of Separation

Kurt Johnson

The right for right's sake is the motto we should take for our own life.

Felix Adler

INTRODUCTION

In this article, in context with the other contributions to this book, I want to examine the spectrum of religious experience, especially as it is codified within organized religions, and comment on what attitudes—especially ethical and ontological—appear helpful to democracy and which do not. Much of the public is actually unaware of the complex sociological underpinnings that characterize religions worldwide and the pervasive roles and influences these institutions have on the equally complex fabrics of the world's many kinds of societies.

So-called democracies (or more appropriately "republics" or "federal systems") are only one of the societal models pervading the world. However, since the subject of this colloquium of the Humanist Institute concerns democracy—what it is and isn't, and what contributes to its potentials as an ethically satisfying system of government and societal living—I will limit my comments to religions as they are at play in the world's democracies or federal systems, particularly the United States.[1]

DEMOCRACY AND RELIGIONS

When one uses a phrase like "democracy and religions" readers are most apt to think of religion only in the context of *organized religions* and their roles within the various experiments now occurring as the world's various forms of "democracy." Most people are far less aware that much of the "moving and shaking" within religions actually occurs at the level of personal or group religious experience and, most particularly, from the activities of myriad religious practitioners and their constituencies, often in the forms of innumerable smaller religious and not-for-profit organizations.

Many of these myriad smaller organizations, practitioners, and constituencies are within the boundaries of larger organized religions (and therein they often define those religion's most active elements). However, many are not. Considerable numbers are independent or autochthonous organizations, while others are groups actively working to define "the cutting edge" of what is going on in religion or religious experience (an activity of tremendous moment in this time of instantaneous and global communications).

Importantly, in the United States (and the West in general) many of these active practitioners and their constituencies represent "imported religions," that is, extremely dynamic elements of religious activity, imported into democratic or other Western settings (and therein often adapted or redefined). The actual roots or origins of many of these groups are from elsewhere in the world, from other cultural or historical settings, particularly those of the East.

One of the most dynamic developments in recent world history has been the influence of religious traditions moving about the world and being adapted to or redefined in new social and cultural settings. Equally influential have been religious traditions, previously suppressed by closed societies, finding burgeoning new life within the world's more open societies. The influence of His Holiness the Dalai Lama and Tibetan Buddhism, or of the Baha'i tradition as liberated from closed Middle Eastern societies, are good examples of the latter.

In regard to the former, examples abound in many forms of Buddhism and Hinduism which have arisen in the West, while a near antonym of this phenomenon has occurred with the export of evangelical Christianity from the West to the East.

If anyone doubts the veracity of such observations concerning the "ripple effect" grassroots religious activity has in the world, one need only point to quite contrasting examples: the Christian "religious right" in the United States and the coercive militias of various regional or local Islamic clerics in the Middle East. Such constituencies and their leaders often represent very singular points of view. However, one can also point to major influences which arise from yet other kinds of groups—those concerned with "diversity," "holism," or "peace," as in many influential groups whose roots are, to use very generic terms, Buddhist, Hindu or even "New Age."[2]

CONCEPT-BASED RELIGION, BEHAVIOR-BASED RELIGION, AND THE DEMOCRATIC IDEAL

It is often not recognized by the wider public, often thinking only in terms of societies and the organized religions within them, that the entire collage of religious activity in the world can be basically divided into two categories containing groups with quite starkly contrasting "tones" when it comes to moral and ethical implication.

One basic category includes religious activities or organizations which ground their views in various exclusive claims—either about how reality is put together or about history (this category would include many "literalist," "deterministic," "divinely revealed" or "fundamentalist" views). The other category contains activities or groups that are not interested so much in concepts or beliefs as in moral or ethical behavior. Overall, one category contains religions that are concept-oriented; the other contains varieties of religion more oriented toward simply eliciting moral or ethical behavior. Obviously, there is a degree of overlap between the categories; however, the difference can further be clarified by pointing out that although concept-oriented religion may mandate moral and ethical behavior as well, when "push comes to shove" the proper belief concept (i.e., "right belief ") cannot usually be abrogated in favor of simply high moral or ethical behavior (i.e., "right behavior"), that is, "creed" overrides "deed." Oppositely, with behaviorally oriented religion, it is the quality of resulting behavior that is usually considered most important, aside from any argument about concept, that is, "deed overrides creed."[3] The latter viewpoint, of course, was key to the founding concepts of most of the ethics and values-based communities, many of which constituencies makeup the Humanist Institute. Similarly, generally Buddhist-based critiques cited here (along with those from the Advaita ["nondual" in Sanskrit] Vedanta [Hinduism]) are also non-theist in nature.

It is important to point out that this is not an abstract concept. The division in overall ultimate moral tone between religions of these two categories became starkly apparent, for instance, on a CNN program (*Larry King Live*) immediately after the attack on the World Trade Center and Pentagon on September 11, 2001.

Among a panel of religious leaders chosen by CNN—to discuss the behavior of terrorists as well as the social conditions that engender terrorism—the question arose from representatives of behaviorally oriented (mostly non-theist) religions whether the representatives of the concept-oriented religions on the panel (mostly theist or "revealed" religions) indeed believed that persons with "wrong beliefs" were doomed to either "suffering in this world" or, ultimately, to "hell" in an afterlife. Although representatives of two concept-based religions were politely apologetic to their co-panelists about their answers, they did confirm, yes, their belief was that the others on the panel were doomed to either worldly suffering or ultimate hell. Interestingly, the representatives of the behavior-based religions pressed their question, pointing out that, from a "bigger picture" (regarding all humankind), this view of ultimate suffering or hell did not appear to make moral sense. As might readily be guessed, the panelists from the concept-based religions had to answer that they were bound by divine revelation. It is an old story, of course, but one needing emphasis here in introduction.

Affecting the simple categories used above are a number of generalities quite well known to students of the sociology of religion which are also important in introduction here. They further qualify simplistic elements in these categories by (1) taking into account various fundamental and dynamic factors also at play with and within religions and how they affect societies and (2) pointing out that certain effects of organization simply result from various structural rules common to all systems. Reviewing these briefly allows some further insight into the workings of religious practice over time and how religions and dynamic religious practice affect societies.

One of these properties is the inevitable transformation of religious practice over historical time, including the process of the codifying of religious experience in organized religions. The very act of religious activity becoming organized or codified initiates a process of defining that religious practice *away from* some, or even many, of the holisms that may initially be at its roots. For example, the most simple holism— being unconditional or advocating embracing openness—will inevitably begin to fade with definition. In all systems there is usually a direct correlation between degrees of organization and degrees of codification because this is how all organization works. Further, there is often an observable direct correlation between the degree of "Deity-base" (i.e., "Theism") in a religious practice and the degree of codification or organization because deity-based systems are hierarchical by nature. Oppositely, those religious groups maintaining holistic, eclectic, or more unconditional views (as in teaching only "love" or "ethical behavior") are more apt to be more diffusely organized and less codified.[4]

Overall, no amount of essential holism, eclecticism, or embracing openness in initial historical teaching can stop the process codification or organization over time because all systems evolve toward complexity and departmentalization. The fact that religious practice exists in a societal context will add extra impetus over time to define and thus separate. This ongoing factor has caused even the non-theistic or behavior-based religions (like various "enlightenment-based" religions [most generically, for example, Buddhism and Hinduism]) to also become organized and codified religions within various social and cultural contexts over time. This process also reflects an observation of sociologists of religions regarding the social "potency" of a religion, that is, what I will call here "hot religions" (ones that still maintain their evangelical thrust) versus "warm religions" (ones that have been around long enough that they have departmentalized themselves within their social context and moved toward a more quiet accommodation with others). Returning to the example from the CNN post-9/11 broadcast, the two religions still insisting the others would go to hell were coming from "hot religion" ("only we are right"), while those urging accommodation might be looked at as coming from more "warm religion" ("we can agree to disagree.")[5]

Most important to the considerations in this paper, however, is that within this historical process there is always a significant counter-current. Amid the collage of history there is always a constant upwelling of "refreshed" or "renewed" experience—from the practitioners and their constituencies, which come and go with every generation. It is a historical pattern, organized or not (often called "renewal" or "reform"), in which groups within even the many organized religions, but particularly those at the "cutting edge," make a dynamic and persuasive return to the most basic moral or ethical roots of their traditions. Thus, although on the one hand it is impossible to change basic patterns of how religious experience will always tend to organize and codify in the linearity of history, sociologically it is also impossible to prevent the constant emergences of refreshed approaches, or renewals, which aim to return to fundamental holisms (basic teachings of universal love and understanding). The latter, when seen in the largest view, underpin the moral and ethical fabric common to nearly all of the world's religions and ethical practices. Of course, relevant to the discussion here of religion and democracy is that these same holisms anchor the values fundamental to the world's various experiments with "democracy," as in the "inalienable rights" in America's Declaration of Independence—"life, liberty and the pursuit of happiness."

Concluding the discussion above, more defined religious experiences or activities are also more apt to adopt more fixed approaches to various sociological or political issues while, oppositely, frequent upwelling or "renewal" or "reform" emphasizing the basic holisms underlying such religions are less aft to take fixed approaches (and thus, support more "democratic" praxis) within their societies. In modern religious parlance, the holistic type of religious experience or activity is often referred to as the "approach from the Heart," one in which the role of equanimity has primacy.[6]

MORAL HEROES AND HEROINES

The observations above become extremely concrete when one considers the kinds of persons cultures have often deemed as "heroes" or "heroines," that is, persons who somehow inculcated deep heartistic values in ways that were socially transformative within their own societies or cultures. Very often these have been historical persons who emphasized basic values—like the view that humankind is one whole, one family, without "separation."

Although everyone's heroes may differ, it is likely that lists of superior moral beings would include persons like Mahatma Gandhi, His Holiness the Dalai Lama, Mother Teresa—or perhaps others like Martin Luther King Jr., Nelson Mandela or Kofi Annan—to name only a few. Given considerations early in this article inevitably linking religious and social activity, it is also not surprising that the lives and social influence of such persons touched both the religious (or ethical) and sociopolitical arenas of their particular society or culture. This point is key to understanding what will be referred to in this article as the "critique of the language of separation."

THE LANGUAGE OF SEPARATION

Regarding the phrase "language of separation" most persons will think what is being referred to is the separation of church and state, as built into the federal or republican system devised by the founding fathers of the United States. This constitutional aspect of the federal system of the United States is one element in the interplay of religion and society in our American system (and some other republics or federal systems), but it is not the "language of separation" which will be referred to here.

"Language of separation," as used herein, refers to a general "critique" of Western "democracies" (and their operating modalities) which has arisen over the last years from a number of writers among the more dynamic "cutting edge" of world religions which draw primarily on the world's great "Wisdom Traditions" (particularly those rooted originally in the East but now widely practiced, with much variety, in the West).[7]

Although it is important to anchor this discussion with some academic rigor, as could be done, for instance, by quoting from a recent review by Roy Money of David R. Loy's *The Great Awakening: Buddhist Social Theory*:

> The delusion of dualism . . . is similar to the Buddha's teaching of no-self. . . . this continual struggle with a subject-object dualism is one of our main sources of suffering. The ending of social dukkha [Buddhist term for suffering] would require a process of realizing our "interpenetrating nonduality with the world." Only then could we transform our dualistic and dukkha-producing institutions.[8]

a non-academic, more popular approach, is far more useful here and, for that, I will turn to the publications of a more popular writer whose work I have adapted to some degree for a number of speeches and talks I have given recently around the ethical societies of the American Ethical Union.

First, however, it is further enlightening to introduce this critique by characterizing its subject—that is, the particular "language of separation" that characterizes much of the discourse of today's American politics. In his very insightful book, *Moral Politics*, George Lakoff notes that much of the success of the current United States President George W. Bush stems from his and his supporters' success in communicating a certain metaphor (with which they themselves may actually identify)—that of the "strong father figure" who in familiar terms (or even clichés of "Americana") portrays himself as the strong icon of safety, confidence, and "protecting our way of life."

Lakoff notes that, in fact, much of American politics in recent decades, especially since the era of mass media, has involved the "selling" of such metaphors to the public as part of the praxis of political persuasion. In the past, other such successful metaphors have included the "Camelot youth" of the Kennedy era (wherein serving humanity suggested, among other things, joining the Peace Corps or VISTA); then the metaphor of the "entrepreneur" or "independent achiever" who can build the "American dream" (as in the Ronald Reagan era); and, more recently, the "populist" or champion of the common man or consumer as in the likes of Ralph Nader, Jerry Brown, or Ross Perot. As Lakoff notes, the tastes change with the times and the times can also change quite quickly.

The language of the current American administration is one with perhaps the strongest language of separation used to date: good guys versus bad guys, champion of liberty versus axis of evil, civilization versus barbarism, and so on. Interestingly, these metaphors are not reserved expressly for overseas "enemies" of the United States but also often used, in slightly watered-down tone, on the political opposition within (as in "soft on security," "weak on terrorism" etc.). If viewed at a certain "base level," this kind of language typifies the language of separation; it appeals to persons whose simple, common emotional needs include a strong need to feel safe, confident, or secure about their lives. As Lakoff points out, it is also quite possible that the purveyors of this kind of language actually hold this worldview and are themselves motivated to a great extent by fears this language seeks to allay.

The critique is not saying there is not ample reason to be fearful in the current world climate. The important point is that the language of the "moral heroes and heroines" mentioned earlier in this article is a very different kind of language. The latter, far from the language of fear, is a language about humankind as a single family, a holistic view—what is often characterized, as in Teasdale's words, the "view from the Heart."[9] Further, the apparent moral strength and success of such heroes and heroines suggests that there is important, perhaps even objective, evidence that their discourse itself—based on holism and embracing openness—can have a transformative effect on the social arena. The "presence" of their holistic view, inculcated in their lives and discourse, is precisely what seems to have allowed them to motivate, and conduct business with, their fellow human beings in a very different way than the language of separation.

Concerning the present discussion of religious experience and democracy, the point is that it is such behavior (which we have called and will later refer to as "transformative") flowed directly from deep ethical and moral precepts in the teachings such persons personified: in the case of Gandhi, basic elements of Hinduism; for the Dalai Lama, teachings of Tibetan Buddhism (or Dzogchen); and, even in the cases of Nelson Mandela and Mother Teresa, deeply heartistic interpretations each took from idealist Marxism on the one hand and traditional Catholicism on the other. Again, it is important to point out that these illustrations are not abstract; such heroes and heroines lived out their lives fully within the complex realities of day-to-day life, including those same influences and circumstances that can, and have, produced a-moral historical person-ages as well. These latter could include anyone's list of the world's great historical megalomaniacs, dictators, despots, and the like.

As noted above, in considering this connection between the ideal and personification of it, many examples are informative. However, one that is particularly instructive with regard to understanding the cri-tique of the language of separation is the ethical creed and religious traditions which underpinned the social actions of Mahatma Gandhi. Gandhi's non-violence was rooted in simple, fundamental, modalities of discourse (i.e., "language" in the greater sense of this article) from Advaita Vedanta—"non-dualism" in Hinduism, one religious experi-ence in which the adherent experiences reality as oneness, without a sense of separation. These ideals were taught in Gandhi's time by one of India's most revered sages, Ramana Maharshi (1879–1950).

Ramana taught that, in the confrontational "face-off" of separa-tion—bad feeling, enmity, confrontation, etc. between any two "per-sons" (as in any coupling of roles—spouse/spouse, parent/child, person/adversary etc.)—one "person" or "side" must take the risk of initiating an "invitation," firmly grounded in their own willingness, to "drop the role" that is, in part, causing the separation.[10] The con-frontational role might be, for instance, the perceived position of "better than you," "higher than you," "know more than you," "more right than you," "in control of you," and the like. By this invitation, the inviter suggests to the invitee that a new level, or basis, for rela-tionship must be found—one based on more fundamental and authentic needs, most often shared and heartistic—on which ground a new kind of discourse can ensure. Ramana called this invitation a moving from "invoking separation" to "invoking welcoming."

Gandhi put this basic tenet of Advaita into action, in practice, inviting the British authorities to commit violence against Indian non-violent protestors until such point that the British themselves would rec-ognize an inability to accept this role, as "oppressor," and abandon it through their own moral decision. Historically, as more and more news of atrocities by India's British authorities spread around the world, it became more intolerable for the British to accept this role. Inevitably the British moved to "drop it" and find a new mode of discourse. Without that "invitation," to drop the role—in this case being metaphorically similar to "the lamb being led to the slaughter"— it is unlikely that the independence of India would have played out at that time. This is also probably why the recently popular movie *The Passion of the Christ* (although not seen by this writer) appeared to have such a profound effect on many audiences; many remarked that the actions portrayed by Jesus in the movie invited them to a deeper, more fundamental idea of the tenderness required in successful and fruitful human relationships.

Of course, in popular parlance everyone learns this lesson in dealing with others in day-to-day disputes—if one is willing to make the first step to defuse a situation or find a deeper common ground, where the confrontation roles can be dropped, problems are often more easily resolved.

The example of Gandhi's praxis provides a very good introduction to one popular view critiquing the language of separation which I think is particularly useful. This model comes from the work of David Deida, particularly in his books *Intimate Communion* and *Naked Buddhism*. While Deida has used this model more for describing the dynamic of relationships between individuals, in many speeches and talks that I have given around the American Ethical Union community in recent years, I have found it also extremely useful in describing relationships among societies and stages in history.[11]

Deida suggests it is helpful to view development in "three stages"—not, of course, fixed or arbitrary in any way but as extremely informative for analysis and insight. In my own discussions with ethical culturists I have referred to these three stages as (1) the "reactive," (2) the "accommodating," and (3) the "transformative." Characterizing each of these "stages" is very easy by giving examples, both "big picture" and at the individual level, which readily show their usefulness.

The "reactive" relationship can be readily characterized by adopting some old terminology from the 1980s' "Transactional Analysis."[12] The language of the reactive stage is "I'm OK, you're not OK"; "this is mine, this is yours"; "this is mine, not yours"; "let's compete for it, let's fight over it"; etc. Historically, responding to the inevitably negative results of reactivity, the language of accommodation looks to compromise and diplomacy. It's language is: "I'm OK, you're OK"; "let's come to some agreements here"; "we can work this out"; "we can each 'give' a little"; etc.

As Deida points out, in the life of the individual there is usually a transition from the reactive to the accommodating sometime, perhaps after teenage and into early adulthood where, after one "has been beating-up on oneself long enough" (my words), one realizes there has to be a better way. One comes to an accommodation within oneself, as in saying, "I'm going to start to treat myself better," etc.

Similarly, one can look at the world, for instance, after World War II (especially since it tragically followed the so-called War to End All Wars, World War I), and note that the world also seems to have come to a realization, moving from reactivity toward accommodation (again, metaphorically, "we've beaten on each other about long enough; there has to be a better way"). The resulting world of accommodation has brought us the United Nations, international law, treaties and other international agreements, world courts, and so on—a basic groundwork for accommodation in a world of tense diversity. Such movements toward accommodation have, of course, come and gone in the dynamics of world history for a long time.

The historical examples above are mine, but Deida's insights here come into play once again. What Deida points out is that the language of what I call "accommodation" is indeed an ethical step higher than the language or actions of "reactivity," but both views (or discourses) still imply separation. It is on this point that the messages within the world's great Wisdom Traditions become very significant to this discussion.[13] What could be beyond the level of "accommodation"? This is a question that has certainly vexed the liberal left—why has their praxis not yielded greater result in terms of equanimity and social progress?

As Deida points out, most people living at the level of accommodation cannot imagine anything beyond it. Similarly, the question is apt with regard to the question of what lies beyond accommodation at other levels of complexity in the world. What could be beyond the current accommodating phenomena of treaties, agreements, and arbitrating tools that characterize the still generally competitive environment among the diversity of nations?

A hint at the answer appears to lie in the character and praxis of moral and ethical heroes and heroines which have been pointed out above. What is it that made their discourse and its success different? We remember not only such heros' or heroines' work, we remind ourselves also of their words, as in Gandhi's "be the change you seek" or Nelson Mandela's "to remove your own fear is to remove the fear of those around you." We have some metaphorical sense of them, or the Kofi Annans of this world, as we see their ability to approach a politician or diplomat standing on the opposing side of some issue. We imagine them placing a kind hand on the shoulder of the "other" and saying, in a way that is somehow convincing (perhaps simply by "presence")—"Look, we can work this out another, *better*, way." The ability of such persons, historically, to work at a level that was beyond accommodation—that was transformative—stands out. If it did not, such persons would not assume a compelling stature and the allure that they do—not only in their lives but in oft-read books, popular movies or televisions shows about them or, in fact, simply in legend. For instance, at a critical juncture in Roman history such charismatic, holistic, persuasion is credited the Bishop of Rome (Pope Leo I) in AD 451 when he reputedly walked into the camp of Attila the Hun, alone and unarmed, and convinced Attila to turn his armies back from sacking Italy's perennial city. Details may be legend, but it is said that Attila was moved by Pope Leo's courageous advocacy for his people—that it reminded Attila of the role he himself had played in protecting his people from the Mongols and Chinese.

What is characteristic of the approach of such heroes, real or embellished, is that their behavior provides insight into language without separation—what Ramana Maharshi, Gandhi's model, called the "language of welcoming." It is pretty simple at base, in fact, simply the "golden rules" of every culture, the teaching of "humankind is all one family," as rooted in nearly all the great religious and ethical traditions. As Ramana pointed out in his *Talks*, if all the great religions had stuck to their most simple and universal teachings, instead of elaborating additional exclusive claims, religions would not have become a force for harm in the world.

The kind of activity that allows for tremendous equanimity and altruism, often fostering climates of harmony and peace, is what Deida calls "third stage behavior"—or what I have called the "transformative." At the individual level, most of the Wisdom Traditions refer to this transformative stage as "awakened awareness," in the sense of the loss of the sense of separation as "non duality," or, in some parlances, as "enlightenment." It is a climate, or state of being, in which the full range of human potential can be acted on "artfully," as Deida says, without purposeful harm being a consequence. There is no doubt that we have seen this quality in individual human persons. If not, there would be no history of moral heroes and heroines, saints, and the like. Either that part of history is absurd fairy tales or there is a basic truth to it. The question is whether this extraordinary modality of behavior has greater application—to relationships, families, groups, societies, and so on. The tendency, of course, is to think that such a views border on silly utopianism, with the evidence being the ample failures among utopian experimentation. Yet, it seems to follow that if transformative behavior is so obvious in the lives of some individuals, and it is a scientific principle that evolution (or expansion of success or fitness) moves (e.g., recapitulates repetitively) upward from one level of organization to another in a hierarchy, there remains the possibility of transformative behavior more fully working within the social, or more organized, arenas. Even if not, it does not appear to be a "stretch" to imagine the possibility of more transformative individuals acting in the world.

Whether or not one argues the rational possibility that transformative behavior might be able to move beyond the level of so-called awakened individuals—the historical phenomenon of moral heroes and heroines— there is considerable movement afoot, within the burgeoning "spiritual and self-help" community of mass media, and within the dynamic renewal elements upwelling in any number of organized religions and religious institutions, to begin the persuasive introduction into the public conversation that the fundamental language of separation must be abandoned. At least the invitation must be made, and made persuasively, to the public.[14]

In this regard, one of the most influential books, probably because of its Roman Catholic roots, has been Bro. Wayne Teasdale's *The Mystic Heart: Finding a Universal Spirituality in the World's Religions*. This book, in the footsteps of many others in that tradition (like Thomas Merton's classic *Contemplation in a World of Action*) that have addressed the role of spirituality in a world of action, suggests precisely (as previously quoted herein) that civilization is moving toward a culture with a "heart." Teasdale reminds his readers that every positive change he himself witnessed in the post–Vatican II era came from the ability of groups of people (and their representatives) influencing parochial religious policy, and influencing world religions by ecumenical dialogue, to become transformative in their behavior and motivate others likewise. And, Teasdale's analysis of the specter of world religions is precisely a map of the contours of ethical behavior that are possible through the myriad particular gifts that each of the great Wisdom Traditions brings to the table. Colleagues in the non-governmental organization community at the United Nations say that Kofi Annan calls people's attention to Teasdale's view, and his book, as the best way to understand how religions and ethics-based traditions can have a transformative affect in the world.

It appears that there is a widening array of practitioners and religious and values-based constituencies who want to point out precisely to the average citizen that the nature of the use of language itself has a profound influence on resulting societal behavior.

Examples come to mind in current American affairs. Did the language of polarization (and resulting fear) used to promote the Iraq war "set conditions" in which acts bordering on torture, or including torture, appeared to have been condoned by certain American authorities? Will fear inevitably erode America's traditional views on the universality of civil rights? Will there, in fact, be a backlash against language of separation, as currently widely used by the Bush administration in purveying a view of the world divided as "good" and "evil." Are movies like *Bowling for Columbine* or *Fahrenheit 9/11* results of such a backlash by critics, phantasmagoric or not, to try to point out fallacious or counterproductive behaviors or perceptions? Will there be more questioning of the standards of fact versus "spin" in American discourse? Will such questions amount to the kind of ground swell that, at various times in American history, have led to major pendulum swings toward more truly democratic and equanimous forms of praxis? Certainly, in the year 2004, we find ourselves in what appears to be a pivotal conversation in this regard.

"Language of separation" has a profound effect on societal behavior. However, it appears unsure whether a counter language of "welcoming" might produce an opposite effect. It is seldom tried in public discourse. Yet, the negative results of separation language are easily recognized among history's many great horror stories—like Nazi Germany or Stalinist Russia—to name only two. However, Americans have been slow to identify the lesser, but still insidious, incremental effects of this kind of negative language on their own society and political process. Similarly, with regard to the role of religious plurality, and the role of religious groups who try to assert influence on American politics and culture, it is apparent that the kind of religious experience, and resulting language, appears to either have a positive influence on fundamental democratic ideals or a negative one in which, instead, there is movement toward positions that are anti-choice, and in that sense, anti-freedom.

Religious experiences, and organized religions, which teach separation or divisiveness by the very nature of their experiential modality, work against democracy and the democratic ideal. This appears true no matter what day-to-day ethics they may claim to teach for the individual, a point made by the aforementioned essay by Joseph Chuman in the American Ethical Union's *Dialogue* magazine. Therein, Chuman listed four kinds of religious experience which, by nature, "do not violate the human conscience" at its deepest level (which I take to be very similar to the language previously quoted herein by religious writers Teasdale and Vaugh-Lee with regard to the standard called "Heart"). Although I do not have space to elaborate Chuman's categories here, they included "Nature Mysticism," "Reverent Agnosticism," "Deweyan Idealism," and "Non-Instrumental Holism." This list might not fully parallel my own (I do not have one) but at least anchors the views of the present article strongly in the tradition of Humanism.

Religious experiences, and organized religions, which teach holism or basic ethical precepts, without any exclusive experiential or historical claims, aid healthy democracy. It would be tragic indeed if the very religious groups and experiences that pride themselves on being the underpinning of "the American way" actually became those who historically, simply by their innate language of separation, eroded this great, and indeed rare, democratic experiment. "The right for right's sake," quoted at the beginning of this article from Felix Adler, the founder of Ethical Culture, becomes a blessing or a curse depending on the interpretation of "right." If "right" is a quality based not on concept but only on the objective proof of actual moral and ethical behavior, it appears possible that the world might move from a praxis of simply "accommodational" behavior (which, by its implying "separation" is doomed to limitation) to that which is truly transformative. The character of the latter appears to have been objectively exemplified by the lives of many historical persons revered by various traditions as moral and ethical heroes. Paralleling Adler's admonition "The right for right's sake is the motto we should take for our own life," it is worth remembering the words of one of Ramana Maharshi's great successors, Sri H. W. L. Poonja ("Poonjaji" or "Papaji") who said, "The condition for freedom is to want freedom and freedom only."[15]

ACKNOWLEDGMENTS

I am grateful for discussions at the gathering of the Humanist Institute faculty in New York City in May 2004 and particularly to Joseph Chuman for forwarding his comments in the Spring 2004 issue of Dialogue. In furthering those discussions here I greatly thank Lama Surya Das of the Dalai Lama's tradition for suggesting works in the area of Buddhist social theory, David Deida for permission to freely adapt from his writings on "the three stages of growth," Melanie Freas for comments on Sri Aurobindo, and Pamela Wilson (in the lineage of Ramana Maharshi) for discussions concerning Ramana's teachings mentioned herein, as this article neared its completion. Always, debt is owed to the vision and example of Bro. Wayne Teasdale, whose book subtitled "Finding a Universal Spirituality in the World's Religions" is an abiding inspiration and fully in harmony with the spirit of ethical humanism.

BIBLIOGRAPHY

Adler, Felix. *Life and Destiny*. [1926, out of print] as quoted in: Friess, H. L. *Felix Adler and Ethical Culture: Memories and Studies*. New York: Columbia University Press, 1981.
Aurobindo, Sri. [The] *Life Divine—U.S. Edition*. New York: Lotus Press, 1985.
Berne, Eric. *Games People Play: The Basic Handbook of Transactional Analysis*. New York: Ballantine Books, 1996.
Bush, Marabai. "Conversation on Contemplation, Religion, Politics, and the State of the World." May 5, 2004, New York City, made available by Lama Surya Das (Dzogchen Center, Cambridge, MA), 2004.
Deida, David. *Intimate Communion*. New York: Health Communications, 1995.
———. *Naked Buddhism*. New York: Plexus, 2002.

Dialogue. New York: American Ethical Union, 2004.

Ethical Culture as Religion. 1995. Pamphlet of the Washington Ethical Society (member of the American Ethical Union).

Ethical Culture Review of Books. www.aeu.org [referring to citations of footnote 7 herein].

King, Robert H. *Thomas Merton and Thich Nhat Hanh: Engaged Spirituality in an Age of Globalism*. Continuum Publishing Group, 2003.

Lakoff, George. *Moral Politics*. Chicago: University of Chicago Press, 1999.

Loy, David R. *The Great Awakening: A Buddhist Social Theory*. New York: Wisdom Publications, 2003.

Maharshi, Ramana. *Talks with Ramana Maharshi*. Carlsbad, California: InnerDirections Publishing, 2000.

Merton, Thomas. *Contemplation in a World of Action*. South Bend, Indiana: University of Notre Dame Press, 1999.

Poonja, H. W. L. *The Truth Is*. New York: Weiser Books, 2000.

Teasdale, Wayne. (Foreword by H. H. the Dalai Lama.) *The Mystic Heart: Finding a Universal Spirituality in the World's Religions*. New York: New World Library, 1999.

Turning Wheel, Spring 2004 [referring to citation of footnote 8 herein].

Vaugh-Lee, Llewellyn. *Working with Oneness*. Inverness, California: Thomson-Shore Inc, 2002.

Walsh, Roger. "Perennial Wisdom in a Post Modern World," paper based on a talk given to the Western Buddhists Teachers Meeting, Mt. Madonna, California, 1995. Made available by Lama Surya Das (Dzogchen Center, Cambridge MA; posted at InterSpiritual Dialogue Web site, www.isdac.com, under Resources, Buddhism).

NOTES

1. This subject has had considerable recent attention in religious circles. For instance, in reporting a dialogue among six "leaders" representing a number of religious traditions, Mirabai Bush, Executive Director of the Center for Contemplative Mind in Society, noted the following major questions, among others: can religious experience restore the conversation/concern on the ethical dimension of social life? how can we change the abuse of religious belief in guiding public policy (e.g., the aggressive political use of religion versus authentic religious experience)? who speaks in public for the wisdom within the great Wisdom Traditions? what is the proper relation between church and state? What did the founders intend? how is the popular misunderstanding being manipulated?

2. For instance, a recent book, *Thomas Merton and Thich Nhat Hanh: Engaged Spirituality in an Age of Globalization*, traces the roots of this cross-fertilization between East and West as it has influenced both religious experience and the role of religions in societies, East and West.

3. Emphasis on "Deed versus Creed" is, of course, one of the most oft-noted originating motivations behind Felix Adler's founding of Ethical Culture (as stated, for instance, as "Deed before Creed" in "Ethical Culture as a Religion" (pamphlet, 1995, Washington Ethical Society); however, there is little difference between that emphasis and what is stated by David R. Loy in his *Buddhist Social Theory* (see text of this paper); in Loy the emphasis is completely on the question of how religious teachings either do, or do not, contain a "language of separation," that is, as stated in more depth elsewhere herein, the "continual struggle of subject-object dualism as one of our main sources of suffering." In a recent article in the American Ethical Union's *Dialogue* magazine (May 2004), Joeseph Chuman of the Humanist Institute has elucidated the kinds of ethically oriented religious experiences that "do not take us out of a naturalistic framework nor violate a humanist conscience."

4. Again, see David R. Loy, as cited herein, wherein the individual context of suffering ("dukkha") in Buddhism is extended to the "dualistic and dukkha-producing institutions" or societies. Or, see "Perennial Wisdom in a Post Modern World," by Roger Walsh, MD (psychiatry), as cited herein.

5. It is interesting that this precise quotation is also used by Mirabai Bush, as cited herein, wherein she quotes Helen Twokov, the founder of *Tricycle Magazine* (*The Buddhist Journal*), as saying that "such compassion seemed to be rare in American life as it gets more polarized."

6. Catholic monk Brother Wayne Teasdale in the very influential book *The Mystic Heart: Finding a Universal Spirituality in the World's Religions* specifically uses the word "Heart" (and its derivatives) to refer to a values-based shared recognition among all peoples as to their hoped-for world with ideal social conditions for all. He said, specifically of paradigm shifts now happening in the world, "they are preparing the way for a universal civilization: a civilization with a *heart*" (p. 5).

7. A number of the books I have recently reviewed in the Ethical Culture Review of Books (www.aeu.com) are books addressing this "critique" in various ways. These include Wayne Teasdale's *The Mystic Heart: Finding a Universal Spirituality in the World's Religions*, Dasarath's *Freedom Dreams*, Lama Surya Das's *Letting Go of the Person You Used to Be*; Catherine Ingram's *Passionate Presence: Experiencing the Seven Qualities of Awakened Awareness*, and Lewis Richmond's *A Whole Life's Work*. In addition, there are more "academic" discourses concerning this view, as in David R.

Loy, *The Great Awakening: A Buddhist Social Theory*, as cited herein, or the work of David Deida (loc. cit.) from which herein I adapt a number of ideas.

8. *Turning Wheel*, Spring 2004, p. 39.

9. This language is also used by the modern-day Sufi writer and social leader Dr. Llewellyn Vaugh-Lee, who, in his book *Working with Oneness*, refers to "the heart of the world" of which he quotes from their great literature, 'I am He whom I love, He whom I love is me' is stamped within the heart. . . ."

10. This theme is elaborated in various sections of Ramana Maharshi's most well-known book in the West: *Talks with Ramana Maharshi*, wherein the application to various social situations arises from questions and answers between Ramana and those visiting him, in his later years often social or religious leaders from many parts of the world. Gandhi himself often spoke of Ramana.

11. The useful parallels to social and historical questions do not come as a surprise since Deida's teachings stem particularly from non-dual Hinduism and Buddhism. Specifically, in the former, a particularly influential teacher, Sri Aurobindo, who wrote prodigiously on social and political matters as well, articulated in one of his spiritual classics, *The Life Divine*, the view that individual sentient beings are a microcosm of larger processes in time and space such that patterns and processes such as evolution, in the macrocosm, are actually recapitulated (at least symbolically and metaphorically) in the personal internal journey (or path) of each individual.

12. See, for instance, Eric Berne, MD, *Games People Play: The Basic Handbook of Transactional Analysis*.

13. Specifically referred to here are the religious experiences of "non-dualism" or "no separation" enumerated by Bro. Wayne Teasdale in *The Mystic Heart*, among them Advaita Vedanta in Hinduism, Dzogchen, Pure Land and other Buddhist experiences, Sufism in Islam, Kabbalah in Judaism, infused contemplation in Christianity, awakened Shamanism, and "awakened" or "nondual awareness" in non-religious contexts (for the latter see the writings of Australian scientist John Wren-Lewis).

14. Such an "invitation" was made at the 2003 United Nations Forum on Indigenous Peoples by cultural anthropologist and Andean indigenous religious practitioner Oscar Miro-Quesada; he pointed out that the dominant language of that forum was often "victimization" and "blame" and invited a more holistic, welcoming, language which, he said, typified the experiential roots of the indigenous Andean religious traditions (as in the name of his own supporting organization—Heart of the Healer). It was hard to gauge the result of that invitation, but it was certainly heard.

15. *The Truth Is*, Sri H. W. L. Poonja.

7.

Democracy's Destroyers

Robert B. Tapp

L et me start with a historical note. Shortly after its founding (and before the Cold War started), UNESCO began an ambitious project defining "democracy." The report was edited by the distinguished philosopher Richard McKeon.[1] The most interesting overall conclusion was that no one rejected "democracy" anymore. Not even the Soviets. No one from among the UN members! There were (however!) enormous differences in the meaning imputed to the term. In the USSR it was claimed that "economic democracy" was paramount, while the Westerners highlighted "political democracy." Rereading that volume today, one is struck by this irony—and cautioned about easy definitions and terminologies.

As we are writing these papers, the naive assumptions of many of our leaders and neighbor-citizens regarding the desirability of democracy are becoming frighteningly clear. All humans do *not* want it, nor does it readily emerge from the ashes of war-shattered cultures. Nor can it be imposed by force. Nor will it emerge from rootages in many of our world's traditional religions. Nor can we assume that all citizens of democracies, when on military and colonial ventures, will act democratically. Case histories? Iraq, Afghanistan, the former Yugoslavia, Somalia, North Ireland, Angola. . . .

The historic record of Christianity is little more encouraging. As

A. D. Lindsay carefully argued many years ago, democracy at most emerged from the tradition of left-wing Calvinism—not from any mainstream version of Christian faiths.[2]

Even more important for our consideration is the new UN Development Program report "Democracy in Latin America: Towards a Citizens' Democracy." Only the Spanish text was available at the time of this writing, but it presents a devastating review of the status of democracy in that part of the world where US hegemony, since the creation of the Monroe Doctrine, has ruled supreme. Not only have we typically been content to support and deal with oligarchies and dictatorships in the Latin world, we have failed to give real support when these authoritarian rules were effectively overthrown.

Our fiascoes go way back. Occupations of Haiti. Invasions of Nicaragua. Support of Batistaism in Cuba so strong that we failed to prevent Castro turning to the USSR in despair—to list only recent misadventures. Overtly and covertly we blocked democratic changes in almost every country south of our borders. We armed and financed right-wings, winked at pseudo-democracies in Argentina and Mexico. Even today we covertly undermine elected leaders in Venezuela and Haiti. This bi-partisan failure to encourage and support democracies in "our part of the world" surely renders suspect most of the present rhetoric. Our behaviors do not show that we believe in and want to foster democracy or that we believe it to be the universal human birthright.

Secretary-General Kofi Annan, in hailing the UNDP report, said:

> Opinion polls tell us that today only about 50 percent of Latin Americans prefer democracy to authoritarian rule. That is very sad. More important, it is wrong. The solution to Latin America's ills does not lie in a return to authoritarianism. It lies in a stronger and deeper-rooted democracy.

This report again reminds us that democracy is a very fragile and recent human development and one that can never be taken for granted. The official UN summary describes this in more detail:

> Just 43% of Latin Americans are fully supportive of democracy, while 30.5% express ambivalence and 26.5% hold non-democratic

views, according to opinion surveys conducted for the report in 18 countries in the region; more than half of all Latin Americans—54.7 percent—say they would support an "authoritarian" regime over "democratic" government if authoritarianism rule could "resolve" their economic problems.

Since 2000, four elected presidents in the 18 countries studied were forced to quit before the end of their terms following steep drops in public support.

The first generation of Latin Americans to come of age in functioning democracies has experienced virtually no per capita income growth and widening, world-record disparities in the distribution of national income; in 2003, 225 million Latin Americans had incomes below the poverty line.

59% of the political leaders consulted for the report said political parties are failing to fulfill their necessary role.[3]

This kind of political alienation, whether a new thing or a regression to historic cultural patterns reflective of the medieval European heritage, further illustrates the need to attend to the deeper cultural factors that are necessary to sustain democracy.

"This shows that democracy is not something that has taken hold of people's minds as strongly as we had thought it would," said Enrique Berruga Filloy, Mexico's ambassador to the United Nations.

The report says that while unhappiness with political leadership has a long history in Latin America, the people now complaining are faulting democracy itself.

Voter turnout is falling across the region, especially among the young, while civil unrest is on the rise.[4]

This dismal kind of public opinion has emerged even as the "objective" conditions for democracy had been expanding enormously

Democracy's progress is reflected in the Electoral Democracy Index (EDI),[5] a compound measurement prepared for the report that combines four variables: the right to vote, fair elections, free elections, and elections as a means of access to public office. The average EDI (whose value ranges between zero and one, where zero indicates the complete absence of electoral democracy and one the maximum) for

Latin America rose rapidly from 0.28 in 1977 to 0.69 in 1985 and 0.86 in 1990, climbing further to 0.93 in the year 2002.

Important as these structural possibilities are for developing and sustaining democracy, the turnout percentages must also be noted. Some Latin countries had once viewed voting as legally mandatory—to be proved via a card stamped at a polling place. But now even that dubious law can be circumvented when dictatorships fold. Disappointment with the results of democracy, as indicated in the UNDP statistics, leads to a drop-off in actual voting. Putting this more politically, cynicism trumps democracy.

The report also sets out broad goals for developing Latin democracy:

- Democracy implies a certain idea of the human being and of the nurturing of citizenship;
- Democracy is a form of organization of power that implies the existence and proper functioning of the State;
- While the electoral system is a key element of democracy, the latter cannot be reduced to the mere holding of elections;
- Democracy requires full civic participation, that is to say, the full recognition of political, civil and social citizenship;
- Democracy in the region is a particular historical experience that must be understood and judged in terms of its specific characteristics.

THE MILLENNIUM PROJECT

This Latin American study grew out of a too-little publicized UN project aiming at certain world standards to be achieved by 2015:[6]

Goal 1: Eradicate extreme poverty and hunger

Goal 2: Achieve universal primary education

Goal 3: Promote gender equality and empower women

Goal 4: Reduce child mortality

Goal 5: Improve maternal health

Goal 6: Combat HIV/AIDS, malaria and other diseases

Goal 7: Ensure environmental sustainability

Goal 8: Develop a Global Partnership for Development

These UN goals, with all the negotiating and compromising that they necessarily embody, clearly move beyond the simple functional meanings of democracy into social and economic and scientific realms that are structurally basic.

THE RULE OF LAW

While it is almost a commonplace among scholars that the rule of law and judiciary independence are essential to democracy, these have been low on the priority lists of most advanced nations when they deal with the less-developed world. Cultures differ widely upon the contents of any "natural" law—some seeing it as directly flowing from a divine law and some seeing it more as a part of a nature to be scientifically studied and understood.

ACCESS TO INFORMATION

A much more ambiguous factor is the role of information and the functions of media. Jefferson, in 1787, said,

> This basis of our government being the opinion of the people, the very first object should be to keep that right; and were it left to me to decided whether we should have a government without newspapers, or newspapers without a government, I should not hesitate a moment to prefer the latter.

But he said that in a situation where literacy was widespread, reading newspapers was common, and the competition among news sources lively. Our times are different. Many more of our US neighbors learn whatever they learn about their society and world from TV rather than newspapers. And network TV, having trivialized its audience, can become even more trivialized in its future programming. Our college students (the "leaders of tomorrow") do little better.

TRANSFORMATIONS OF MEDIA

Moreover, it has been clear for some time that TV is an entertainment medium, not an educative one. Less obvious are the ways in which corporate values affect content. Expenses must be met, and this is only by advertising. The audiences served by public television and radio are minuscule. The dominating networks both create and serve their markets and very effectively lobby legislatures to eliminate barriers to their increased consolidation. Periodic attempts to allocate public interest segments typically fail.

Media students have noticed interesting changes over time. Sports involvement, of course, is the most obvious. Some older readers may remember pre-TV times when about the only sport that was really professionalized was baseball. Younger viewers can be captivated by a wide variety of sports, including wrestling—that have finally, by now, even opened to women participants.

"Celebrity" covers a myriad media attractors—film, pop music, TV, sports. Networks evolve to cater to these wants—E, MTV, BET, VH1, ESPN.

"Reality" is the newest genre competing for attention. Labor costs drop, of course, when ordinary persons replace actors and stars.

Events leading up to the Iraq invasion, the war itself, and the early stages of occupation made this quite overt misinformation quite clear. If journalism depends upon access, then access depends upon currying favor. The Pentagon creation of "embedded" reporters (and its rejection of those few journalists who attempted independence) was a new step in controlling the news. The censorship of images of dead bodies, friend or foe, was a clever advance on the grisly images shown during previous military encounters.

The rationale for that war (weapons of mass destruction) was little probed by journalists and certainly was not subjected to widespread media attention. Even when they were not found, continuing searches for them persist.

Can the Internet fill this gap between information and entertainment? That has been the dream of some reformers, and the information-sharing success of Web sites such as MoveOn have been cited as examples. Supporters of this theory may note that more than half of US adults have broadband access either at home or at work.

This pluralization of potential sources of information may be hopeful in preserving a democratic society, but the issue of dissemination still remains. How will the word get out to the general populace in ways that catch attention and invite critical reflection? Paul Krugman coined a great phrase to describe this lag between discovery of information and the time and processes that ensure before the information gets "traction with the broad public."[7]

There are, alas, already signs that profitable computer games attract more viewers than do the information sources. This suggests that commerce will trump progress once again. Is the main lesson that people will get what they want? And that competition for changed wants is an arena where the lure of profits trumps education?

VOTING AND NON-VOTING

Media alone cannot be blamed for the fall-off of political participation. The relative satisfaction of basic needs is certainly a factor. Satisfied citizens may well become less concerned about perceiving or feeling the need for changes. And the vocalization of an educational system, from kindergarten through university, must bear some of the blame.

The comedian Mort Sahl has recently taken to the stage again and sees changes here within his own lifetime:

> [T]hrough it all, Mr. Sahl has maintained optimism. That's what he worries is now in short supply, especially among young people.
> "You can see it in the movies," he said. "Their movies resonate with people disappointing them, parents, lovers, children, as if the

net result of all your effort will be disappointment. Sometimes they think I'm conning them when I talk about justice and true love. They think they're slogans. But in the last analysis, people are sustained by believing in something."

For Mr. Sahl, the crucial distinction is between cynicism and skepticism. "It's the noncourageous among us who become cynical and say nothing is possible," he said, "which gives them a convenient out, because if you're a cynic your heart can't be broken."[8]

The rise in cynicism is, of course, not limited to Latin America. It is commonplace to view recent US voting drop-offs as similarly caused. "We the People" becomes "We the Few (and Fewer)." Until recent years, lowered voter turnout always played into the hands of conservatives and incumbents. Today, this may no longer be the case for reasons that we will be examining.

ROLES PLAYED BY WEALTH

I want to emphasize now the roles played by wealth in shaping and in undercutting democracy. My focus is on "wealth" rather than "income" for the same reason that economists use—it is a truer measure. And it makes more sense semantically than "poverty"—although in many ways that term refers simply to its inverse.

Some time ago sociologists began exploring the components of "class" as it functioned in actual societies. In our society, for instance, income based on gambling does not move one as high in the perceived class structure as would income based on salary. Even those lines begin to blur when recent corporate shenanigans are taken into account.

FREEDOM AND EQUALITY

Enlightenment thinking focused on two values—equality and freedom. Particularly in the United States and France, the term "citizen" referred to persons declared to be politically equal. Those with this new status would be able to determine their own destinies by voting, freed from any domination by church or crown. To be sure, large numbers were excluded on the basis of gender or slave status and by variations of economic discrimination in the thirteen states. Even for those groups, there came to be a certain amount of equality before the law. Freedom included freedom to speak and to assemble. But certain forms of freedom, for instance, religious freedom, were sharply restricted by local and state customs and laws. Sabbath laws activities restricted Sunday activities; blasphemy rules restricted speech and publication.

Especially in the United States (where one could claim the "practical Enlightenment" took root), the abilities to change presidents, governors, judiciaries, and legislatures made the expansion of initial democratic values possible.

The forms of representative democracy that emerged in the US experiment persist to complicate the present. From the beginning the Senate was based upon equal representation for each state, while the Congress was based upon equal representation for each citizen—more populous states having more representatives. The hard fact of regionalized slavery complicated this since each slave counted as three-fifths of a human but had no vote. That Orwellian solution meant that all residents were equal but Southerners were "more equal."

As political democracies of England and the US shifted to capitalist economies, the tensions between these values became much more apparent. Industrialization came to involve urbanization. And that meant not only the loss of small-town rootings that constrained so much of human behavior. In the US, the immigrations resulting from political crises in Europe and the labor needs of new industries created potential Catholic voting blocs in formerly Protestant cities. And the exercise of individual freedom not only created middle classes but enormously expanded the gaps between rich and poor. That trend continues into our own time—and not only here but throughout the developing world as well.

Democratic equality has never meant the absence of all differences. What it meant initially was equal access to the law and to the change processes of society. This was a significant development from the Protestant Reformers' idea that sinners stood equally damned in their distances from a perfect divine judge. The Enlightenment doctrine of Progress created the difference. Instead of inhabiting a world of rigid divine orders, humans were now seen to be the shapers of their societies along rational lines, based upon the reasons that were their universal possessions as humans.

What must be pointed out repeatedly (and from metaphoric rooftops) are the ways that democratic societies have expanded their awareness of barriers to equality. "Equal opportunity" theorists have focused on discriminatory uses of gender, age, race, origin, religion, region, language, class, wealth, health, sexual orientation, and from such studies have come changes embodying those expanded moral visions, thus enlarging the meanings of Equality. The Millennium goals of the UN cited previously are a good illustration of the present state of this process.

Past democrats have found ways to reduce the polarizations of wealth that emerged with some exercises of human freedom—progressive taxation, encouragement of philanthropy, inheritance taxes. On a deeper level, societies need to valorize other uses of freedom than entrepreneurism. Public servants, scientists, scholars and teachers, health workers, environmentalists, artists of all kinds are essential to the common good.

MASSES AND ELITES AND EXCELLENCES

I have been calling naive those who think that humans automatically want freedom and self rule. Readers of Dostoevsky's parable of the Grand Inquisitor will know what I mean. And those journalists who worry about opinion on "the Arab street" are saying the same thing. With the UNDP Report mentioned above, we need to add "the Latin American street." And we had better not ignore "the US street."

The risk, of course, is that societies at every level of development are open to trivialization, what Alan Riding calls "massification":

Since World War II, however, has come the massification of culture. In response Europeans have tried to reinforce national and regional identities, to hold onto their languages, foods and folkloric traditions. But given the option of American-style entertainment, they show little interest in one another's arts. It may simply be lack of information: European newspapers offer poor coverage of their neighbors' art scenes, and television is not much better, with the exception of the French-German network Arte. Whatever the reason, artistic endeavors that do cross borders today reach few people.[9]

To describe the alternative as "elitism" conjures up too many unsavory past associations. So too "expertism." Perhaps we should try "excellences," keeping the term pluralized. Critics and innovators of all kinds are essential to the development and sustenance of democracies. Even pop culture makes its lists of "top tens." We need to help persons do the same in all fields of endeavor—both as a motivating theme and as an educating theme.

DE-UNILATERALIZING—AND GLOBALIZING—THE US

The naïveté of defining democracy simply as voting, and assuming that everyone wants the same thing, is daily exploded by events around the world. The desires for religious conformity are too strong to ignore— whether described as theocratic society, a Muslim state, Hindutva, a Jewish state, a Buddhist state. And those labelings are misleading since they overlook the extreme pluralisms within most religious traditions. How significant is a "Christian" label that must include Protestants of a variety of persuasions, Catholics, Orthodox, plus growing and independent sects?

Democracy, strictly speaking, designates the "shift in power downward," to use Fareed Zakaria's widely read designation.[10] The significant issues, of course, are the comparative sets of values held by those "formerly above" and those newly empowered. Replacing an arbitrary monarchy with an educated but repressed underclass is one thing; replacing a benevolent oligarchy (not necessarily an oxymoron) with a revolutionary fundamentalism is quite another. In many recent cases, the choices have been yet grayer. How should one compare the Pahlevi shah with mullah Khomeini? Or Soviet dictators with the Afghan Taliban? Or the Saudi princedom with whatever Osama bin Laden would substitute?

This process could, less admiringly, be described with Alan Riding's "massification" or simply "vulgarization." Whatever the chosen term, democratization seems inevitable in the long run. The real question is what can hedge it. I have suggested that equality needs to be balanced with excellence. On mass levels, this is obviously recognized in sports, pop music, and cinema. The youngest child can come up with his or her list of "ten best." What education should be doing is to widen the exposures to all human genres of achievement. Top scientists, top poets, top architects, top statespersons, top diplomats, top historians, top musicians, top social reformers, top engineers, top ethicists, top psychologists, top dramatists, top novelists. Good education will reach beyond the present and local. We might even celebrate Matthew Arnold's great declaration that culture is "to make the best that has been thought and known in the world current everywhere."

Humanists should be engaging in a fourfold task. First, to stress the prescience of those Deists and Masons who not only created "we the people" but managed to craft a constitution that omitted reference to any god and freed the consciences of individual citizens.

Second, to keep alive the interpretive concept "civil religion." While humanists may not want to use it themselves, it is certainly the right key for understanding such phrases as "under God," "in God we trust," "so help me God." While these phrasings persist, they make no technical sense since there have never been serious agreements among Christians as to the nature of this "God" or his dictates (cf. Protestant vs. Catholic on Lord's Prayer and Ten Commandments). Nor has there even been a functional recognition of any "Judeo-Christian tradition." On the latter point, reflect on centuries of anti-Semitism and conversion activities by Christians toward Jews. Sensitive scholars such as Jacob Neusner have long decried the truth of the elision.

Third, humanists should be stressing the current diversity of the US population in terms of religious identifications and the presence of significant blocks of non-religious citizens. The political founders could only dimly have anticipated this, but their structures made it possible for such variety to emerge without continual intergroup warfares. In fact the major civil war of the nineteenth century served to split most of the major religious denominations rather than be a war between them.

Finally, and of equal importance, humanists should be underscoring the enormous advantages of such a secularized state in maximizing the abilities of all citizens to pursue happiness as they define it, respecting the lives and liberties of their neighbors.

RESPECTING THE LIVES AND
LIBERTIES OF THEIR NEIGHBORS

In a globalizing world, everyone is our neighbor (and the term "citizen" is too open to local interpretation). Putting it this way suggests a vast, if implicit, social contract where the only restrictions that should be enforced would be upon those who have restricted their neighbors. This choice of simpler language would make it easier to commend democratic practices to a wider audience.

Nevertheless, the simpler word carries a heavy load of assumptions. How can I respect your liberties if I do not know your values? How can I relate when your values conflict with mine? How can I respect someone's life and liberty if I have not reflected enough on those terms to understand that they denote rights—to food, shelter, education, health, movement, expression?

At these points, our long historical experiences indicate the restricting roles of religions and ideologies. Suppose Church X says, "Error does not have the same rights as Truth." If "true" is only their arbitrary decision, no respect is involved unless everyone makes the same arbitrary decision. Or if Church Y says that "Infidels do not have equal rights to Believers," the same simplistic designating is involved. If Church Z suggests that "Suicide in the right cause will earn you Paradise," only those who believe in such transcendental realms will agree.

Surveying the present situation could easily lead to pessimism regarding this humanist agenda of knowledge-based democracy. Theocratic religions are capturing both attention and power. They claim access to a non- and supra-natural reality not knowable by ordinary means. Moreover, they move toward various apocalypticisms suggesting that this higher realm is about to establish its dominance over the world of ordinary experience of ordinary human beings. And, most disturbingly, they suggest that apocalyptic times necessitate a suspension of ordinary moralities.[11]

This "special morality for times of crisis" can be seen in the more popular "Left Behind" series where the times between "Rapture" and "Final Appearance" are filled with violence and slaughter that would normally be forbidden by any "Christian" ethics.

For most of the last century, most sociologists of religion indulged themselves with a "secularization thesis" where the spread of a science-based education would erode traditional faiths that had traditionally served to endorse primitive moralities. The story is more complex, especially in the US. Not only have fundamentalisms survived; they have been flourishing.

Various explanations have been adduced. Some argue that most of us are wired for versions of supernaturalism and that only a relatively small minority can live without the transcendental anchorings. One is reminded of Martin Luther's "Man hat Gott oder Abgott" (humans need either god or idol).

Others contend that a proper education in the humanities will help people transcend the more arrogant and virulent forms of religiosity. One can certainly argue that current university educational diets (which inevitably trickle down into lower schools as well) are humanities-starved—shifting to various training systems linked to the lucrative fads of the moment.

Still others argue that more science education would free students from supernatural temptations. It is clearly the case that science education in the US has become weaker. And particularly evolution teaching, the lynchpin of much of science, has been brilliantly undercut by fundamentalist forces.

My own position would add to this more education "about" religions. Perhaps better educated foreign-policy makers, and their CIA, would have avoided those mistakes in Palestine, Iran, Indonesia, and Afghanistan that strengthened the worst in Islam. Better knowledge of Islam would have warned against close alliances with Saudis and Pakistanis. Certainly better education regarding Islam would have avoided the stupidity regarding democracy in Iraq. Some sophistication regarding Guatemala would have avoided support of an evangelical Protestant tyranny. Comparative religions may be our best insurance against bigotry, as well as being our best argument for the necessity of a secular society in which all ideologies must compete without state support or favoritism.

NOTES

1. United Nations Educational Scientific and Cultural Organization [from old catalog] and Richard Peter McKeon. *Democracy in a world of tensions*. Paris, 1951.

2. A. D. Lindsay, *The Essentials of Democracy* (Philadelphia: University of Pennsylvania Press, 1929).

3. From the UN press release: http://www.undp.org/dpa/pressrelease /releases/2004/april/0421prodal.html

4. Dean Hoge, *New York Times*, Apr. 22, 2004—summarizing report released in Lima, Peru, April 21.

5. Developed in a 2003 paper by Gerardo L. Munck and Jay Verkuilen. Available at http://www.asu.edu/clas/polisci/cqrm/APSA2003/Munck-Verkuillen_APSA_ 2003.pdf

6. http://www.unmillenniumproject.org/html/about.shtm.

7. Paul Krugman coined this useful phrase in a April 27, 2004, column in the *New York Times*. He was noting that it took David Kay's public statement to firm the public awareness that the WMD stories about Iraq were fallacious.

8. Bruce Weber, "Mort Sahl, Still Simmering After All These Years," *New York Times*, Apr. 27, 2004.

9. Alan Riding, "A Common Culture (From the U.S.A.) Binds Europeans Ever Closer," *New York Times*, Apr. 26, 2004.

10. Fareed Zakaria, *The future of freedom: Illiberal democracy at home and abroad*, 1st ed. (New York: W. W. Norton, 2003).

11. See the 5-volume Fundamentalism Project by Martin E. Marty and R. Scott Appleby (Univ. of Chicago Press) and the post-final volume in which they shifted terminology to "strong religion": Gabriel Abraham Almond, R. Scott Appleby, and Emmanuel Sivan. *Strong religion: The rise of fundamentalisms around the world* (Chicago: University of Chicago Press, 2003).

8.

Is Democracy a Rational or a Mythological Concept?

Andreas Rosenberg

W hy is an analysis of the concept "democracy" important in terms of its origin from either rational considerations or as an interpretation of a specific mythos? Starting with the beginning of this century, the concept "democracy" has become a slogan. A slogan we have stitched on a banner, under which we march in our effort to persuade or force all nations to accept what we see as democracy. We also feel that this is the answer to their problems, whatever these are. We consequently ought to know what we are selling and what the intrinsic nature of our product is.

The scope of this paper is quite narrow. A wide review and discussion of the voluminous literature is reduced to answering the following question: which, if any, of the attributes of the concept "democracy" can on purely rational grounds be considered to render democracy superior to alternate styles of government? We do not talk about preferences for different forms of government shown by populations in the past or the postulated moral values of this or that government form, neither do we discuss analysis of the problem by other investigators of democracy. We do not talk about efficiency in producing goods for short-term pleasure or the ability of a democratic nation to vanquish other nations. A democratic government may, of course, satisfy some of these criteria for excellence, but for me superiority means a long-term advantage in the process of the evolution of the organization of humanity, a Darwinian concept.

If we ask one of our citizens to explain what democracy is, we often hear that this is the best form of government and that it is the form of government prevalent in United States.

How is this government, then, different from other governments classified as non-democratic? The answer often is, paraphrasing Abraham Lincoln, a government of the people, by the people, for the people. This is a very poetic statement that, however, approaches truism. All governments manage the common affairs of the people. This is the definition of the function of a government and the managing is certainly carried out by humans and not by dogs or aliens.

More precisely, the question we raised was whether the label "democracy," as generally accepted in the Western world, describes either a rational system of governance, preferred because of its theoretical and practical merits, or a mythological narrative, depicting idealized dreams of mankind. Do these dreams provide one narrative among many that provide the necessary but arbitrary ideology for one possible form of government?

The other major forms of governance that developed from the primitive family and tribal structures—theocracy, monarchy, and autocracy—can easily be shown to be based on mythological narratives.

In theocracy, the plan for governance is defined and those governing are chosen by revelation from higher, extra-terrestrial powers. The Divine justification for these choices is based on some form of mythical logic. Classical examples are the Abrahamic religions that are based on the assumption of a world which is only temporarily governed by humans until the return of the rule by the original power, the Creator.

Monarchy is a hierarchical secular system linked to the theological mythology. The world of humans is divided into two parts: material and spiritual, the latter being the abode of the Divine. The power structures in the material and spiritual worlds are mirror images. Whether the structure of the spiritual domain, the mythology, was created by copying the monarchial structure of the material world or vice versa is in this context irrelevant. The simplest and cleanest case of the linkage between these two domains is the monarchy of Japan, where the emperor is declared a descendant of the Sun God, the ultimate extraterrestrial power, linking thereby the two systems. In Western monarchies, taking the French pre-revolutionary monarchy as an example, the hierarchy in the secular world with a monarch at the top is authorized through a divine mandate from the hierarchy in the mythological world. Such an absolute mandate is the basis for the legendary utterance "L'état c'est moi" (I am the State) attributed sans cause to Louis XIV.

Autocracy in its different forms often originates from a simple power grab by an individual; however, it is always justified by referring to its own mythology, where the narrated story does not have to take place only within a purely mythological, spiritual realm. The military dictatorship (a clear case of autocracy) in the former Soviet Union was based on the myth of an ideal Communist State, a clearly materialistic story from our daily world but a myth anyhow. Adolf Hitler's autocratic rule was based on the myth of racial purity and supremacy. In some cases, the autocracy is disguised by tradition and the formal power structure appears not to represent the autocracy. In the very late Roman Republic and the early Empire, the trick was to separate formal legislative power and executive power, the former residing in traditional assemblies of the governed and the second residing de facto in the hands of an autocrat, Augustus. This was necessary because, as often in human affairs, the influence of the mythology, in this case glorifying the elected assemblies of Romans, was stronger than the practical and rational necessity for a central executive power to govern the burgeoning empire.

We might want to add to this list another societal model: technocracy—the rule by purely pragmatic technicians, striving to reach the absurd goal of the highest possible productivity. This model replaces humans with goods produced as the basic unit of society. In technocracy, humans appear peripherally and only as users of these goods. The justification of technocracy is based on the myth of an earthly paradise created by never ending flow of goods from the Horn of Plenty of Technology.

Although not realized anywhere yet, technocracy forms a threatening picture in our imagination and anticipation and looms large in our artistic vision of the future. The books and movies such as *Brave*

New World by Aldous Huxley or *Metropolis* by Thea von Harbau and
Fritz Lang have been replaced by the daily adventures of the cartoon
figure Dilbert. Such threatening images are the basis for the visceral
fear of the excesses of free market and global capitalism—and maybe
form the strongest force for idealization of past and appreciation of
traditional historic forms of government.

Compared to these systems, democracy—representing governance
by elected officials—seems to represent a simple and rational model
for government. However, looking at the states that we by consensus
define as democratic, we see large differences. Take England, for
example. It is a monarchy with an aristocracy and no written constitution. Still we define it as a democracy. When it comes to the United
States, we find that some of its founders did not consider it to be a
democracy at all. James Madison writes as Publius in *The Federalist
Papers*,

> The error which limits republican government to a narrow district
> has been unfolded and refuted in preceding papers. I remark here
> only that it seems to owe its rise and prevalence chiefly to the con-
> founding of a republic with a democracy and applying to the former
> the reasonings drawn from the nature of the latter. The true distinc-
> tion between these two forms was also adverted to on a former occa-
> sion. It is that in democracy the people meet and exercise the gov-
> ernment in person, in a republic they assemble and administer it by
> their representatives and agents.

Thus, both a republic and a monarchy can be democratic, and consequently, democracy, as we define it today, is not the blueprint for a
total government structure but describes common characteristics of
some forms of government. The majority of the population associates
democracy with personal freedom. However, we have to remember
that the guarantees for freedom are based on laws issued and followed
by any form of government and the feeling of personal freedom
depends on what you consider essential for such freedom. Rousseau
published his revolutionary tract during the reign of an absolute
monarch who denied the justified petitions of redress from utter
poverty by the majority of Frenchmen. The democratic Athens con-

demned Socrates to death for speaking freely to the youth of the city. Personal freedom is not a necessary consequence of democracy!

We can describe the popular conception of democracy and its equivalence with personal freedom using the words of a *New Yorker* cartoon, "That's the wonderful thing about democracy. You and I can stand here and shoot the breeze and you don't know who the hell I am, and I don't know who the hell you are." But this kind of laudable feeling of freedom is not uniquely linked to democracy. In order to understand the precise meaning of the label "democracy" better, we have to carry our analysis further.

We can determine what democracy represents by comparing nations considered to be democratic but with different government structures. When comparing United States and England, we see that what is common is a system of electing officials through universal suffrage in these elections. Elections and all further decisions by the elected body are determined by vote where the majority wins, the minority loses. The laws according to which the elected officials govern can be and are quite different for these two countries.

We can separate the functions of democratic practice into three major areas:

Operations selecting the Governing structures and individuals;
Maintenance of Governance;
The rules for Governance.

We are accustomed to calling the first *the legislative function*; the second, *the executive function*; and the third, *the juridical function*, all defined by the French Enlightenment philosophers.

So far so good. What I have outlined here is present in most appropriate textbooks and, I am sure, well known to most. Democracy seems to be basically different from all other forms of government by the apparent absence of mythological justification. This uniqueness has led to the popular conception that although democracy is not perfect, it is fully justified in the absence of another viable alternative to governance except those based on different mythologies.

So, operationally defined, democracy represents a mechanism for decision making whether it is a direct decision through plebiscite or an indirect through elected representatives. The decisions are not arbitrary but restricted to alternatives allowed within a system of laws established by the same mechanism. This is a very rational process.

The argument developed here seems at first glance to answer satisfactorily the question posed in the title of this paper. However, if the democratic form of government existing in United States is a fully rational system, why do we have a whole section of our juridical system busily interpreting our laws in the light of the words in our Constitution, comparing them sentence by sentence and using purely text-critical methods? Such methods, often classified as representing the science of hermeneutics, have been and are still used in the interpretation of religious dogma in the light of the unique words of the Scripture defining Christianity. The question whether women should be allowed to participate in governance is not decided by any rational arguments but by the words of Paul in his letter to the Corinthians, "Let women be silent in Church, they are not to be allowed to speak." Why are we in a similar vein looking at words in our Constitution and interpreting our civil laws as if the words in Constitution were inspired by divine revelation? Do we believe that the Spirit of Democracy appeared to Madison on the way to his Damascus and dictated to him the text of the Constitution?

We have here to insert the caveat that admittedly the Supreme Court has over the years changed the society to a more tolerant and inclusive one; however, this has taken place mostly by purely hermeneutical means, reinterpreting the unchanged text. The number of amendments has been very small. Whereas society has seen radical demographic, economic and technological changes during the last eighty years of the seven amendments introduced, six deal with details of voting, and one repeals the Prohibition. The statements of the Constitution, which deal with how we shall live and share our privileges and responsibilities, remain unchanged, echoing with the cadence of ancient poetry:

> Man the master, ingenious past all measure
> Past all dreams, the skills within his grasp
> He forges on, now to destruction
> Now again to greatness. When he weaves in

The laws of the land, and the justice of the gods
That binds his oaths together
He and his city rise high. . . .   Sophocles, *Antigone*, lines 406–12

The problem of approaching the Constitution as a myth lies within the logical structure of democracy. The democratic process, if studied using the vocabulary of science, can be characterized as a calculus, a formal, logical system of reasoning. Such a calculus is based on basic axioms (self-evident truths) chosen arbitrarily and propositions that can be derived logically from axioms and propositions already derived. The calculus and axioms we are most familiar with are connected to the description of the three-dimensional space we live in. The story of cubes, circles, triangles and angles and calculation of the hypotenuse according to Pythagoras is based on axioms describing the concepts of point and line and the properties of parallel lines. The propositions that can be derived from them are many, allowing us to navigate the seas and construct skyscrapers.

In political calculus (and democracy is a political calculus), propositions become well defined in the English language and appear not only as mathematical symbols. In political calculus, however, axioms such as "liberty" or "justice" have many definitions; consequently, the conclusions are not unique anymore, so we cannot call them propositions, implying testable uniqueness, but they become corollaries and therefore a less sure consequence of a proposition or if the axioms are even more ill defined, the conclusions become guesswork—conjectures.

The corollaries and conjectures of the political calculus purportedly addressing the same problem, although logically correct and consistent with each other, can lead to many possible solutions to problems, solutions that may contradict each other. Why is it important to understand the difference between conjecture and axiom?

If a conjecture is not useful for our political deliberations, if it does not support our point of view, we can derive an alternate one by giving the axiom a slightly different interpretation. However, we cannot abandon the axioms themselves without changing our understanding of the meaning of what the whole calculus that we call political democracy represents. Democracy was defined by our choice of axioms, so in order to derive a new more agreeable conjecture, we have to give the unchanged axiom a new meaning. If the axiom states that decisions are made by voting—one person, one vote—a possible reinterpretation defines the person more restrictively, for example, by lowering or raising the age when one becomes a political person.

The pivotal point in democracy we practice today, the governing axiom, is the absolute power of the majority. If we consider voting as the quintessential pillar and axiom of democracy, and it seems that this is what we are doing in United States, then a better name for our governing system would be majoritocracy. Our problems with democracy lie with this specific model and a specific interpretation of the dominant axiom of democracy.

The problem with majoritocracy is not the powerlessness of the minority. The importance of defending the interest of the society as a whole, represented by the majority, against the individual desires or the desires of the minority is inherent in the structure of all forms of democracy. It is a proposition derived from another axiom of democracy, namely, that the society is an organism and the well-being of the organism takes precedent over the needs of the individual. However, the relationships between the society and its individuals are conditional and can be considered contractual. The form of the democratic government, citing Rousseau, represents a social contract. A contract can be rewritten any time following the wishes of the majority.

The problem arises from considering any decision by the majority as final. Thus the legislature can after rational discussion change by vote the basic structure of the democratic government. It can legally abolish the democracy and disenfranchise the minority. Through their absolute power, citizens can abrogate their own power and privileges. This has happened. The rise of Adolf Hitler to power is a clear example of a legislative body which step by step, perfectly legally, voted out democracy in favor of a mythological autocracy. The law, the Enabling Act, which allowed Hitler to move from the position of legally appointed chancellor to dictator was approved by the German parliament with 441 votes to 94. Evidently, the declaration of the will of the majority, a clearly malevolent will, was nevertheless binding. *Vox populi vox Dei* is a major flaw in the structure of democracy.

In other words, we can see that majoritocracy is an unstable form of government. The answer to this problem has been to declare the description of the basic structure of the elective government a sacrosanct document of axioms, making major changes so difficult as to be nearly impossible.

This basically hermeneutic approach is what we see in United States today. It is often associated with the views of Robert Bork, a much maligned and politically controversial but very logical and intellectually honest lawyer. It is quite correct that if protection against tampering with what we consider our basic liberties is to be achieved, one way is to convert the nature of the Constitution and the structure of democracy from a rational contract to a mythological narrative.

Fine, but we have thereby reached a clearly opposite conclusion to our original proposal, namely, that democracy is a rational, operational concept. In order to preserve democracy, we had to convert it to mythology and all mythologies are arbitrary and radically removed from the world their words are applied to. Mythologies are not judged by practical operational results but by concordance with some moral of the narrative, in our case, the mysterious "original intent."

Thus, the advantages of democracy over monarchy that we believed to be found in the inherent rational basis of democracy are not there anymore and we have to judge the comparative value of this form of government by its historical achievements. These achievements refer to applications of the different interpretations of the democratic narrative by different nations. We have opened a can of worms. What is a better achievement: freedom of speech or absence of poverty? Such comparisons are not possible. They are similar to comparing oranges and apples. We have to go back in our argument. Maybe the assignment of the principle of the majority vote in decision making as an axiom of democracy was an error that led us to majoritocracy and astray.

What if the voting mechanism is but an important practical mechanism of governance but not an essential axiom?

Let us go back to history and look at democracy as the Greeks originally saw it.

The first clear definition of democracy as a form of government appears in the funeral oration delivered by Pericles, son of Xanthippus, in 431 BCE. Pericles said, among other things,

> Our constitution is called Democracy because the power is not in the hands of a minority but of the whole people. When it is a question of settling private disputes, everyone is equal before the law; when it is a question of putting one person before another in positions of public responsibility, whatever counts is not the membership of a particular class but the actual ability the man possesses. No one, so long as he has it in him to be of service to the state is kept in political obscurity because of poverty.

He continued,

> We are free and tolerant in our private lives; but in public affairs we keep to the law. This is because it commands our deep respect. We give our obedience to those whom we put in position of authority, and we observe the laws themselves, especially those which are for the protection of the oppressed, and those unwritten laws which it is an acknowledged shame to break.

The definition of democracy continues,

> We do not say that a man who takes no interest in politics is a man who minds his own business; we say he has no business here at all! We Athenians in our own persons take our decisions on policy or submit them to proper discussion: for we do not think that there is an incompatibility between words and deeds; the worst thing is to rush into action before the consequences have been properly debated.

It is very clear where the fulcrum of Greek democracy resides: the equality of all citizens before the law and the absence of an advantage given by birth or money. All citizens are expected to participate in politics and in the discussion of decisions. All decisions are made in town meetings by the members of the community. Some functions of the society can be delegated to elected officials, and the mode of selecting officials is not the crucial problem.

All forms of government have a problem of weighing individual desires against what is conceived to be the common good. Democracy defines as an operating procedure that the common interest is represented by the majority opinion, recorded as vote. Whether this is the best and only possible measure of common interest on all occasions is open to debate. Another possibility for the population is to consult experts, agreeing in advance to their decision. In the republican form of democracy, most choices are always delegated to elected officials whose mandate as public officials is under constant scrutiny of the citizenry and the common interest is indirectly represented by frequent election of officials.

The basic premises for the Greek version of democracy: equality before the law, choice of officials based on merits and not influenced by birth or money are rational principles, assuring the maximum possible number of capable people in the leadership of the State.

It is here that the logical, rational premise for democracy lies. A society that utilizes every possible capable individual and considers every possible alternative to its policies has an inherent advantage over all other forms of society. This purely Darwinian advantage represents a non-arbitrary axiom. It is based on a more basic principle than politics, namely, that of an advantage in evolution.

The operational procedures of ascertaining the will of the majority and equating it to the best choice for the community are practical, alternate procedures open to modification if the results of their application do not prove successful. Majoritocracy is thus not a basic concept that is necessary for Greek democracy; it does not touch the basis of a society of equals taking their responsibilities as a duty. Consideration of the Greek form of democracy reveals that the voting procedure, although important in recording popular opinion, was not an axiom defining democracy.

In history, the axiom of equal access to leadership, on the other hand, has recorded many examples of success resulting from broadening the basis for leadership recruitment. The Napoleonic military machine and the American Civil War and Revolutionary War achievements represent maybe the best-known cases.

When we go back in history, the next time democracy comes up in a major context is during the Enlightenment. This does not mean that democracy was forgotten during the centuries between the Greek civilization and the age of Enlightenment. The medieval Icelandic Althing, although a beautiful example of democracy in the North, did not have a major influence because Christianity and Islam, the dominant religions, considered the structure of government on earth fixed by mythology and translated the Abrahamic hierarchy in heaven to the complementing monarchy on earth.

It is Rousseau who in his book *The Social Contract* introduces the two concepts that thereafter dominate democracy, namely, "the common good" and "the will of the people." Montesquieu made the concept of "the common good" into a Platonic moral concept, not any more definable by practical results. The still more diffuse "the will of the people" is there to justify the revolution but came to justify the terror. Voting is there not to choose between practical alternatives but to learn the will of the people. When the new president of United States after being elected with a miniscule majority immediately fires a huge number of officials, it is clearly not any more for the purpose of assuring good and experienced leadership; it is to demonstrate the absolute power of the will of the people. From there, it is only a short step to laws whereby people will be executed by the will of people because they hindered the progress of the common good as defined by those judging them. Montesquieu himself had grave doubts about the ability of the society to define the common good. The division of and independence of legislative, executive, and juridical function is not prescribed by some new corollary derived from the basic axioms such as the "will of the people" and "the common good." It is there to guard against the will of people if it becomes arbitrary or dogmatic. These two nebulous concepts of the Enlightenment, unfortunately, convert the Athenian concept of democracy, a practical, rational arrangement, to pure mythology. The interpretation of a mythos—one may call it a search for the original intent—converts democracy into an ideology.

Of course, there is always a crisis of democracy at hand. All ideologies or religions, as a rule, are in a continuous fight against heresies popping up here and there. Unless you slavishly copy word by word the story defining the ideology, you are producing a new narrative. The mythological narratives are open to limitless interpretations, and what is the canonical interpretation and what is a heresy is indefinable. Limitless number of Supreme Courts can spend limitless hours in such a debate and spin endless new narratives.

If the discovery of the common good was very difficult and often controversial, the problem with the will of the people is much worse. How to determine what the will of the people is, outside the rare occasion when all the members of a small community make a unanimous choice, has been relegated to counting opinions or votes. In opinion polling or voting, the will of the people is equated with the majority opinion. It is, scientifically speaking, a thoroughly inadequate way of proceeding. If we submit to a hundred people the question whether we should choose alternative A or alternative B and we get 52 choosing A and 48 B, we declare alternative A to be the will of the people. This is a curious way of defining a property supposed to characterize all the people. Is the will of the people an average will? By counting, we have only found out that the chosen alternative has a 52 percent chance of being the will of any given individual. For some type of choices such as selecting a large number of delegates, the more advanced democracies of Northern Europe try to correct for this uncertainty and assign delegates proportionally to the number of votes received by the parties. However, if the question is whether we should build a bridge or a tunnel, such proportional interpretation is not possible. You cannot build something that is 52 percent bridge and 48 percent tunnel.

The classical example of a dilemma with the will of the people was the plebiscite in Sweden about the choice between left- and right-hand traffic. The majority voted for retaining left-hand traffic. However, the elected officials reasoned that with the advent of the European Union and increasing intercontinental traffic, a shift to right-hand traffic would represent the common good and overruled the will of people. In a country with true majoritocracy, the will of the people would have won on ideological grounds.

The English parliamentary system, in no ways an advanced democratic country in the sense described here, has made a great effort to reduce all choices in decision making into a binary form. You are either for or against this proposition. The choice is either right or wrong.

Of course, the binary choice cannot be blamed on the English. The whole classical logic is based on rules of deduction from propositions that are either true or false. It is closely linked to the branching structure of our mental thought trajectories and probably represents the most effective algorithm for the human brain. The problem is not that the system of reducing choices into two alternatives and deciding by majority is a bad or unsuitable system. It can function very well in any system of government. A king can poll his advisers before a decision as effectively as a parliament can count votes. The problem is that this practical and approximate way of choosing between alternatives is equated with the mythological concept "the will of the people." The concept does not evidently represent some kind of sum of the individual wills but some unique primeval force associated with the community. The logic here is not different from Friedrich Nietzsche's elevation of the individual human "will to power" to the role of an important force working in and molding our society. Thus, the will of the people becomes, like the will to power of an individual, an explanation of the necessity and a justification for the appearance of expansionist, empire-building societies.

Further reference to the will of the people becomes also a justification for any oligarchy, the domination of the society by small groups of dedicated people who when obtaining power believe that they formulate the will of the people. Jesuits, communists, fascists, fundamentalists, we all know their claim of representing the will of the people.

The founding fathers of America did, for their day, an astounding piece of work in the Constitution; however, not surprisingly they had to make compromises for the sake of unity. Thus, equality before law and advancement by merit is included but with notable exceptions. Unfortunately, due to the large surface area of the country, difficulties in communicating and recording the wishes of the population led to an elaborate system of elections of delegates, that shifted the focus from creating a society of equal opportunity and law to the detailed rules by which the will of the people can be delegated. This change, we may call it a paradigm shift if we borrow from Thomas Kuhn, allows the celebration of power of the elected individuals to replace the celebration of equality. This despite that the Constitution, as clearly expressed in the Preamble, is designed to establish a more perfect union, justice, common defense, and general welfare—all aspects of the community. The individual is promised only liberty by the Constitution!

Unfortunately, despite the presence and the reverence for the Constitution, libertarian philosophy supporting the adoration and appreciation of the individual at the expense of the society has gained ground since the creation of the Republic. This has resulted in the neglect of the principles of the Constitution and has produced an unwillingness to curb individual demands for the good of the community. In fact, the government, the expression of the community, is considered by many only as a framework for the greatest possible pleasures of the individual. We see this in the general unwillingness to fund the government and the tendency to privatize many functions of the government, thereby replacing common good as the driving force with individual profit.

This definitely is a grave error. Individuals are mortal; it is only in the community that the immortality of the human race resides. The simple wisdom "You cannot take it with you" is correct. However, you can leave your genes in the gene pool and transfer your knowledge to generations to come. For this mechanism to function, you need a strong community. The emphasis of individual pleasures is in direct contrast to the aims of the original Greek and the later democracy of the Enlightenment that both stress the need for a strong community. This, despite the great appreciation of individual creativity and heroism among ancient Greeks, was the source of the strength of the remarkable Greek civilization. Let me cite Aristotle in his *Nicomachean Ethics*, "For while it is desirable to secure what is good in the case of individual, to do so in the case of people or a state is something finer and more sublime."

What we have in United States at present can perhaps best be described as an oligarchy, the rule by a class of individuals with enough resources to buy directly or indirectly the necessary votes to choose them as representatives of the will of the people. The resources are not only money, although it plays a large role, but family ties and relationships to organizations as well as an image (the ability to act the role). For those groups securing their power, it is essential that democracy remains a purely mythological tool. Remember, all autocracies and oligarchies turn to mythology in order to justify their hold on the power and uphold the exclusion of large parts of the population from participation in the leadership of the country.

Democracy, on the contrary, should strive to use all or the maximum number of individuals. It is an egalitarian and tolerant society. These are rational principles, chosen to provide the community with the best possible resources. Democracy cannot be allowed to develop into mythology open only to hermeneutic interpretation. Democracy must have the ability to respond rationally to changes in the circumstances within the society.

What we need today is to reaffirm the unchangeable basic principles chosen on rational grounds. First, equality in the eyes of law; second, the ability for any individual regardless of background to advance solely on merits; third, the independence of the Constitution from any mythological narrative—be it religion or any competing ideology. I would add to this something that is not in the Constitution but has appeared as the decisive tool in the evolutionary progress, namely, the right to pursue knowledge. There is no such thing as forbidden knowledge.

The rules governing the application of these principles, such as the rules of elections, are derived propositions and thus rank below the basic principles. They can and should be changed according to the needs of the advancing society. The ones I would downgrade in importance are the nearly religious adoration of the ballot box and the belief in the mythical concept of "the will of the people." A simple first step toward redefining the application of democracy is to change the elections of representatives from a winner-takes-all basis to the election of party representatives on a proportional scale. The reason is that with the advance of technology, because of the size of the country and the population, the candidates appear to most people only as images on the screen. Looking at the advances of technology, we know that it will soon be possible to present a totally synthetic, virtual candidate. The step from actors and pop stars to animated figures is quite possible. The selection of officials according to past merits and future promise will then be totally replaced by the ability to buy a personality, a designer politician.

A political party may be dominated by a few politicians; however, its political platform represents a practical concept and will in proportional elections assume a much larger role for the electors. We have, however, to realize that the proportional representation, although better reflecting the electorate, can lead to difficulties in forming stable governments as new governments can be introduced and voted out maybe weekly—a process we saw happening in France between the First and Second World Wars. This, of course, can be avoided by clear separation between the legislative assembly and the executive function along the lines of the present system in United States. The role of the majority in voting can and should be used to ascertain the opinion of the population; however, the requirements for majority should change, demanding a greater degree of consensus. Most important is to choose at least half the judges of the Supreme Court from lay population, shifting the focus from text-critical studies of the Constitution to envisioning the future of the nation as well as we can and trying to change our laws with time to provide the best conditions for future growth along the lines defined by the preamble to the Constitution.

In summary, a fear of change has forced us to codify and convert the clever system of decision making, democracy, into a mythological narrative. We should dethrone the mythos of "the will of the people" and the absolute rule of the majority and return to the rule of equality and the participation of all people according to their ability in the government. We would, thereby, restore the ancient glory to democracy and allow it to become a rapidly changing system of choices based on rationally chosen axioms and logical arguments designed to advance the evolution of mankind on a rational basis. In such a capacity democracy is unique and immortal!

What remains is to answer the question how democracy relates to humanism.

Humanists have embraced democracy in their manifestos but without clearly defining which propositions we agree with and which ones in the practice of democracy today that we don't consider to be in concordance with the principles of humanism. Clearly, the conversion of the ballot box to something akin to the Ark of the Covenant points to an ideological interpretation that we should have difficulties agreeing with.

On the other hand, reading Pericles' description of Athenian democracy, we could exclaim that he is reading from the absolute First Humanist Manifesto.

I feel that the reorientation of the basis of democracy more toward the Athenian form would practically fuse humanism with democracy. The problem with democracy, as it is practiced today, is that those advocating democracy as the only acceptable form of government have lost sight of the basic axiom of equal opportunity of participation in governance and converted the rational narrative of democracy into mythology—leaving us only with the name without its original content.

REFERENCES

Madison, J., as Publius in *The Federalist Papers* (1788).

Pericles in Thucydides, *The History of the Peloponnesian War* (ca. 400 BCE).

Rousseau, J. J., *Le Contrat Social* (1762).

Montesquieu, C. S., *Le l'esprit des lois* (1748).

Nietzsche, F. *Der Wille zur Macht* (1910).

Kuhn, T. S., *The Structure of Scientific Revolutions* (1962).

Aristotle, *The Nichomachean Ethics* (ca. 330 BCE).

9.

Democracy and Biology: Genesis and Fall

Philip Regal

"THE WORLD IS TOO MUCH WITH US"

The world is too much with us; late and soon,
Getting and spending, we lay waste our powers:
Little we see in Nature that is ours;
We have given our hearts away, a sordid boon!
This Sea that bares her bosom to the moon;
The winds that will be howling at all hours,
And are up-gathered now like sleeping flowers;
For this, for everything, we are out of tune;
It moves us not.—Great God! I'd rather be
A Pagan suckled in a creed outworn;
So might I, standing on this pleasant lea,
Have glimpses that would make me less forlorn;
Have sight of Proteus rising from the sea;
Or hear old Triton blow his wreathed horn.

William Wordsworth

AN ANTHROPOLOGICAL AND DARWINIAN CONTEXT FOR THE GENESIS AND FALL OF DEMOCRACY

L et us begin a discussion of modern democracy with its biological and cultural foundations.

The American ideal of modern democracy depends very much on the idea of freethinking, rational analysis, and free communication among responsibly autonomous individuals. This phase of democracy was preceded by older and related principles of small-scale tribal democracy based on interpersonal respect for personality differences, for intellectual and physical talents, and on collegial inclusive participation. Democracy was a plain fact of life for over 99 percent of human history, during which our species gathered plant material and invertebrates and hunted game in small migrating bands.

The formation of hereditary ruling classes and the formation of the non-egalitarian hierarchical civilizations among sedentary peoples has been quite recent and geographically localized. For example, though tools improved substantially about 1.5 million years ago, this was still in the context of hunting and gathering life, and agriculture and settlements were only known from about nine thousand to ten thousand years ago. It is not clear that even the earliest known organized permanent settlements at Jericho and in Turkey had become politically stratified.

Hunter/gatherers have found security and pleasures in one's fellows, who are both one's friends and one's allies in social pleasures, work, and defense. Functional adaptation and survival require that children must grow up having learned to do unto others as one would have others do unto oneself, or become outcast—and socially dysfunctional groups could crumble as materially functional entities.

Straw men and red herrings. One should be extremely careful not to jump to the simplistic conclusion that I will in any way suggest that hunter/gatherers have an inborn genetic instinct that dictates or compels individuals to behave "virtuously."

It would be easy to try to read between the lines and *imagine* that I am implying this. Cognitive psychology explains that old mental pigeonholes tend to structure perception. Literate people today have been influenced by hundreds of years of polarized human nature issues, and notably the critics of Rousseau have insisted that he was advocating that there were and are "noble savages."

One's brain may well automatically but wrongly see the "noble savage" straw man in what I have started to outline. So I advise caution.

It is worth pointing out at the start that the fantastic "noble savage" stereotype was not only not advocated by Rousseau, but he did not construct it. Learned society had long before been ideologically conditioned to oppose populist ideologies and had been rehearsed to charge at "noble savage" windmills—as is done today. Human nature issues had already for centuries before Rousseau and thereafter in the popular mind down to our own time been oversimplified, polarized, and misrepresented.

The noble savage notion actually was formed from odd combinations of Christian chivalry, the Adam and Eve story, and Germanic mythology, especially in the late Middle Ages around the time of the Crusades. The Church promoted the idea that the uncorrupted child of nature, the wild man, had innate virtues of honor, passion, courage, and strength that he could best develop by enlisting in the army of Christ and submitting to the goals of the Church. The modern avatar of the medieval wild man myths would be the noble Tarzan, raised by nature and king of the jungle.

A politically charged subgenre of noble savage models later used the belief in Adam and Eve as an ideology, at least by the time of the Peasant Revolts of the 1300s, to argue that all people were created equal by God and are thus basically good if they use their free will properly. Thus in principle communities could govern themselves and did not need the hierarchies of crown and cross to rule over them. The nobility responded to this populist revolutionary ideology with their own simplistic elitist repressive ideologies. For example their polemicists insisted that the Fall had thoroughly corrupted human nature so that there was no longer any good inherent in us. Thus people needed to be ruled by church and crown. John Calvin and Thomas Hobbes are the most familiar thinkers on this side.

Thus, Rousseau was trying to get his rather nuanced analysis understood in a fierce ideological cross fire that had been raging for centuries.

Rousseau did, however, not base his theories of human nature on actual "savages." He instead retreated from the city and, like Thoreau later, used personal introspection and observations of rural people to speculate on what human beings might *want* out of life *if* they lived in a purely hypothetical unstressed state of nature, and without the shaping effects on their minds of militaristic, wealth-driven, and intellectually competitive societies.

Rousseau concluded that individuals would not want a war of all against all and to reduce all things to possession as the Calvinistic and Hobbesian factions had insisted, but people would want to live in peace, have warm and trusting friendships, be left free to have meaningful contemplation and conversations, decide their affairs for themselves, etc. Clearly Rousseau was attempting to distinguish between how people *actually behave* and navigate various social landscapes and how they *might prefer* circumstances to be according to their inner natures if they were sufficiently free of outside influences and distractions and were allowed to be introspective and have thoughtful discussions.

The dynamics of genetics/learning that are involved even when puppies do not bite hard or will get angry and may even lose trust when bitten hard are not well understood. So the genetic/learning dynamics involved when humans cooperate or get angry when they are deceived and exploited are surely not well understood.

But it is clear that upbringing matters enormously for both dogs and humans. There has never been any scientific reason to jump to the conclusion that humans have an instinct *to behave* toward others automatically in a "democratic" manner. There is no more scientific evidence that primitive people are driven by nature to act nobly than that European aristocrats are driven by nature to act nobly.

But humans do seem to have some sort of universal *expectation or desire at the receiving end* to be treated fairly, to have their autonomy respected by others, to have congenial social relations in the end. Even hardened criminals with extremely cynical views of human nature *want* friends and lovers and get angry if they are betrayed. And small children get angry and hurt if they are trying to play and one violates congeniality and cheats.

Thoughtful observation illustrates that even the strongest human *desires* can not possibly translate automatically into appropriate actions. Our bodies tell us when we are hungry and when we are full, but desires for food do not translate automatically into knowledge of how to fish or snare a rabbit or how to cook game. Hunger is not a philosophical proposition or even a learned "meme" for most people, but how best to get fed is debateable and requires learning.

Plain observation shows that children have to learn how to accomplish congenial relations in their particular culture. They must learn how to earn fair treatment and how to express their autonomy in ways that others will respect and that are effective. The teenaged body may scream with sexual desire, but desire does not instinctively dictate how to act socially—how to treat others. A randy boy must learn by word of mouth or trial and error how to not get slapped or ostracized, or even arrested for date rape.

Band and tribal cultures from time immemorial have in a sense developed ways to practice what we call today "reverse social Darwinism"—ways to control angry and selfish feelings within the community and between neighbors. Orthodox social Darwinism proposes to the contrary that selfish competition should be encouraged because supposedly it is the force that automatically leads to progress, and cooperative pleasures and social ideals beyond the immediate family are superfluous.

Reverse social Darwinism comes to an opposite ethical/political conclusion: if nature red in tooth and claw is indeed a cosmic force within us and tearing to get out, then we must use reason to overcome this destructive force and keep it within.

John Locke elaborated a form of reverse social Darwinism in *Two Treatises on Government*. It is quite obvious that we surely have the capacity to kill each other off, but most individuals with a minimum of common sense can also see that allowing free run for our anger and selfish passions would put everyone at risk and destroy the possibility of social harmony. In Locke's version it is in our natures to desire this social harmony, but we have to use common sense to figure out how to accomplish it.

The statistical fact is that only a minority of human cultures have come to esteem acrimonious or injurious conflict. These are characteristically societies that sustain themselves by military or economic conquests or that have long been forced into readiness for active defense.

But even in these "warrior societies," particular arenas where conflicts are acceptable and esteemed may be circumscribed. I was fascinated, for example, to see how the diverse warrior cultures that are densely packed into the highlands of Papua New Guinea have developed ingenious customs to minimize the frequency and intensity of conflicts between neighboring tribes. They easily trade with their enemies and on most days by far there is no fighting.

Of course, life within any community is never problem-free. For a variety of reasons not all individuals do learn and practice the civil behaviors that are appropriate for their cultures. Many have not learned civility and the best rational skills, simply because of family or social breakdown, dysfunctional parents, mental illness, etc.

Indeed many in our own competitive "free market society," and not simply stereotypical little leaguers, are actually being taught by parents and peers—as I have long been hearing in discussions with students—"Hey! If you can get away with it, why not?" They are being taught selfish competitive individualism and not civility or about how to make democratic society work.

I have an illustrated children's book in hand. *A Child's Machiavelli: A Primer on Power* by Claudia Hart has page after page of advice such as, "You gotta be tough. People won't really like you then, but they're probably only your friends 'cos they think they can get something off you." Of course, it also gives advice on when and how to hide your toughness, make people think that you are a nice guy, etc.

It might seem that no parent would be open about such things. Some will buy it as a joke, and others will say they did, but in any event, people certainly do try to raise their children to be what they consider to be functionally adaptive in their particular subcultures. Certainly many children get at the very least many mixed messages in our highly competitive yet highly religious society from parents and peers.

The present essay in any event is not about mythical "noble savages" or about the endlessly polarized nature/nurture issue! There is a great deal that can and should be understood about mammalian biology and anthropology without getting sidetracked by that facile old brouhaha.

The realities of daily life, survival, and adaptation are in any event cooperative and collegial for hunter/gatherers. Not much if any deep philosophy or formal political theory is needed for them to see that cooperation among peers is the primary challenge for individual adaptation and the satisfaction of needs. It is plain that there are inevitable interpersonal misunderstandings, conflicts of interest, and personality quirks and that there are no alternatives to working these out collegially within the band according to custom, experience, and reason.

Status has depended more on interpersonal evaluations and respect for demonstrated individual talents and skills than on ancestry and inherited formal "positions of authority." Typically there is not slavery. Male and female spheres of power tend to be balanced. People value personal autonomy.

In some cultures hereditary clans may be assigned particular responsibilities and powers. Different sorts of responsibilities and authority are usually assigned to different clans, and thus there is an overall balance of power among clans.

Hereditary clan powers should be flagged for our attention, however. They are probably the innocent seeds from which ruling classes sometimes have grown in cultural evolution, and band/tribal democracy has been lost. It is obvious how imbalances of power could sometimes develop by *deceit* and/or from real or perceived *necessity* in time of crisis. It would be possible for military or priestly clans to conspire and combine and take power, especially when the larger group becomes psychologically vulnerable due to cultural breakdown and/or goes out of control due to disruption from war, plague, over-population, ecological disaster, etc.

Simple local idioms of custom, cosmology, and common sense about how individuals in communities of our quite social species should treat one another have nevertheless been quite serviceable for an unimaginably long time in bands and tribes below the organization level of hereditary chiefdoms. Tribal people do to be sure use various idiomatic forms of *formal reasoning*. I have compared the strengths and weakness of these relative to Western idioms of rationality in *The Anatomy of Judgment*.

Whispers from within. When today we long for democracy, or fear or mourn its loss, or struggle with a sense of alienation from those around us, why do these regrets and sad feelings rattle about in our brains? If our species was forged on the anvil of a war of all against all, where do the seemingly maladaptive and irrational desires for society, peace, and harmony come from? Do such feelings simply reflect romantic notions invented by Enlightenment philosophers, or is there a contribution from our biological and cultural evolutionary past as social hominoid apes and as bipedal hunter/gather hominids?

Desires for respect, warm interpersonal relationships, collegial cooperation, and personal autonomy do seem to be rooted in our evolutionary history. So if longings such as these that are so closely tied to modern democratic aspirations are splashing about in the complex soup that is our nature, how have they so often been lost and/or subverted historically by poor judgment and tyrants? What is it about our brains and natures that allows democratic sentiments to be lost or twisted back against us by repressive cultural forces?

To begin with, it must be understood what the fundamental fact that humans are mammals implies in terms of brain and behavior, including our vulnerability to anti-democratic political manipulation.

Humans are mammals. There are few if any people who can happily be like lizards—content with solitary individual satisfactions, like simply filling their bellies and warming their bodies in the sun. We are not selfishly individualistic reptiles. Humans are mammals, and mammals are all social and have social needs, and the human species is the most highly social of all mammals. Plato, I sometimes suspect, learned to observe like a zoologist from his student Aristotle late in life. He keenly observed in the *Statesman* that we are a herd species, even more social than dogs, and quite like livestock. We are a herd species, and the statesman must recognize that he must therefore be a type of herdsman. Then, in his following and last book, his rather totalitarian *Laws*, Plato described how the herd should be herded.

Thomas Hobbes, often held up as the father of political science, was to the contrary quite off base zoologically and anthropologically. He proposed in *Leviathan* in the earliest seventeenth century that his original human, his atomistic man, was solitary, selfish, and unfit for society and yet intelligent enough to draft a social contract. Hobbes described a fictitious species of intelligent territorial lizards or crocodiles, not a mammalian species—certainly not a primate species and certainly not the ancestral human.

Our reptile brain, layer one—A basic site for individual survival functions, as well as for anti-democratic manipulations. Mammals are not reptiles, but all mammals including ourselves *retain* certain reptile features from our reptilian ancestors in our skeletons and soft tissues. Evolution has preserved the *entire* reptile brain as the foundation tissue layers, nerve centers and pathways, and the biochemical machinery of our own brain core.

The simple reptile brain that *is* the core of our own has served crocodilians, turtles and their kind splendidly for hundreds of millions of years for solitary and selfish lives that involve little more than feeding, copulating, fighting, and fleeing.

While our reptile brain core serves even us well for simple survival functions, it is a double-edged sword for humans. When its centers are strongly aroused they can overwhelm us with powerful and fundamental emotions such as fear, hatred, and lust that it is difficult for reason or love to control.

When anti-democratic forces manipulate people, they commonly mobilize strong emotions related to primitive and basic functions that are situated at this level, such as fear, sex, safety, hunger, and competition/jealously.

Brain, layer two—A site for social survival functions, and a target for political manipulation. The evolution of mammals from reptiles has added a second quite distinctive and elaborately constructed new layer over the old reptile brain. And humans even have a third new layer over this second. There is a good popular discussion of this "triune brain" in *The Dragons of Eden* by Carl Sagan.

What new biology is the complex second layer good for? This second "paleomammalian brain" contains the elaborate nerve connections and centers that are involved in (among others) social behaviors such as nurturing of young, play, affection, and bonding.

Neuroanatomy aside, anyone can understand that lizards, snakes, and turtles make different sorts of household pets than do dogs or even cats. Such mammals have neurological machinery for bonding, play, and the rudiments of social communication and can easily become "part of the family."

Thus social beings did not first appear on the face of the earth as the result of a rational contract that was drafted when humans developed grammatical language and decided to end Thomas Hobbes' fabled war of all against all.

This second brain layer is again a double-edged sword. We value social tendencies such as love, loyalty, and compassion and they are adaptive for mammalian life. But these also feed conformity and the herd mentality, which can work counter to freethought and objective reason.

Moreover, anti-democratic forces commonly manipulate the circuits at this evolutionarily old level when they manipulate not only the herd mentality, but fears about one's children, friends, and community, or offer true or false promises of social status and praise, or entice people into religious, political, nationalistic, ideological, etc., social networks which can then be controlled.

The neomammalian brain, layer three—A labile imagination/communication organ. Democracy and the recurrent needs and urges to defend self-government and political freedoms require yet greater biological complexities than elementary mammalian bonding and affection.

There is a wide variety of hunter/gatherer and tribal democracies, with observably complex kinship systems, beliefs, rituals, and customs. The functional organization of each cultural system involves imagined concepts that are constructed and communicated through abstract symbols.

The abstract symbols and concepts are functional social tools that societies have invented and use to make, communicate, and perpetuate rules of conduct and idioms of identity. The various sets of symbols and idioms of logic give the stability of "meaning" to these and to traditions. They become terms of discourse that are referred to and are manipulated logically to resolve the inevitable conflicts of interest and misunderstandings that can arise between individuals and families especially in complex human societies, which demand a zoologically new level of interpersonal expectations. The cultural sets of symbols and concepts involved for example in maintaining divisions of labor, technical skills, kinship systems and interfamilial relationships and obligations, morale, etc., are astonishingly more diverse than have been observed in any other mammal.

This new level of functions has neurophysiological correlates within a third brain layer, the "neomammalian brain" that has developed in the great apes and notably in humans. The tissues in this layer are heavily involved in the complex human systems of abstraction and symbolic communication.

One might think of this newest layer as a sort of highly flexible cognitive filter, gate-keeping and processing the flow of information between the environment and the low brain layers. The filter, at least in humans, consists of imagined worlds and is flexible in the sense that it has the potential to build virtually an infinite variety of them.

One can think of imagined worlds as individual and group "cognitive maps" and as including idiomatic vocabularies, grammars, religious, ideological, philosophical, and scientific and other highly labile cultural perspectives. The imagined worlds can take on realities and powers of their own, much as maps on paper do, with their place names and political boundaries. Similarly, middlemen in economic markets can take control in those markets over both producers and consumers. The reptile and social brains below must "know" the greater world through the products of the symbolic brain above, much as the consumer sees only the retailers and packaged goods not the actual system of production of raw materials and of manufacturing and distribution.

Moreover, even the "self" is necessarily an abstract object that is defined through a filter—in terms of the idiosyncratic habits of perception, cognitive maps, symbols, and logic of the third layer. "Know thyself" has proved, when taken with unqualified seriousness, to be perhaps the most profound challenge ever uttered.

On the positive side, this third-layer capacity for abstract cognition, imagination, logical manipulation of information, and communication has allowed humans to develop, experiment with, modify, invent, and exchange an enormous variety of social and material technologies and to spread across the planet from the tropics and deserts to the arctic ice sheets.

Neuroanatomy and neurochemistry aside, daily experience shows that humans have exceptional powers to generate mental images. These have meanings that arise from and translate into the common social currency of idiomatic languages, beliefs, myths, philosophies, etc. Plain observation also shows that images and symbols, in turn, have been necessary for the functioning of elaborate kinship systems, customs, and reasoned arguments. These embody diverse cultural rules for interpersonal relationships, that assign diverse cultural idioms of responsibility and labor, and provided diverse intellectual tools for the mediation of disputes and the reform of anti-social behaviors.

Thus, the mediation of the idiomatic cultural dynamics of human interpersonal interactions can be thought of as one critical function of the organ of imagination and thought, largely through devices of communication such as gestures, the arts, ceremonies, logical systems, and verbal language.

Imagined concepts, the symbols for classifying and communicating them, and logical systems for their manipulation and mediation have culturally and individually assigned cognitive shapes and boundaries that are *not inherently* fixed. A word like "freak" or "bridge" or "freedom" will easily conjure up different images and associations even to different people who speak the same language. And languages are so diverse culturally that it is clear that specific details can not be prescribed by genetics.

The open-ended nature of sets of symbols gives them enormous flexibility as tools or vehicles that can organize information and hold diverse social systems and patterns of material production together and keep these functioning over time in ways appropriate for a diversity of particular ecological situations. Languages have features that offer the potential for stability and yet hold open the option of adaptive flexibility.

One can think of any given imagined world of concepts, symbols, and conventions of information processing as being mathematically sort of a culturally evolved "strange attractor" that defines and describes the phase space in which the trajectories of individual components in an adaptive dynamical system move (in ways that often may superficially seem to be random, patternless, and disconnected).

What does this analogy mean in more ordinary terms? Imagine a cloud of moths (the components) fluttering around a candle (the attractor). Individuals behave much the same but not exactly the same. Thus the overall pattern of their collective behavior has a pattern of stability, but individual behaviors vary considerably.

Thus, mathematically speaking, cultures have "fractal properties," and this should help one to visualize structure that has persistent properties but that is not static or made up of deterministically regimented components.

Beyond stability and flexibility, the potentials of the third brain layer have a negative side and thus constitute yet another double-edged sword. They are extremely difficult for sound reason to control.

On the negative side, many individual and cultural dreams for the future have turned out to be misdirected follies. And imagination commonly feeds and even inspires denial, distraction, and self-deception, which can easily override objectivity. I have discussed such matters in detail in *The Anatomy of Judgment.*

There is a wonderful painting by Francisco de Goya titled "El sueño de la razon produce monstros." Goya was a great supporter of the Enlightenment, and the title is usually translated as "The sleep of reason brings forth monsters," which is true enough. This translation puts reason in a very positive light and is in the spirit of Voltaire's wonderful saying, "So long as men believe absurdities, they will commit atrocities."

But "sueño" is a deliciously ambiguous Spanish word and can mean either sleep or dream—as in "la vida es sueño" (life is a dream). So some assume that Goya meant, "The dream of reason brings forth monsters." This, too, would have been a profoundly important point to a thinker of the Enlightenment.

Individuals certainly do dream up reasons to rationalize their hatreds, crimes and foolishness; to escape responsibilities; to deny realities; and the like. "Reason" is not a fixed thing that some people have and others do not, with an "essence" that is always good and never bad. Reason is a work in progress for those who seriously aspire to develop it in the best sense and do not simply imagine that one can buy and wear the mantle.

Reason can be used at the service of the selfish reptile and the conformist herd brain layers within us arguably even more easily than it can be used to control them. This is in large part because people, including most scientists, do not fully grasp the implications of the fact that we are the products of evolution. They may accept the elementary idea of natural selection, for example, and yet not appreciate that these brain layers exist and what this means for us.

Democracy aside for the moment, humanists should pause to contemplate the general problem for an individual. We cannot truly be rational and choose good lives for ourselves if we do not really know ourselves. We cannot fully know ourselves without considering the general properties of the brain and how they interact with culture, as I began to outline in *The Anatomy of Judgment.*

Moreover, we cannot fully know ourselves when we lie to ourselves. Self-deception is an enormous obstacle to self-understanding (as discussed, for example, in *Self-Deception and Self-Understanding* by Mike H. Martin). What parts of "us" benefit and what parts suffer when we rationalize and flatter our egos and inflate our dreams unrealistically? What games does this third brain layer so skillfully play with our consciousness and how, to what end, and with what effects?

Let me suggest that in a sense our cultures are essential mental fictions of the third layer. They provide script outlines and roles and describe the stage and basic lines, etc., and human survival has long depended on taking these "fictions" seriously. Thus they become in fact true artifacts with material existence. That is, *Homo sapiens* imagined a new level of *material reality* into the biosphere some eons ago. Survival in each case depends on taking given fictions seriously because the fictions are functional and adaptive.

Thus, getting back to the question of self-deception, is it possible to challenge our own scripts and whatever defenses insist that they are real and still survive for the better? Clearly it is for some people, and yet others must turn back at some point or stop and make a safe homestead. Socrates' words "know thyself" scarcely hint at how much difficulty and painful self-examination, and in many cases risk, they ask of those who would take them seriously.

Martin quotes Adam Smith, "This self-deceit, this fatal weakness of mankind, is the source of half the disorders of mankind." I would put the fraction higher because I would include not only the follies generated from within each individual but the vulnerability of masses of individuals to political manipulation.

Senseless wars have been possible from the dawn of recorded history because great masses of individuals have been flattered by their leaders into believing that God should naturally love them more than he loves the other side. It is impossible to count the millions who have been slaughtered and crippled, the civilizations destroyed, the land ruined, the treasuries bankrupted, the misery inflicted, the resources depleted because it has been so easy to inspire people by flattering their egos with a sense of superiority, destiny, or invulnerability.

In terms of anti-democratic political manipulations, reason has also been used to persuade masses of individuals in effect to give up a

range of freedoms and to commit terrible crimes against humanity—
from the "science" based dreams of National Socialism and Stalinism,
to the absurd rational teleological dreams of Dr. Pangloss and the
breathtakingly disastrous rational dreams of modern development
economists.

Conceited reason will flatter us that we can accept propositions
based on half-truths, or even on completely tentative truths, so long as
they seem logical. It has been common throughout history for manip-
ulators to lead people to specious conclusions with token facts and a
lot of superficially logical argument. Astrologers for example can cite
solid facts—they can exactly predict the positions of the heavenly
bodies, and it is fact that individuals do have different mixes of personality traits.

So the issue of how to use reason and the other remarkable properties of the third layer well has been enormously difficult and decid-
edly non-trivial. It has occupied much of both Western and Eastern
intellectual thought. Great thinkers, such as philosophers William
James and Jean Piaget in the modern era, tried to develop a psychology that was worthy of philosophy and democracy. But it has
proved easier for university administrators to give tenure and for federal agencies to offer grants to large numbers of scientists who study
and teach about pigeons pecking at corn, feline brain waves, and criteria for matching personalities to the job markets.

Goya was a brilliant and provocative artist. I like to think that he
had both meanings in mind and intended exactly to provoke us to think
about the double-edged nature of reason and to remain cautious and
alert to the potentials and problems of reason.

The amazing imagined worlds and inventions for reasoning of the
third layer have always been targets for the cooption and reprogramming of individuals and groups in order to alter perceptions and
behavioral responses to serve the interests of others. The third brain
layer can be tyranny's passport to the enormously powerful and lower
layers with their reptilian fears and selfishness and mammalian herd
instincts.

Yet our educational system has failed to properly educate the
average citizen about the nature of one's own mind and its potentials
and pitfalls. Even the average educated and literate person does not

understand these facts so that they can make better domestic decisions, and also in the interests of individual freedom and democratic society, even after course work in psychology as it is taught today.

These imagined worlds are key strategic sites for ideological manipulation because they code and channel and thus can be enticed to recode and redirect the flow of information between the world of the senses and the deep layers of ancient survival reflexes and emotions. It is even possible to create worlds largely in the mind or "on paper" that throw reality out of focus, much as the teleological/philosophical filter of Voltaire's Dr. Pangloss in Candide threw reality out of focus and served the ideological end of maintaining the status quo in his day.

An imagined world is not merely ideas. It is a tuned antenna and a filter that influences perception, where the eyes turn and how long they linger, and what the brain sees and hears in what the eyes and ears tell it. It sets up habits of perception that divide the real world into the idiomatic categories of a particular language and reflects the philosophical landscape and cognitive maps of a particular culture or subculture.

"Give me a child until the age of six," the tyrant Cardinal reputedly bragged, "and I shall have him for life." Richelieu could count on the fact that it takes great and thoughtful effort to do other than continue throughout life to build an architecture of not simply beliefs, but of habits of perception on previously established foundations. People with a particular filter in their brains pay attention to certain external and internal things and dismiss others, and the unenlightened brain will give those things that it does focus on and those that it dismisses different meanings according to its personal and cultural cognitive maps.

GENESIS: THE BIOLOGICAL AND CULTURAL ROOTS OF *MODERN* DEMOCRATIC ASPIRATIONS

The adaptability and survival of human individuals has long been tied to their functioning within cultural "phase spaces" that have been democratically negotiated among the members of given small bands over time. In this sense democracy and freedom have been expressions of the collective interests that individuals necessarily have in local group adaptation and family survival.

Individual freedom cannot, though, have been a black-or-white matter, because freedoms exist in a cultural context that has been in effect "negotiated" and thus freedom necessarily involves compromises. "Negotiation" could have been implicit by "satisficing." Satisficing means that, in contrast to a calculated optimization, people or animals may simply try different things until a satisfactory pattern has been found. Picture a culture in which people have learned or "negotiated" among themselves unconscious habits to avoid collisions on a crowded sidewalk by swerving to the right or left as the case may be. One might say that individuals must actively (if unconsciously) "negotiate" to create and maintain a suitable social environment in which they and their children, friends and allies, can adapt and survive—and perhaps this image can help one to visualize the gray zone in which idioms of necessarily relative freedom have long taken shape.

Bands of hunter-gatherers and tribes prior to the development of hereditary chiefdoms have been democratic in the sense that they have been self-governing. The Inuit/Eskimo film *The Fast Runner (Atanarjuat)* (2001) illustrates how members of a band in effect must and do work out extremely messy and dangerous interpersonal problems among themselves, and cannot appeal to police or courts. Families and tight communities even in our own society do work out most of their interpersonal problems without police or courts and without killing each other, even if the process can get messy.

Our bonobo, chimpanzee, and gorilla cousins are also democratic in the broad sense, though obviously they do not have ballot boxes (as "democracy" is too often conceived of). But while life in these ape cultures is more involved than is commonly appreciated, they are nevertheless much more simple than human cultures. Evidently the non-human primate mechanisms for bonding, conflict resolution, and communication will not allow them to divide labor, teach technologies, designate interpersonal relationships, visualize taboos, mediate disputes, etc., at the levels of complexity and with the stability that human adaptation has required.

Respect for both individual and group differences. Small-scale tribal democracy works to respectfully integrate the inevitable bio-chemical and experiential differences between individual personalities and perspectives.

Large-scale modern democracy must accommodate both individual differences of these sorts and also multicultural differences. What is common in both cases is an understanding that differences in temperament and perspective are incvitable but that they can be woven into a workable society.

Democratic republic. American large-scale republican democracy developed out of the merging of diverse traditions of self-rule in the early colonial communities.

Many of the European immigrants to the colonies that rebelled had been refugees from various European wars to suppress peasant self-rule and thus brought with them living traditions of local village organization, resentments against various aspects of tyranny, and optimism for self-government. The Reformation revolts against elite classes, in turn, had been closely tied to an apostolic revivalism that was optimistic about the ability of local communities of Christians to follow the fundamentally egalitarian, indeed sharing and commune-istic, community teachings of the Gospels.

Populations in various parts of Europe had been enjoying various degrees of freedom and self-rule for some time for diverse reasons in addition to any opinions that the Gospels mandated communal living and social equality. Mountainous terrain made Basque and Swiss regions difficult to conquer, for example. In the Netherlands, self-organized communities proved to be effective in maintaining the dykes and the below-sea-level polders.

It has become increasingly apparent that European village traditions of self-government and common lands were not, however, simply produced by apostolic Christian texts or geographic idiosyncrasies but had deep cultural roots in the earlier Paleolithic societies. This should not in the least bit be surprising considering that democracies have been common among widespread *small-scale societies* on all continents.

Technical principles of American republican democracy were also learned by Europeans living in contact with self-governing Amerindian tribes and confederations.

There had also been a republican or anti-mercantilist spirit in Europe among those merchants in Europe and the colonies who were campaigning against royal monopolies and for various forms of self-rule.

Thus, the modern republican democratic spirit involved the practical realization that diverse people not only *should* find ways to respect each other's differences and live together but also *could* do so without being ruled by an authoritarian monarch or dictator.

Yet history shows that anti-democratic forces have subverted democratic aspirations more by "twisting meaning" and slowly modifying traditions than by trying to negate the feelings outright. All sorts of tyrannies have called themselves "democratic" because people like to believe in their minds that they are free, whether or not their freedoms are in fact substantial.

People have commonly been made to believe that they are free even while their freedoms were being taken away. This is possible in large part because common sense tells people that total individual freedom is never possible in a society, and there are always trade-offs with the implicit idea that freedom will be maximized by the trade. As John Locke argued long ago, common sense tells us that if everyone were free to kill others, then no one would be safe.

So we all accept restrictions on our freedoms even in democracies. Anti-democratic forces merely convince a critical mass of people that they make the best possible bargain when trading off various freedoms for presumed "freedoms" of "stability," various perquisites, etc.

I am going to take it as a biological given that democratic *aspirations* are biologically rational sentiments for *Homo sapiens*. Efforts to subvert them will thus cause more problems than they solve over the long run. So the proper course of action for humanists should be to find ways to make the concept of democracy work.

FREETHOUGHT AND MODERN DEMOCRACY

Obviously people cannot question and freely decide whether they have in fact negotiated the best bargain unless they are truly free to think their circumstances and alternatives through rationally. The ideal of *modern* democracy has been intimately tied to specific ideals of *freethought*. This is the case because modern democratic *formal ideals*, republican or monarchical, owe considerably to the European Enlightenment struggle against tyranny's censorship, suppression of free speech and assembly, and control of education.

At the same time and earlier, the diverse Christian groups protesting the rule of Rome and its allies had been asking for and sometimes fighting for religious intellectual freedom. The Reformation and the more secular Enlightenment thus overlapped and intersected in ways too complex to discuss here.

The tyranny of church and state (Catholic or Protestant) had long kept its alliances in power by keeping the European mind and emotions in chains, encouraging a general superstitious mentality. More specifically the psychological technology of oppression dictated that suffering would be rewarded in an afterlife, and that disobedience to the culture and its guardians would be punished in hell. Critical reasoning and empirical observations of the real world were developed and promoted to break the chains. The leaders of the Enlightenment also realized that they would have to hone reason to balance liberty, equality, and fraternity against the messiness of the inevitable diversity in individual temperaments and perspectives.

Enlightenment freethought did not historically imply intellectual anarchy or carte blanche for insanity. Freethought was yoked to the progress that science had been making in applying Aristotelian logic to the careful empirical study of nature. That progress, in turn, had surfaced out of the profound interest in nature and worldly affairs that characterized the political and intellectual currents of the late middle ages, Renaissance, Reformation struggles, and the revitalization of ideas from Pagan antiquity.

The formally reasoned arguments for freethought and democracy, such as ideas from Locke and Rousseau, had fertile social ground in which to grow in North America. American democracy had a strong basis in community experience and values and was not simply about the voting procedure of filling out a secret ballot—so-called free elections. It involved a rich mix of old social skills and traditions of assembly, participation, discussion, and respect for at least one's fellow citizens qua citizen-neighbors. Some historians argue that the so-called American revolution was actually a *rebellion* against European authority rather than a true social revolution such as the French engaged in over many decades.

It is remarkable that this model of democracy, including intellectual freedoms, was importable to the large-scale American society, where, flawed indeed, it was developed and work as well as it did for as long as it did and in a republican context. The large-scale modern model has even proved in some cases to be exportable to other large societies in the modern world and in some cases improved.

Considering the history of human biological and social evolution, though, it is not daring to suggest that the widespread appeal of this model for modern democratic political systems and freedoms has been due to the fact that it resonated with something very deep in the human psyche.

The idea that there is a natural endowment of feelings of egalitarian entitlement makes sense even if the Creator was natural selection and not a supernatural god.

DEMOCRACY'S POLITICAL LINGUA FRANCA: SECULAR PRAGMATISM AND SCIENCE

People have been forced to develop languages for trade and intercourse across cultures, such as Melanesian Pidgin English and the Mediterranean lingua franca, Latin. English is commonly the international lingua franca today *not* because it is easy to learn or inherently virtuous, but for purely practical reasons.

"Scientific thought" has proved to be a practical sort of conceptual lingua franca for civic affairs. It provides systematic ways for placing checks on superstitions, superficial impressions, and undisciplined emotional impulses—potentially unfair and destructive "irrationality." For example, our courts have rules of procedure and rational criteria and high standards for the validity of material evidence and we aim for a rule of law that is consistent with empirical experience as well as logic. We no longer punish people because one "feels" that they are evil or because God inspired an inquisitor.

The adoption of secular scientific models in civic discourse has been the practical outcome of centuries of awful experiences with discourse based on the supernatural beliefs and religious dogmas of religious cultures. Of course, certain moral principles from the Western religious tradition have remained even in the modern secularized cosmology. For example, modern secular society rejects the older Biblical standard of an eye for an eye in favor of the newer religious ideas about contrition and redemption, and likewise it voices egalitarian ideals that echo the Gospels, charity for the unfortunate, the Golden Rule, etc.

Discourse based on supernatural inspiration or dogma has sparked inquisitions, torture, religious wars, and the subordination and abuse of whole classes of people. Despite its ideals, religion on an historical scale has not by itself produced as much fairness, justice, peace, and equality as it has produced destructive zeal.

Of course, dogmatic secular ideologies can also produce insane destructive zeal, including those that have claimed to be purely scientific and rational, such as National Socialism and Stalinist Communism. Secular beliefs that claim to be rational can in fact be irrational, and so secularism is not in and of itself a guarantee of sane humanism.

But if and where secular beliefs remain open to proper applications of evidence and reasoning, then there can be systematic safeguarding. However, constant and careful vigilance is necessary.

"Science" can be ideologically co-opted. For example, *economic* dogmatisms and zeal, which insist (against both evidence and close scrutiny) that their claims are scientific, have produced enormous destructiveness, inequities, and inhumanity on a global scale. "The newest and best" schemes for economic reform commonly have turned out to conceal the foraging of the same old voracious wolves in the fuzzy new sheep's clothing of mathematical equations and elegantly argued (if oversimplified) promises.

Theists and other believers in supernatural claims worry that the science that provides rational models and information for the lingua franca of secular democratic discourse is inherently atheistic. I would point out that science is not inherently atheistic. Modern European science began centuries ago as a search for the mind of the divine—early Catholic and Protestant scientists believed that nature followed the commands of God's laws, and they set out to learn God's mind. Then after centuries of looking science found no clear evidence for the Judeo-Christian God or any of the gods that have been hypothesized in various cultures. It was forced to stop articulating in its lingua franca the belief that the laws of nature must be divinely mandated. Thus the scientific lingua franca today cannot include gods as either causes or substances in nature because the idea simply did not pan out even after centuries of searching.

But this conceptual and communication development is not the same as deliberately excluding the very possibility that there are gods of some sort that have material influences that have escaped detection even after centuries of looking. The situation is logically parallel to the legends that Montezuma's treasure was hidden in the southwestern United States. There is no evidence that it exists or where it might exist, and though people have been looking for a very long time, no one has found it. Thus it might possibly be there, as many treasure hunters strongly believe, but it would be incorrect to bring the legend into negotiations about property values. Personally I would not invest in an expedition.

At the same time, the secular lingua franca based on Aristotelian logic and empiricism that was refined was found to be quite useful for reasoning about practical matters among people with different supernatural cosmologies. It was realized that this could provide a healthy alternative to inquisitions and religious wars.

The recognition of the importance of science to democracy does not, of course, mean that there is no place for *private* religious beliefs in democracies as civic entities. The main problems with religion *for modern democracies as social entities* can come when zealous religious factions try to take over and replace the secular lingua franca or dominate multicultural societies.

In short, democratic societies learned to use the secular lingua franca for discourse on community matters. But this is a practical use of secular terms and concepts, and it does not mean in and of itself that private atheism is certifiably correct or that private religious beliefs are certifiably wrong. Science and logic can only say that centuries of studies of a plethora of major phenomena that were long thought to require gods can instead be explained by "automatic" natural causes. This leaves a residue of questions and feelings that rational individuals must come to grips with in terms of their own personal philosophical studies, and critical self-analyses of their emotions and intuitions.

A major challenge for humanism. Neither science, atheism, nor secular ideologies provide foolproof guarantees against inhumanity or sloppy thinking. Scientific half-truths and misapplied concepts have become the common persuasive weapons of ideologues and the slick lawyers and public relations people that they work with because of the fact that science has become the lingua franca that they must twist to get their way.

Modern democracy thus has a tremendously vital interest in watchdogging science and scientific language to try to purge it of ideologies and political/economic cooption.

THE FALL: THE COOPTION AND CORRUPTION OF DEMOCRACY

Satisfactory democracy is rare in modern large-scale societies. Few humans today live in self-governing hunter-gatherer bands or democratic tribes. Humans in the modern world everywhere yearn for freedom and democratic self-rule, but true democracy, based on the simple biological logic above, is not common in complex societies. These instead typically have institutionalized hierarchies of political/economic and/or religious or ideological power.

Moreover, not all modern humans do yearn for political freedom as much as they yearn for security. Perhaps many more believe that they are quite free when in fact they live in various forms of bondage to others, even though they have not given their *informed* consent or participated equitably in the formation of the conditions that define their own circumstances.

One important biological reason behind these facts is that there are many ways that people's perspectives and values can be and have been manipulated since at least the rise of hereditary chiefdoms and the great civilizations.

For one thing, the symbols and patterns of communication that had long before become essential to human adaptation can become overloaded and "jammed." The neomammalian brain can become so confused that it becomes useless in working out the true long-term interests of the individual. This can result from any number of general causes such as the corruption of language, lack of educational enlightenment, social breakdown within and between families, information overload, etc.

The traditional habits of community organization tend to get lost in highly mobile societies, for example, passively, if only because people are too busy to get to know each other very well. People may make up for this in part by choosing emotional bonds with celebrities, but one cannot work through difficult personal and intellectual issues with a movie star.

In principle, though, people could invent new alternative ways to maintain community and teach these in schools. Yet in fact democracy tends to be taught in schools too much as *procedures*—for getting bills through Congress, etc.—or as some simple idea about values that centers on "equality." When this is the case, the students may never grasp why freedom of speech and assembly and separation of church and state would be critical to the functioning of meaningful democracy in large pluralistic societies. The impression is left that these are nothing more than "birth rights" to each solitary individual—simple gifts, individually owned property—to be taken or disposed of at one's individual whim. They are not understood to be delicate tools to allow one to function as a proper integrated social being in a nurturing social environment.

The information processing of the neomammalian brain can also in a sense, metaphorically speaking, be "hacked" and large numbers of individuals can thus be reprogrammed for the benefit of smaller numbers. The third-layer filter then serves to stimulate the lower brain layers to function in ways that favor the manipulator. For example, politicians have used the message "enemy" to cause the neomammalian brain to tell the paleomammalian brain to break its social bonds with neighbors and choose new allies and to tell the reptile brains to fear and attack the designated enemies.

The only way to protect against such things is through self-examination as one grows up and by learning one's own vulnerabilities and to deal with them and with the challenges through critical reasoning. This is difficult because it takes intelligence, patience, emotional fortitude, and courage.

It is also difficult because aggressive ideologues and evangelical religionists are busy indoctrinating by telling us how to reason critically. Creationists, as an extreme example, promote a species of "critical reason" that allows them to ignore the bulk of empirical science and conclude that the world was created in six days. Flat-earthers also believe that they are using critical reasoning. But these only illustrate one colorful area on a spectrum.

Proper education could help, but several factions are fighting to control our educational institutions. The control of education and media have been major objectives in the Culture War in the United States and elsewhere, and the challenger culture warriors have made great strides.

Denial: A major obstacle for democracy. No one knows if lizards or kangaroos engage in denial and rationalizations, but apparently not the elaborate self-deceptions of humans. Denial is very likely a neo-mammalian brain layer function. Tyrants always provide options for denial and rationalization and people commonly accept their offers. Denial is comfort food for the mind. It may be universal. My sense is that it has something to do with protecting worldviews and habits that have proved adaptive and have served as "behavioral/emotional gyroscopes" for individuals and cultures.

A common tactic throughout history has been to tell people that they are free when in fact their freedoms are being taken away. *Arbeit macht frei* was in hindsight simply ludicrous in the context of Nazi concentration camps. But most Jews had proved vulnerable to denial as their freedoms were taken away bit by bit. The German leaders understood that people will deny that they are in trouble until it is too late, even until the gas floods through the fake showers.

Once people begin kidding themselves, the next inner lie comes easier, and then the next, and so on. Similarly, the denial of the chemical or sexual addict, the cornered politician or student, or the discredited scientist can stretch out into astonishing distortions of reality.

When are we free and when do we have a true democracy as we believe? Some people will be satisfied with very little because they do not want much. And others will be satisfied with very little because they think that they have more than they really do have.

Media and education. The threat to democracy from the steady concentration of media ownership in the United States has been endlessly discussed, as has been the failings of education to instruct students in critical thinking and in the ways of the world. The media world is largely a virtual world, only loosely connected to the breadth and depth of the real world. Humanists should give these issues considerable study, and there are abundant books and professional journals on the subject.

The character of the people. Machiavelli argued cogently that there can only be true self-governing republics where the people have a mix of pride, courage, and a sense of excellence that he called *virtù*. But if they do not have *virtù*, then a strong leader must take control in order to maintain stability.

There is surely some truth to this. In fact, people generally will accept imposed stability if the alterative seems to be anarchy and may even welcome it. So one technique of tyranny has been to encourage instability, or at least the *image* of chaos, so that people will welcome control by a strong leader. Some of this could be seen in the documentary film *The Revolution Will Not Be Televised.* The government of Venezuela was taken over in a coup in 2002. The perpetrators even bragged on camera that they had created a bloody incident to associate mobs with the democratically elected government and thus give the economic elite an excuse to arrest the president and dissolve the Assembly. (Once the deceit was understood, there was popular outrage, and President Chavez was later returned to power. According to the film, in effect Chavez had instructed his people in *virtù*.)

The *virtù* to maintain freedom might be lost passively for various reasons, but it has also been subverted actively by ideologies, as well as from deliberate disinformation and meddling with circumstances.

Symbolic meanings are easily reprogrammed. The very features that have provided both adaptive stability and flexibility for individuals in small groups are vulnerable, as has been discussed. A powerful imagination capacity with only limited structuring properties and open channels of communication makes for a double-edged sword, from the perspective of human adaptation.

Systems of inter-individual information organization, processing, and communication can degrade due to various causes. Thus, while one could argue that an authentic collegial democracy was once "the natural state of humankind," it has not been the natural/normal state for "civilized" people for most of written history. The large-scale experiments in democracy and the liberalizations of freethinking that formed during the Enlightenment have been a relatively new and unusual chapter in the history of large-scale cultures.

Modern freedoms in large-scale democratic societies have been under assault by an epic Culture War in the United States and some other parts of the world notably since the 1970s. So it is timely and urgent to expand here briefly on the fact that any open system of information processing, storage, and communication can be deliberately jammed, hacked, and/or reprogrammed.

The history of civilizations with written records is a chronicle of top-down psychological manipulation and control. It is generally agreed by scholars that *all* the major civilizations developed under theocracies. Freedoms of conduct and thought obviously have been restricted where there is institutionalized political hierarchy, and certainly where beliefs have been imposed by those who hold power and where the beliefs are not subject to major discussion or negotiation by those who are ruled.

The twentieth century saw the rise of destructive hierarchical secular ideologies, where political theories were imposed with the assurance that they were firmly backed up by science and that they were in some way democratic because they somehow were "for the people."

It is easiest, of course, to use as graphic examples the paradigmatic, failed, or passé examples of reprogramming rather than the successful and more immediate examples of thought control that remain in shadows. In the paradigmatic Orwellian example, peace was redefined to include what was previously understood to be war. The rusty signs over the gates of various concentration camps offered "arbeit macht frei"—work makes for spiritual freedom. Maybe this was a comfort at the time to those outside the camps—but in this case probably most of the workers inside, at least, were not fooled, nor are we in hindsight.

How many oppressive nations today are called the "Democratic Republic of This-or-That"? More subtly but quite commonly, lies can be passed along as pristine truths with a clear conscience because potential doubters get confused into believing that the lies embody some hypothetical "higher truths." Subsidized and coerced trade can be called and thought of as "free trade" because its proponents are allegedly "for freedom." It is permissible to execute innocent people now and then because the institution of capital punishment supposedly provides a deterrent and hence social justice.

Ugly realties are replaced and obscured by attractive ideals as smoothly as a magician can change a watermelon into a rabbit. Critical thinkers can mock the idea that you'll get pie in the sky when you die, but various forms of pie-in-the-sky promises to the masses have been very filling meals for a great many elites throughout history.

Today's people often seem to be ruled by bumper sticker slogans and by the catechisms of economic and other ideologies and faiths that do not actually serve their own long-term interests as much as they have been led to believe.

This emphasis on widespread deceptions today in societies that have struggled to develop self-conscious democratic ideals is not to deny that individuals in small bands and democratic tribes doubtless did sometimes exploit the open properties of the programming of human consciousness. Some surely did take malicious control of their larger group, and surely there have been psychopathic and manipulative shamans over the course of human history even in these small-scaled societies. The line between respect, leadership, and exploitation can be difficult to discern at any scale of society.

But as Rousseau observed long ago, when people are raised together, and live their entire lives and pass the generations in very small groups, and care for children in common, they tend to be much more transparent to each other than we are in our much more complex world. So various types of checks and balances have been possible in small bands that are less powerful in large-scale societies. In our world, people commonly do not know even members of their immediate families as well as they imagine.

DE SADE, DEMOCRACY, AND BIOLOGY

Philosophically inclined people will be comfortable in focusing on the very real threats to democracy in our times from ideologies. Modern sociologists will want to discuss the very real threats from the conflicts of interests that develop within societies. Anthropologists may wish to focus on the very real fact that some societies more than others encourage aggressiveness and political hierarchy because this is adaptive in terms of their needs to fight military and/or economic wars, etc. But as a biologist I would be remiss if I did not at least mention how these quite real causes can interact with biology and with the promotion of obfuscating biological ideologies.

Anthropologist Geoffrey Gorer culled through the rambling writings of the Marquis de Sade to produce *The Revolutionary Ideas of the Marquis de Sade*. De Sade, Gorer detailed, championed an intriguing biological theory for why democracy fails. And in a preface to the 1934 edition the distinguished biologist J. B. S. Haldane wrote that Sade's theory is scientifically plausible and worthy of serious further study.

The premise is that people cannot live respectfully as equals because some individuals will by their nature have needs to dominate others in a sexual context and even to see others suffer. For various reasons they cannot satisfy these needs directly, and so they will use deceits to gain power over others in ways that do not appear outwardly to be sexual. Their "inner demons" will also cause them to abuse their power in small or great ways that do not appear outwardly to be sexual.

Sade's theory in part involved what biologists would call today *frustration aggression*. This is a well-known biological phenomenon, where ambiguous mixes of rewards and punishments will dramatically raise the levels of hostility and aggression in rodents, sheep, humans, etc. *Displacement behavior* is a related behavioral phenomenon where the frustration of a behavior can cause aroused energies to be redirected to attacks even on other species (example: kicking the cat) or inanimate objects (hitting a wall) or to sex (raping a child or cellmate).

Apparently Sade was not specific about why it is in the sexual nature of certain individuals in the first place to need to dominate and hurt. Nevertheless, *some individuals* have to take control over others *outside of an obviously sexual context* and pervert efforts at democracy. So Sade's solution was to encourage such individuals to face up to their suppressed aggressive and dominating sexual inclinations and act them out in the bedroom and the brothel cathartically. He hoped that his sexual fictions would help redirect frustrated libidos toward more private vices and away from public abuses of democratic egalitarianism.

One reason that such suggestions may seem outrageous today is that thinking about human sexuality too often has an orgasmic bottom line in mind. For example, human sexual satisfaction is often equated with coitus, orgasms, climaxes, and "peak experiences."

But human sexual satisfaction is more complex than the animal act and in fact has a variety of faces that can mix idiosyncratically. There can be lots of orgasmic human sexual *activity* that nevertheless lacks in love, in steadily growing intimacy, in play, in honest communication, in abandon, in tenderness, in whimsy, in fantasy and experimentation, or that has an undercurrent of guilt. Humans can surely have sexual *desires* that are rejected or even ridiculed by spouses and potential partners and even by their own conscience and consciousness. Even a Don Juan can be sexually frustrated in one or more of these ways. And one might not have all the sexual partners for which one lusts. But too often people think of sex simply in terms of "getting it," and this is not a very useful perspective scientifically for understanding inner turmoil in humans.

For the sake of discussion assume that de Sade did have the germ of a valid insight that could not have been profitably pursued with eighteenth-century science. And to avoid misunderstanding, let me add that I think his *solution* looks quite naive from today's perspective. It might possibly work for some individuals, but for others it could amount to trying to put out a smoldering fire with gasoline.

Nevertheless, this discussion does draw attention to one of the great threats to modern democracy. The general threat is that we know each other so poorly that driven and charismatic individuals can rise to power, and they can too easily have mildly or severely pathological personalities.

Psychopathology need not have anything to do with sex, obviously. And there was an interesting literature developing on psychopathology and power in the days before most university research became federally funded. But the points raised by De Sade and Gorer do make the point graphically that there can be threats to democracy that it is not socially or politically correct to discuss publicly. Yet threats in this category must be included for completeness. And I suspect that every reader will be able to visualize at least that there are many possible links between various aspects of sex and the determined lust for economic, political, and various other forms of social power.

Another "biological" threat has to do with the spread of biological ideologies, and ideologies, of course, are the constant enemies of the critical thinking that democratic aspirations require. The pathological person will want to portray himself in the most favorable way, both for self-esteem and social effectiveness. For example, he would violently reject the suggestion that he is driven to social power because he is sexually frustrated, pathological, etc. For this reason, ideologies that portray his mentality and behavior as *natural* and even heroic are immediately appealing.

Moreover, social theory predicts that a social system "will not want" individuals to understand the psychological dynamics that lead them to serve that system. The beliefs that support the system must be labeled "truths" and not "ideologies." For example, National Socialism would hardly have wanted the population to understand that it was promoting anti-Semitism as an outlet or scapegoat for their frustrations. It packaged its messages as scientific facts.

British scholars have been rather candid in explaining how the harsh English "public schools" reflected a general system that helped to train leaders who maintained the British class system and colonial domination throughout the world. In *The English Vice: Beating, Sex and Shame in Victorian England and After*, Ian Gibson details how upper-class boys were indoctrinated into sadomasochistic flagellation and humiliation for so long and to the degree that even British politicians have spoken fondly about their memories of the rod in open defense of the tradition against proposed reforms.

This theater of cruelty was not instructing sexually vulnerable boys *openly* in the nuanced dynamics of dominance and subordination or telling them the personal advantages of supporting a class system in which they could discretely act out their cultivated tastes. It was "building character" and making future leaders "tough" for God and country, and teaching subordinates to "love and respect their betters" for the sake of social stability. Clearly these were functional aspects of the *ends*, but they are labels that obscure scientific understanding of the *means* that this society developed to pursue those ends. And if a society makes it taboo to discuss means in objective terms and openly, then where does this leave critical thinking and its place in democracy?

My field of biology has been plagued by ideological spin as in the case of eugenics, social Darwinism, biological determinism and related popularized distortions. For example, a spin on legitimate Darwinism has been used to justify "scientifically" the aggressive businessman, the warrior, the ambitious politician, and install them as the gold standard for human nature. We hear that such persons are all simply "alpha males" doing what alpha males by nature are "supposed" to be doing. Any contributing cultural factors such as normative social expectations and values, peer and parental pressures, frustrations, neuroses, and institutional customs allegedly are supposedly trivial and can be forgotten. Differences between cultures can be waved away by reductionism—arguing that *in essence* people are all *basically* the same (without justifying critically what, if anything, "essence" and "basically" would mean scientifically or the practical implications of cultural differences).

Social Darwinism has been used to disempower, marginalize, humiliate, and exploit whole classes of people and whole cultures to lesser or greater degrees. It is an example of how the democratic aspirations of a people to search for mutual tolerance and respect and critical thinking can come into conflict with the pragmatic functional requirements of their economic system and elites, and with the ideologies that support these. This ideology has helped to confuse public discussion and understanding. It has encouraged biological dynamics in society that have been unhealthy for democratic principles and aspirations.

SELFISHNESS AND THE CORROSION OF DEMOCRACY

Homo sapiens is a social animal, and popularizations that reduce human nature to mere selfishness or self-interest are not sound biology. Furthermore, such doctrines can be corrosive to democracy. Democracy implies society for *the common good*, and mutual respect is an essential component.

But there have been efforts to redefine democracy as the freedom to make and keep profits that will produce a "commonwealth," in the sense of individuals who identify with each other simply because doing so will produce economic prosperity, or common *wealth*. Those who controlled wealth realized at least by the seventeenth century that they need populations of social mobile competitors with desires and values that would allow them to be controlled with money. Desires for fairness and community were manifesting as demands for public charity and compassion for the poor, better working conditions, public education, etc. The opposition to these was busy promoting ideas that eventually were called social Darwinism. They insisted that selfish individualism was the fundamental essence of human nature and therefore right. Ignore the poor because they are simply "unfit" by nature.

This ideology ignores several facts. And one is that human potentials are too multifaceted to reduce to a single dominant "human nature." We have selfish and self-involved dimensions to be sure. But we also have social dimensions. We have contemplative dimensions.

Augustine observed long ago that man is motivated by three loves—love of self, love of one's fellows, and love of God. One should strive for a harmony between these three loves or motivations, for problems in individual and social life arise from imbalance.

The major problem that Augustine saw among humans was that too often there was too much *self-love*. A modest amount of self-love is necessary for self-maintenance, but too much results in a neglect of compassion and responsibility for others and too little selfless contemplation about the universe.

Augustine's three loves translate easily into modern secular humanist terms and make good sense from the perspective of modern zoology. The secularist can better understand the cogency of Augustine's insight by putting aside the idea that by "God" he could only have meant a man in a white beard or some such supernatural being. "God" would have meant a variety of things to sophisticated religious thinkers of the fourth century, in addition to a divine personality, much as it does today, and some of these translate easily into modern secular terms and concerns for contemplative understanding and/or secular cosmologies.

For love of "God" substitute secular words that imply imagined third-brain-layer idiomatic constructions such as a sense of or a passion for a higher reality than one's uncultivated self—perhaps a passion for "understanding." Imagine idioms of respect, commitments, and/or ideals that rise above egoism, selfishness, and nepotism. Substitute "the Good," for example, or venerable traditions and laws, a concept that some things must be right and wrong in an unquestioned (not necessarily philosophically unquestionable) sense. Substitute "philosophy" or disciplined reason if one likes. Substitute secular democratic or progressive principles and ideals—beauty, hope, justice.

Wearing my zoologist's hat, and with "the soundtrack off," *Homo sapiens* is a species with individuals that, like any lizard or snake, are deeply self-involved but that, like any dog or bison, also have strong mammalian needs for social contact and affiliations.

But *Homo sapiens* are also deeply involved in zoologically unusual things that vary conspicuously from one culture to another and that make much more sense with words, with "the soundtrack on." If one tunes into the elaborate chatter and learns to decipher it, one learns that potentially all behaviors are influenced in addition by implicit and explicit learned idiomatic ideas, values, and habits of perception, logic, and communication.

And humans are intensely interested in arranging the settings, people, and events around them into characters and scripts, so to speak, in their individual and group minds. The fact that everyone gossips, and that literate people are drawn into films and novels "to see what develops and how they end," is a symptom of this tendency.

Perhaps concepts of gods and other spirits arise because they are useful script elements. But the tendency to need to make up scripts implies a larger biological phenomenon than simply fear, guilt, faith, hope, or bartering with deities.

So all of these are human nature—the selfish dimension, the social dimension, and the contemplative dimension—and it is easy to see how they would have been adaptive in the evolution of human societies. A healthy democracy will respect all of these and not urge its citizens primarily to focus on pursuit of selfish desires.

But the leaders of our nation have promoted ideologies of self-interest for decades. It could be a coincidence that scandals have been spreading in business and government, that there is crime in the streets, that universities are increasingly managed by opportunists, and that people are losing faith in our institutions and in the very notion that we have a healthy democracy. But on the other hand, ideas and role models do have consequences.

"I'D RATHER BE A PAGAN
SUCKLED IN A CREED OUTWORN . . ."

Many in the world hunger for material security and consumer goods. But many of those who possess these have found the culture that goes with them to be disappointing. There is widespread disaffection with a competitive society of winners and losers where more and more of life is being commodified. Social relationships and culture too often are subservient to economics, and communities are fragmented or dysfunctional. Stress, dysfunctional families, and chemical and other addictions are epidemic.

Ideologies insist that the competitive and commodified way of life is based firmly on rationality and that this is the best of all possible worlds. Is it any wonder that there is a thirst to explore the irrational? And what are the implications for democracy of this thirst?

The thirst to explore irrationality and find a different/better world is a double-edged sword politically.

Experimentation with irrationality is often linked to efforts to rebuild community—whether communities based on biblical religion or on "new age" revivals of non-biblical Eastern and pagan ideas and rituals. Efforts to rebuild community per se could contribute to a strengthening of democracy.

But these social movements (linked loosely to what are sometimes called the postmodernisms of reaction and resistance) often contain great anger at the modernist status quo. They want to tear it down, and this would throw out the baby of good reason and the progress of the Enlightenment along with the dirty bathwater of the ideologies that claim falsely to be rational and that claim to represent the Enlightenment.

The angry and evangelical religious conservative movements have become the political pawns of the very elites who have contributed so much to shaping the competitive and commodified modern world. Thus they have become frontline soldiers in the Culture War. They battle for their generals against rational analyses that would elucidate the nature of the modern tangle and the erosion of democracy.

The "new age" factions have been more diffuse and difficult to manipulate. And philosophically their doctrines have not been conditioned to make them obedient to power. These elements and their desires for community explain why many of them campaign aggressively for democratic principles.

On the other hand there are "new age" factions and "postmodernists of resistance" who have become so extremely negative about Western civilization and Western rationality and science that they tend to be intellectually nihilistic and unsupportive of practical political compromises.

CAN DEMOCRACY SURVIVE GLOBALIZATION?

These challenges to democracy interact with a shift that has been taking place away from the grounding of capital largely within political jurisdictions. Moneyed elites have been exploiting the potentials of rapid mass transportation and global communication to escape local oversight.

Corporations want for themselves the rights that individuals have in our justice system. But it is important to understand that they resist being bound to the expectations of civility that individual "good citizens" are expected to shoulder.

Multinational corporations have learned to play national and local governments off against each other. They have learned to threaten to move their operations unless governments compete to give them reduced regulation, subsidies, etc. Americans, for example, still think that big "American corporations" are necessarily American, whereas a given corporation will claim to be American in Washington and German in Berlin and appeal to patriotism in each capital.

Citizens are disempowered when they do not understand such manipulations. People around the world have been seduced by such appealingly simple slogans as "a rising tide raises all ships." It turns out that while a rising tide may lift some ships, it can also sink fragile boats, erode shorelines, and wash away sand castles and homes.

Corporate literature details that the nation-state can and must be redefined. The nation state is in effect being transformed into an administrative entity to provide labor and the training of experts, subsidies, sites of production and administration, to keep populations in order, and to provide international policing for economic interests.

The use of corporate money to influence elections, politicians, and bureaucrats is well known and has even become a notorious issue. There is no reason to belabor it here.

Thus, the power of citizens in democracies to control their own affairs through local and federal governments is being steadily diminished.

STONE BY PATIENT STONE

The challenges to democracy today seem overwhelming. But historically the challenges were also overwhelming. The combined force of Church and State left people for centuries with virtually no legal rights, censorship of information, incarceration and physical torture, and fear of the most terrible hell imaginable. The elites relentlessly tried to control both mind and body with every available physical and psychological instrument. But as Will and Ariel Durant characterized the Enlightenment:

> Year after year patient plodders brought a stone to the rising pyramid of knowledge, and in a hundred cities curious men tested hypotheses with experiments. Slowly the area of the supernatural shrank, the sphere of the natural and secular grew. It is a dull, impersonal, fragmentary history, and the greatest drama of modern times.[1]

Confucius observed that the journey of a thousand miles begins with a single step. Lesser known writers understand this as well. Even when other paths seem blocked, we can begin to take significant steps by ourselves.

The structures that oppress us are like everything in this world. There was a time when they came into being and there will come a time when they will die. Our task is not to crush them violently, but rather to build something beautiful ourselves. We begin in our families, with our spouses and our children. We build respect and dignity and democracy there. And in our communities. That is where we have to begin. (Mario Fárez, indigenous leader, Ecuador)

NOTE

1 Will and Ariel Durant, *The Story of Civilization*, vol. 7 (New York: Simon and Schuster, 1935), p. 579.

10.

Ensuring the Future:
Democracy and Education

Harvey Sarles

INTRODUCTION

Ensuring the future of democracy is always a tricky and problematic endeavor. In order to preserve democracy, it is not sufficient to proclaim its necessity or its greatness. We have to participate, remain involved, develop, and update our analyses and understandings. And we have to educate each new generation to the ideas and importance of democracy, even as the world and times change—perhaps especially as the world and times change. How can we see the present and create a positive and democratic vision of and for the future?

In this moment of history, the times are changing quickly and radically! Precipitated by the introduction of new technologies, the vastness of change affects America, the world, all and each of us in various ways. Importantly, the very nature of work is changing: as large a change as the Industrial Revolution—perhaps greater.

The rapid rise of television, computers, the Internet, medical drugs, and others also helped to create a concentration of wealth and power which has real possibilities of shifting a liberal democracy to oligarchy, monarchy, or worse. We seem to be running a modern version of the "gilded age" in our collective thoughts and outlooks, with money as the mantra of being and success.

Technological and political changes have also set off a range of new *conceptual* currents. These range widely—from globalization, to gender issues, to the ways in which we locate and create meaning in our lives. We find ourselves, in the midst of all these changes, without much sense of anchorage or stability, afloat in the rough seas of what's new, each day. And our outlook has been affected and redirected in many ways that range from obscure to unclear in our ongoing thinking and analyses.

It has also become increasingly difficult to sense that the idea of progress is available in our lives. Progress, driving the powerful idea of a democracy of "we the people" has eroded, particularly with the threats of terrorism rending us vulnerable to various enemies: clear or vague. But the sense that things will get better, that we can create a world which will provide more or deeper meaning to our being, is less and less available to us. Progress is, at most, a mixed metaphor, not a direction toward the future.

In response to the felt changes, this is a time of powerful reaction. Looking to the past rather than the future, there is the philosophical, political, and religious temptation to look to the ancient thinkers as still possessing the genius to take us to better and safer times. We look for permanence, for surety, in such times, as the idea of democracy simply fades.

It was a time, not very different from the present when John Dewey began his efforts to change education, to attempt to rethink and "reconstruct" philosophy, ideas, the world—to move us forward into the future of a participative democracy: the Progressive Age. Can we move forward in these changing moments toward a new Progressive Age, and help ensure the future of democracy?

I. THE PRESENT AGE

On a bookcase in my office at the University of Minnesota is a sign (viewable only by me) which says: "I touch the future. I teach."

In a world in which teaching is given short shrift, in which education is primarily toward credentials and career, we have to wonder how much thought and appreciation is being given to the idea and importance of the future. In this time of concentration on the present, and some increasingly strong urges to look back to ancient times for the very sense of what is real, the notion of democracy seems much at risk. The perennial question, posed most clearly by Dewey: how to teach students to understand and participate actively in a continually changing-evolving democracy?

While this country pushes the idea, more the word—DEMOC-RACY—upon the entire world, its meanings and actuality seem adrift, caught up in pressures of electioneering and public relations.

Democracy needs, as Dewey said repeatedly in many contexts, to be rethought and brought into practice in every next moment: with those who are newly grown and those who are newly arrived in our world, engaged in its analysis and practice. How do we move "forward" to ensure the future of a participative democracy?

The obvious temptation is to deal within quite narrow political struggles in terms of very short time dimensions, to see which issues sell on a given day, or appeal to a narrowly reactive citizenry: did the president? Will the other side react? Jobs and the economy? War and empire in this global framing? And in the current world where public relations fed by television, spin, and appearance rule the temper of these times, it is a distinct worry that the concepts and practices of democracy will fall under the radar, even as all sides invoke it to promote whatever they are trying to promote in any instant. Democracy has become a promotional icon.

But what are these times? Are they as different as the technologies which have come to center, perhaps rule, our activity and thinking: television, the Internet, transportation, just to begin?

What conceptual changes, what their dimensions, have occurred with the technologies? They certainly seem large, immense in many senses. I wonder, for example, if the power of the Pill to sunder the very relationship of sex and procreation has affected much of our thinking about all relationships and the very meaning of our being: gender, marriage, just to begin. How is democracy in these actual and conceptual times, when the very definition of personhood is less and less clear?

We have become a celebrity culture, money and fame ruling the thoughts and activities of much of our population, particularly shaping the concerns and activities of the young. Education toward democracy, in a time of the "gilded age" of concentration of and upon money and fame, doesn't much enter the thinking of most of our students. Get a degree, get out into the world, make a lot of money . . . retire early and enjoy. Democracy . . . ?

Most of America is witnessing a very large immigration: witnessing but not experiencing, not much trying to educate toward understanding and analysis of the democracy which it praises. During the previous period in which this occurred, a law severely limiting immigration was in effect for forty-one years (1924–65), passed in a huge reaction to a changing ethnic America. Most of us don't know, don't much appreciate this history or the pattern which may enable us to see what is occurring right now, beyond the political polemics which gather most of our attention.

Another pattern: the current development of new technologies mirrors the last "gilded age," when the "robber barons" were able to concentrate money and power very mightily. This is happening right now in many industries (computers, oil, pharmaceuticals, etc., and probably most important—the media). Yet, last time, the end of the nineteenth century, the moneyed age was eventually replaced by a progressive moment. How did that occur? Can we help make it occur this time?

One seductive temptation in this moment of rapidly changing history is to look backward to the conceptual worlds of texts and time to tell us who we are, and are to be, rather than to look "inside" and find the means and vision to go forward. Plato conceptually "stopped" the world and the neo-conservatives following Leo Strauss find this most tempting. The Old Testament, New Testament, the Koran inspire many of us to look for our being and meaning in the ancient thinkers who appealed to us outside of our being and experience. Note the appeal and rapid rise of evangelical and fundamentalist thought and action.

Change, when it grows at the great pace we are presently experiencing, feels to many like "chaos." Thus we are tempted to try to stop the world and return to some idea of how it was . . . when things seemed good or just about right. Or the genius of former times seem larger and more teacher-ly than the actual teaching of those of us who attempt, most days, to touch the future: a diminishing of the present, a reduction of the possibility of future democracy.

This is to proclaim that these times we are in now seem precarious, fragile. How fragile, how precarious, again needs thought toward actions to enable us to move truly toward the future of being and an engaging in democracy. There are those who think America is currently "imperiled," others who tend toward tagging ideas as "conspiracies," and wonder if we are moving toward a fascistic state. Others provide the analysis that we are in some long-term patterns in which future is not very good.

But the perspective of "doom and destruction," the temptation to seek conspiracy around every next corner, feeds upon itself and also seems to frame the idea of the future most narrowly. Everyone we oppose we tend to dismiss with terms like "kooks and crazies"— which any and every opposition seems to use to describe their chosen opponents. Ha! What jerks, how "dumb" the "selected" president is! We haven't heard much about how clever he is, able to maintain his public composure. Not much possibility of discussion in these contexts, mainly polemic and contestation.

II. SEEKING MORE UNDERSTANDING OF AMERICA AND DEMOCRACY

How do we go about "ensuring the future" of democracy? Take a broad and hard look at these times, try to infer the similarity of current and historical patterns, go deeper and to the beyond of the changes which are occurring!

Consider, for example, the vast implications of the Pill, which has literally changed relationships between sex and procreation and is shifting our thinking about gender. Get amazed by the idea of the astronauts looking back at the earth from the moon in 1969 and being able to imagine the entire earth in any and every moment. Rethink the power of television: its speed, its ubiquity, its power to enter and frame our thinking being overtaken by money more than by the need to educate. Note the rise of robotics, seeing the characters on the tube selling toys to kids of all the ages. Appreciate the vast movements of peoples and money making the very idea of the "nation" fragile and mysterious, and the impacts of their ideas, for example, in healing and spirituality.

This is just to begin the discussion that we think in a quite different conceptual framework than when last we thought much about democracy and the future in the Deweyan progressive era of early last century. Trying to redefine and understand our boundaries, we have to place our temptations to shout conspiracy and blame in some positions on hold, and rethink who we are, how we see the world, and how others see us.

First, we need to ask: how "good" are these times? The very idea of America, its practices, its being, its idea of itself seen in global and historical contexts, actually seems quite good—most days.

Appreciate crossing the street with much traffic and feeling generally secure that everyone will yield. Riding my bike down the main street in Minneapolis, with three lanes of traffic one way and buses/taxis the other, is challenging conceptually, but actually not difficult within the marked bike lanes. This is my homely metaphor for a shared world in which there is generally a reasonable respect for most everyone else. Our daily world is not a very "dangerous" place, but mostly safe-feeling. This is not the case for many other peoples, and many people in our own history.

Thinking about other nations and times, and what is this place, recognize that we are all living on Indian land. A century and a half ago, we granted the immigrants 160 acres of land to establish themselves, squeezing the native peoples onto small reservations. But we rarely keep this in our active memories when thinking about how and where we are.

This is a disgrace which, strangely and ironically, provides America's immigrant populations (practically all of us) with some quite large graces. Though we are engaged in the current wars on and with "terrorism," we are essentially "free" of the "histories" which plague most of the rest of the world. No royalty or monarchy to hate or to worship. No twenty centuries of Palestinian occupation of Israel asking to restore an ancient right, no 650 years of battles between the Kosovars and Serbs, no fairly recent histories of colonization still steaming in its blamings: at least inside what we deem to be the

America of this moment. (Outside: there may be much "blowback" for us trying to impose what must feel like colonization to others.)

We need to keep some things actively in our minds. We should remember at all moments that this country is vast and very rich in natural resources. It actually remains fairly empty except for a fairly small number of cities and congested areas.

Most of us who are thinking about the future of democracy are not living "on the edges" but need to consider the fragility of the lives of many of our citizens. Democracy needs to focus much on whatever we consider the "common good" and what is useful, important, or necessary to have all our citizens partake in it.

Importantly, we tend to infer from our particular experiences to that of the peoples of other lands. But we have differences to which most of us give little thought. Different from most other countries, America's borders are very far away from most of us, actually and conceptually. Very few of us live in the three border cities of the north, or San Diego and Texas towns on the south. We have little actual experience of other countries, languages, and the very different nature of living in other nations and histories.

Such differences remain conceptually distant for most of us in understanding what it means to live in another land, speak a different language, or exist in an economy where most of the people are very poor. Our great neighbor to the south, Mexico (where I lived for an extended period), has a level of poverty which is virtually unimaginable to most Americans. Why?—we need to ask ourselves. Do most of us even see the poor around us: having hired "social mercenaries" to house them, feed them, and keep them hidden from us most of the time?

When we imagine who and what we are, we construct the idea of America from a very narrow "insider's" view. We tend to see ourselves as the proverbial "cathedral on the hill" and raise our sense of being to places far distant from our reality and the realization of the rest of the world. In a moment of rapidly increasing globalization, the America of our ideations is very narrow, actually and conceptually.

In order to truly gain some sense of the threat of terrorism in these times, it is crucial to gain a deeper sense of what and who we are and how we are perceived beyond the applause we grant ourselves for being the "greatest," the "good" not the "evil." What does that mean? Who are we?

There is much about America which is to be praised and appreciated. We live, many of us, quite well and longer. But our thinking about what America is, and how to bring it forward in the contexts of a continually living democracy, is based on a much narrower sense of its reality. Much of the story of America is determined by a few doers and thinkers who seem to have a great deal of control in determining our ongoing sense of reality.

III. THE IDEA OF THE FUTURE

Why should we be concerned about the idea of the future? The first response is that democracy is always somewhat fragile. New generations continue to be born and grow up within a narrowness of experience which, to them, is likely to seem like all of what there is. In this era, as in that of a century ago, there has been a great deal of immigration: immigration toward America, but also away from wherever and whoever they were in their previous experience. The viewings of democracy, its fragility and less-than-stable actuality, is not very apparent to the newly arriving: to incoming adults or to a new culture and language in which the impetus for survival outpaces critical analysis.

When are we? It is always difficult to see the present moment with accuracy and some remove. It is no simple feat to locate ourselves in ongoing history, or to note what is very important, and what is small or temporary. How do we locate ourselves in the present, and toward the future? How do we see the complications and problems of democracy, yet continue to envision a future in which democracy is engaged and engaging?

We have the theorists and commentators on democracy, and the form of government: Machiavelli always springs to mind, as describing the nature of politics, and warning that the very idea of power is central to many thinkers. Democracy is always in some moment of instability and uncertainty, and certain moments seen in the longer ranges of pattern and history should remind us of the fragility of power.

What alternatives to democracy can we sense in the present moment? The pattern of the last several centuries, noted by conservative Kevin Phillips in his recent book, *Wealth and Democracy*, is that of concentration of wealth into very few hands. The pattern following Spain, Holland, Britain—next, us—he wonders, is toward oligarchy or plutocracy: too much wealth, too much power calling attention to its ideas of where to go. The pattern includes attention to the rest of our world—now truly global—and lack of attention to our internal structures: jobs, work. Then a grand deflation, poof!

We are just emerging from a technologically driven money "bubble." The pattern of the Gilded Age of the late nineteenth century and of the 1920s seems to indicate that it is quite limited in duration and that we will likely overstep ourselves: whatever that means in the present moment.

Part of this is the expansion of communication: television most powerfully, the Internet: possibilities of a greater democracy, so far turned into the direction of commercial control, an era of public relations determining much of how we are and how we think.

Democracy seems very fragile in this moment of celebrity culture in which the portrayal of character and of truth overrides any necessity to analyze or to more deeply seek understanding of these times. We have to continually find ourselves in the practice of democracy, though always tempted to look at others reflecting in us, to tell us how and who we are.

Public relations determines too much of the world and continues to place the practice of democracy on our peripheries. And the concentration of control of the media, as Bill Moyers and not too many others plead for us to hear, is part of the power which shapes our very thinking. Are we sufficiently strong, have an enduring sense of our own integrity, to shape and frame a democracy? Or do we look to the stars—actually and figuratively—to tell us what we are? Can we hear our own deeper voices, or do we repeat what we are told in the continuously increasing noise, the speeding up, the deepening colorations of the media, of movies, of computer and other games. We must explore our own voices, each of us, to be able to express what we need to say. This is why we need forms of discussion to ensure the future.

Democracy is not easy, never simple, and always in question. The temptation, especially in the midst of rapid change and the very reconceptualization of some of our vital ideas, is to move toward some sense of political closure, looking for clarity less than for certainty.

We are living through some "crisis in meaning." Driven by the pace of change, itself, and by the very deep conceptual changes which some of our recent technologies have fostered, the quest for democracy is never as clear as we may think and hope. The newly grown, the newly immigrated, the experienced and older, those who would and do rule have particularities and limitations of vision which do not seem to project well into the unknowing of the future.

Yet if we do not attempt to project a future vision, the job of ensuring the future is most likely to fall to those whose ambitions of power, money, fame and the rest of the temptations of those who seek them will be shaping the future in their own terms and images.

Thus, our task to attempt to educate students, others, and ourselves in a changing world, to understand, participate, and continue to create a democracy of "we the people."

11.

Democracy in a Time of Terror

Howard B. Radest

INTRODUCTION

a) Confession

Warning: I am a partisan, one of those superannuated types who finds "liberal" an honorable title and not a term of reproach.

Thesis: Godliness, cupidity, jingoism, wealth and greed have come together to exploit 9/11. I do not know if these are "deadly sins," but I do know that this alliance of opportunists threatens the democratic integrity if not the survival of the Republic.

Question: How can democracy survive in a time of terror?

b) Opportunism

No matter the political party, all occupants of the White House, like all successful politicians, have been opportunistic. Although it is called "being realistic," it is a realism that proves disastrous over and over again (in recent memory: Vietnam, Watergate, Iraq; 40 million without health insurance, a multi-trillion dollar debt . . .). Self-serving behavior has become more excessive and more omnipresent than in any other regime in my memory (and that includes the presidencies of

Lyndon Johnson and Richard Nixon). Like an epidemic, it infects the public arena and becomes everyone's moral habit.

Of course, recalling Shakespeare's Mark Antony, "They are all honorable men . . ." and today's "they" (men and women alike) no doubt believe this to be true. Moralism, in other words, serves as convenient and psychological cover for avarice and fanaticism. Opposition is not mere disagreement but radical otherness and evil. A Manichean spirit inhabits the social, political, and religious world. The current scene in which we live and move is comic, ironic, and tragic all at once.

c) Terror

> We have yet to understand that a "war on terror" is a misnomer. Terror has neither beginning nor end. It is all middle! Terrorists are shadows, ghosts that vanish after their work is done only to reappear and vanish again and again. Terror endures since it has no center and since moral and ideological absolutes cannot be compromised. Unlike national interest, terror's demands cannot be negotiated. In turn, we unwittingly come to accept the rules of the terror game. Like our antagonists, we also come to see through the lens of uncompromising moral difference. Terror calls the tune and everyone dances to it.

Terror is a state of being for which we are unprepared and about which we are lied to. We, in turn, embrace the lies and the comfort they bring. In war, we mobilize, suffer, and sacrifice confident that the demand on us is just and finite. In a state of terror, however, we are summoned to a new normalcy, one which includes ever present threat. Suspicion—of strangers, of neighbors, and ultimately of ourselves— becomes our diet. Terror welcomes a crude paternalism and shapes the beliefs, conduct and rhetoric of leader and follower alike.

Terror is the fate of our moment in history. Unlike World Wars I and II and the Korean "war," Vietnam began and Iraq continues the transition from "war" to "terror." Both are, as it were, halfway houses in the evolution of collective violence in the post-modern era.

In an ironic instance of American exceptionalism, we act as if others had not had our experience. I think of Israel, Palestine, Pakistan, Ireland, Kashmir, Sri Lanka, Peru, Spain, England . . . the list is endless. Of course, we have known terror, too, and not just on 9/11—in Lebanon, in the first attempt at the twin towers, aboard the *USS Cole*. But we have understood it as episodic, i.e., we adapted these events to finitude and were blind to their reality. Above all, we felt and now can no longer feel that terror is something that happens elsewhere and to others.

I. 9/11 AND ITS ECHOES

We are a wounded community grasping for a politics of emotional survival. But, wounded people do frightful things, accept frightful things. So 9/11 becomes an excuse, an alibi, for all kinds of behavior.

a) Anxiety

Anxious people strike out blindly, deny the facts, retreat from reality, tell lies to others but above all to themselves. Like the anxious patients in the psychiatric ward, we find shadows everywhere. We *know* that our enemies are hiding, faceless, in those shadows. Desperate to resolve that anxiety of shadows, we are relieved when someone names the enemy, assigns guilt, and promises salvation. Thus the enemy is brought into the light and, with that, becomes available for promising his or her destruction. But it is a charade, and more troubling still, we are untroubled that all of this is a charade. There must be "weapons of mass destruction." Indeed the very failure to find them only demonstrates that they exist and proves the wiliness of our enemies. Hence it is that we welcome the news that we really have enemies out there and that they are evil, indeed, an axis of evil. Thereby, we find assurance of our virtue in the knowledge that the enemy is alien, that the enemy is not like us. Hence, too, we tolerate, even welcome, emergency powers, prisoners without process, national aggression in the name of national survival, the decay of privacy and all the rest. Someone is, as we say with relief, in charge. Consider the elevation of the authoritarian personality, the personality that sees reality in stark black and white, to folk hero status—the New York City mayor, the president!

b) Necessity

Opportunists are grateful for anxious people. They know that anxious people will accept the most repugnant acts in the name of necessity. Thus, told over and over again that we are a peaceable and just nation, we build Pax Americana, seek security through empire. Proudly proclaiming ourselves the only remaining super-power, we announce an era of benevolent, even sacred, world hegemony.

But the opportunists are like the rest of us. They, too, are anxious people. Thus, the ambiguity, even the gallows humor, of our situation. The opportunists also believe and believe in the products of their own opportunism. They are of course lying to others, manipulating, and telling such truth as suits their purposes. But they are also lying to themselves. The agent of delusion is self-deluded.

c) Ideology

State and church combine to explain and justify otherwise unjustifiable behavior. Hence, an alliance of literalism in religion and neo-conservatism in philosophy join in building the agenda of American hegemony. The secular mind celebrates Pax Americana. The religious mind celebrates the holy nation struggling at home and abroad in a sea of heresy yet reassured by the prophecy of ultimate victory. Enemy and friend come to look like, behave like, each other. Terror's mirror is everywhere.

d) Corruption

Corruption appears on a massive scale. We grow accustomed to the multi-billions, witness unashamed greed in the highest places, and gently, oh so gently, protest its justification as appropriate reward for tasks well done. The new dimensions, the size of things—from millions to billions to trillions, from nation to region to globe—overwhelms us, and this, too, multiplies anxiety.

The truths of Iraq, metaphors of the present, await some future historian. Today's Truman Committee does not exist—instead straight-jacketed "commissions" struggle for truth with agendas they did not write and with rules that are calculated to keep them blind; Ed Murrow does not "see it now;" Will Rogers tells no stories; H. L. Mencken writes no broadsides. It is a different time, and war is not war. The pulpit and the press are muted, as it were not merely "embedded" like reporters on the battlefield but everywhere intimidated by bribe and threat and the glories of patriotism. The annoying people are hidden away. After all, to speak in the blunt tones of moral condemnation—to call a lie a lie—is impolitic, impolite, disrespectful of those in the highest places. Of course, the usual suspects still make noises, but they are few. The civil liberties union attends to its task; a random Democrat or two, a dissident cleric or two, an editorialist or two speak out—but, these voices seem embedded, too, trapped in the silences of communal inattention; the muffled voices of loyalty in a convenient wartime. Anxious people cannot hear or see. Anxious people do not want to hear or see. And everyone is anxious.

e) Moralism

On all sides we hear the claim of the good. Ethics becomes a placebo. We are all protectors of virtue. Nietzsche would be proud of prophecy come true, another transvaluation of values. We applaud the true morality, expect to be praised for it, ignoring its deadly casualties. We even invent a soothing language, "collateral damage," to hide the blood and pain of innocents. In fact, we are all trapped in illusions. And, of course, we are all patriots.

Aside—from Mark Twain's "War Prayer":

> It was a time of great and exalting excitement. The country was up in arms, the war was on, in every breast burned the holy fire of patriotism; the drums were beating, the bands playing, the toy pistols popping, the bunched firecrackers hissing and spluttering; on every hand and far down the receding and fading spread of roofs and balconies a fluttering wilderness of flags flashed in the sun; daily the young volunteers marched down the wide avenue gay and fine in their new uniforms, the proud fathers and mothers and sisters and sweethearts cheering them with voices choked with happy emotion as they swung by; nightly the packed mass meetings listened,

panting, to patriot oratory which stirred the deepest deeps of their hearts, and which they interrupted at briefest intervals with cyclones of applause, the tears running down their cheeks the while; in the churches the pastors preached devotion to flag and country, and invoked the God of Battles, beseeching His aid in our good cause in outpouring of fervid eloquence which moved every listener. It was indeed a glad and gracious time, and the half dozen rash spirits that ventured to disapprove of the war and cast a doubt upon its right-eousness straightway got such a stern and angry warning that for their personal safety's sake they quickly shrank out of sight and offended no more in that way. . . .

II. THE EMERGING SCENE

Wisdom: "The Constitution is not a suicide pact."

a) Imperial America

9/11 becomes an opportunity—do we witness the dying Roman Empire's "bread and circuses"? We are warned of an "axis of evil" which conveniently is chosen from the candidates by reasons not made visible. But then, all the gods are arbitrary and hidden, and god's mes-senger on earth is the savior leader, priest, politician, and sacrifice all at once. Strange but not surprising, sadistic crucifixion becomes media imagery. The drama of Satan and God plays out: find salvation at the end of a gun or buy it with a checkbook. Salvation, we learn, has its price, not the biblical tenth or the thirty pieces of silver, but more, much more. But we are assured as was "go on with our lives" it is not too high a price, at least not too visibly high a price. Go on with your lives, we are told, a strange re-assurance that is both enjoyable and suspect.

b) Clients, Not Allies

We learn that imperial powers have clients, not allies. The sad cynical name of "Iraqi Freedom" and the embarrassment of a "Coalition of the willing" are empire's metaphor. The concert of nations emergent out of the blood and death of two world wars is dismissed from the stage of history, whether it be the environment at Kyoto, the world court at The Hague, weapons inspection at the UN. This is not the old isolationism disdaining "foreign entanglements" but the new rulership. Super-powers command obedience, allow no competitor, have no superior. And lo, we are the only super-power left!

c) The Royal Lie

It's an old story, as old as Plato's *Republic*, as traditional as diplomacy's "reason of state." But now we invent entire armies and weapons—weapons of mass destruction, the elite guard—turning vicious petty ogre into fantastic world-devouring demon. By postmodern dictate, reality becomes ever more malleable. So Iraq is more than Iraq; its weapons of mass destruction, the immediacy of its threat, its alliance with terrorism are scenarios of conviction. Anxious people need such scenarios and do not let mere fact stand in the way. For the sake of the greater good and awaiting Revelation's "end time," lie becomes truth and deception an act of godliness.

Aside—Senator Robert Byrd (D-WV), May 21, 2003:

> Regarding the situation in Iraq, it appears to this Senator that the American people may have been lured into accepting the unprovoked invasion of a sovereign nation, in violation of long-standing International law, under false premises. There is ample evidence that the horrific events of September 11 have been carefully manipulated to switch public focus from Osama Bin Laden and Al Qaeda who masterminded the September 11th attacks, to Saddam Hussein who did not. The run up to our invasion of Iraq featured the President and members of his cabinet invoking every frightening image they could conjure, from mushroom clouds, to buried caches of germ warfare, to drones poised to deliver germ laden death in our major cities. We were treated to a heavy dose of overstatement concerning Saddam Hussein's direct threat to our freedoms. The tactic was guaranteed to provoke a sure reaction from a nation still suffering from a combination of post traumatic stress and justifiable anger after the attacks of 9/11. It was the exploitation of fear. It was a placebo for the anger.

d) Preventive War

More of the post-modern. We will make actual war on the basis of imagined threat, trusting lives to an intelligence that at its best—and it rarely is—can only be probable until the event. Fantasy is everywhere . . . but this fantasy sheds real blood.

Aside—From *The Empire Strikes Out* (*The "New Imperialism" and Its Fatal Flaws*), "Putting 'Defense' Back into U.S. Defense Policy: Rethinking U.S. Security in the Post-Cold War World," Ivan Eland, Cato Institute, 2001, Executive Summary, p. 12:

> The United States accounts for about 40% of total world-wide defense spending, up from 28% in the mid-1980s, the height of the Reagan military buildup. That's two and a half times the combined spending of all its potential rivals. But as an indication of its over extension, the United States accounts for only 29% of the world's GDP. Another comparison indicates that U.S. allies are free riding: although the U.S. economy is larger than the next three largest economies on the planet—those of Japan, Germany, and the United Kingdom—$2.1 trillion on the military over the next five years, which will raise annual U.S. defense spending 15% above the cold war average.

e) Homeland Security

The very name is a puzzle and somehow uncomfortably reminiscent, when translated into German, of an unlamented fascism. True, it seems power run wild, an infrastructure for the future of the militarized state. Another part of me, the part that appreciates the human comedy, sees it as bureaucratic foolishness guaranteed to fall of its own weight. Another fantasy perhaps. But even as Homeland Security falls, it has its casualties, too, like civil service protections which were quickly surrendered in the name of necessity, like invasions of privacy that scarcely discriminate between innocent and guilty, that scarcely know the distinction.

f) Rights and Due Process in a Permanent Emergency

Patriot Act I (and II?) turns the politics of suspicion and control into institutions and policies. Symptomatic is the notion of "material support" of suspected terrorist or terrorist organizations. Like some Kafkaesque "trial," intention, the line between error and evil, vanishes. You have done wrong even if you do not know it. Shades of Arthur Koestler's *Darkness at Noon*. We define you; we know you; we find evil in you; we judge you; and we punish you. Perhaps Kafka and Koestler are too serious a reference. As likely, it is Lewis Carroll's Queen of Hearts shouting, "Off with their heads!"

Aside—Coleen Rowley, FBI special agent, Letter to Director Mueller, *New York Times*, March 5, 2003 (letter dated Feb. 26, 2003):

> The vast majority of the one thousand plus persons "detained" in the wake of 9-11 did not turn out to be terrorists. . . . [A]fter 9-11, headquarters encouraged more and more detentions for what seem to be essentially PR purposes. Field offices were required to report daily the number of detentions in order to supply grist for statements on our progress in fighting terrorism.

g) Political Economy

At last, the "military/industrial complex" comes into its own. Eisenhower is dead. Compassionate conservatism is its cover story, the façade of reform without the liberal foolishness of actual reform. Generosity is the claim, but generosity to whom? "Spin" is elevated to a fine art as language deliberately and unashamedly conceals rather than tells. The states starve in the name of "states rights." The environment is dark with the smoke of "clear skies." Water is purified by lead and mercury. Trees fall in the name of saving the forests. Black is white, up is down. And out here where we ordinary folk live, the "spin" is repeated as if it were not "spin" but truth. Thus the lie succeeds. Study your new textbooks—*1984*, *Brave New World*, and *It Can't Happen Here*.

h) Administrative Rulership

Congress and the courts abdicate. The commander-in-chief, after all, cannot be bound by the clumsiness of peacetime. But in a time of terror, emergency is permanent as terror is permanent. The logic is inescapable; abdication is the only responsible act.

Aside—George J. Annas, "Bioterrorism, Public Health, and Civil Liberties," *New England Journal of Medicine* 346, no. 17 (April 25, 2002): pp. 1337–42, p. 1340. A discussion of "The Model State Emergency Powers Act" (Centers for Disease Control [CDC], 10/23/01) and amended (12/21/01) after criticism. George Annas comments,

> Although the revised act can be viewed as a modest improvement, all the fundamental problems remain. Failure to comply with the orders of public health officials for examination or treatment is no longer a crime but results in isolation or quarantine. Criminal penalties continue to apply to failure to follow isolation or quarantine "rules" that will be written at a future time. Physicians and other health care providers can still be required "to assist" public health officials, but cooperation is now coerced as "a condition of licensure" instead of a legal requirement with criminal penalties for noncompliance. The quarantine provisions have been improved, with a new requirement that quarantine or isolation be imposed by "the least restrictive means necessary" and stronger due process protection, including hearings and legal representation for those actually quarantined. Nonetheless, on the basis of a written directive by a public health official, a person can still be quarantined for 15 days before a hearing must be held and the hearing itself can be for groups of quarantined persons rather than individuals.

i) Righteous America

We would never kill the innocent, start a war, drop a bomb, destroy a race. We are the Americans, the guardians of virtue and truth. As our Secretary of Defense puts it, we are not like the "old" Europe— France, Germany. We are not worn and tired. We are the leaders of the "free" world. Need I list the defenders of freedom that line up with us; need I note—"spin" again—that "free world" falls trippingly from the tongue of sheik and dictator? But after all these are our sheiks and dictators, purified by the magic wand of our virtue.

Official religiosity. We are, as we say to ourselves, a god-fearing people. All but some tiny fraction, less than 10 percent, that announce their disbelief. From the beginning we were the "city on a hill." Now we bring it up to date, becoming at last "the light unto the nations," the guardian of global virtue.

Aside: *The American message is heard, but not the way we'd like it to be—a Pew Research Center (June 6, 2003) survey asked the question: "How worried are you that the US could become a threat to your country someday?" Indonesia, Nigeria, Pakistan, Russia and Turkey answered very or somewhat, from 71 to 74 percent; Lebanon, Jordan, and Kuwait (between 53 and 58 percent); and only Morocco with 46 percent found more than half those surveyed who were "not too much or not at all" worried.*

j) Sound Bites

The electorate only seems to care. It votes in fewer numbers and with decreasing knowledge. Beguiled by scandal and slogans and promises, politics becomes its own entertainment. Clinton and Lewinsky are, in today's moment, comic relief. Meanwhile, behind the curtain, the state is bankrupted, and the social contract is shredded. The strategy of tax cuts and military spending guarantees that health care will be inadequate, school buildings will decay, housing will vanish, the urban street dweller will be more numerous. Yes, the child will be left behind as we chant, no child left behind. The pattern—and it is on more than one occasion a "bipartisan" pattern—has emerged over the past several decades. The "safety net" erodes. Obviously—we all nod—the costs of national security must come before luxuries like houses and food and hospital beds and classrooms and all the rest. Dismantle government—which turns out to mean dismantle that much of government as speaks to the needs of people.

Aside—Bill Moyers, *This Is Your Story—The Progressive Story of America*, speech to the Take Back America conference sponsored by the Campaign for America's Future, June 4, 2003, Washington, DC:

It (the increase of public debt and the move toward "privatization") is the most radical assault on the notion of one nation, indivisible, that has occurred in our lifetime. I'll be frank with you: I simply don't understand it—or the malice in which it is steeped. Many people are nostalgic for a golden age. These people seem to long for the Gilded Age. That I can grasp. They measure America only by their place on the material spectrum and they bask in the company of the new corporate aristocracy, as privileged a class as we have seen since the plantation owners of antebellum America and the court of Louis IV. What I can't explain is the rage of the counter-revolutionaries to dismantle every last brick of the social contract. At this advanced age I simply have to accept the fact that the tension between haves and have-nots is built into human psychology and society itself—it's ever with us. However, I'm just as puzzled as to why, with right wing wrecking crews blasting away at social benefits once considered invulnerable, Democrats are fearful of being branded "class warriors" in a war the other side started and is determined to win. I don't get why conceding your opponent's premises and fighting on his turf isn't the sure-fire prescription for irrelevance and ultimately obsolescence. But I confess as well that I don't know how to resolve the social issues that have driven wedges into your ranks. And I don't know how to reconfigure democratic politics to fit into an age of soundbites and polling dominated by a media oligarchy whose corporate journalists are neutered and whose right-wing publicists have no shame.

There is much noise all around us, and yet it is but the politics of silence. . . . The citizen who does not vote does not listen or protest either. Perhaps it is the new Internet politics that will answer to the democratic question in which event we are only a transitional instant. And yet, a skeptic's caution—modern media are notoriously two dimensional, abbreviative, given to signals rather than to meanings. Will that, can that, do for democracy's need?

At any rate, in popular culture and college classroom alike, we learn the language of the single syllable; the grunt is in style. Any message, serious or foolish, must be reduced to sound bite or else it cannot be transmitted or heard. People, as we say, are impatient, have short attention spans. It is as if we were back in nursery school—except that would be a slander on the wisdom of four- and five-year-olds. When news becomes entertainment and a market commodity, is it still worthy of being referenced by the Bill of Rights? . . .

Aside—Senator Robert Byrd, Senate Floor Speech, Wednesday, February 12, 2003:

> One can understand the anger and shock of any President after the savage attacks of September 11. One can appreciate the frustration of having only a shadow to chase and an amorphous, fleeting enemy on which it is nearly impossible to exact retribution.
>
> But to turn one's frustration and anger into the kind of extremely destabilizing and dangerous foreign policy debacle that the world is currently witnessing is inexcusable from any Administration charged with the awesome power and responsibility of guiding the destiny of the greatest superpower on the planet. Frankly many of the pronouncements made by this Administration are outrageous. There is no other word.
>
> Yet this chamber is hauntingly silent. On what is possibly the eve of horrific infliction of death and destruction on the population of the nation of Iraq—a population, I might add, of which over 50% is under age 15—this chamber is silent. On what is possibly only days before we send thousands of our own citizens to face unimagined horrors of chemical and biological warfare—this chamber is silent. On the eve of what could possibly be a vicious terrorist attack in retaliation for our attack on Iraq, it is business as usual in the United States Senate.
>
> We are truly "sleepwalking through history. . . ."

III. INTERLUDE: DEMOCRATIC MEMORIES

Once upon a time—we sentimental liberals talk like that—we claimed to be the "land of the free and the home of the brave." To be sure, it was never an accurate claim, but it was a genuine ideal, something to be turned from promise to truth. In America the "streets were paved with gold," as thousands of immigrants believed, "anyone could be president," all voices had equal access, and hard work would be rewarded. Only forty years ago, in 1963, Martin Luther King Jr. could proclaim, "I have a dream," and the words did not ring hollow nor did they need to be spun. We were, in short, the "American dream" which was not ours alone but the world's. We were that nation which disdained the politics of mere national interest.

Looking back from today's vantage point, we engage the heretical question: were our dreams empty and our claims only a lie? History, as usual, has changed our reading of history. We are a time of miserly dreams. We depose the Iraqi dictator to the undertone of self-interest. Oil, you could hear the cynic's voice everywhere, was really what it was all about, even if that was not so. We are the new Rome, to be sure—the only great power left is our boast—but we are not yet sure whether it is the Rome of the Senate as the "founding fathers" imagined or the Rome of the Caesars.

Democracy is our gift to the world, so much so that we will force the other to accept it or else. But democracy is not found in formalities or achieved at the point of a gun. Tyrants and democrats alike have their elections and constitutions. . . .

The Enlightenment made revolution; we make conquest. Enlightenment's critics, left and right, ask: is democracy but an historic moment which will pass—some would say has passed? Like all other historic moments—Greek city-state, Roman empire and Confucian Mandarin and all that long line in the life and death of civilizations—these must vanish before their successors. Challenge and response, wrote Arnold Toynbee. History does not know an eternal now. No doubt, some future historian, looking back, will point to our belief that democracy is the end of political development and capitalist democracy even the end of history. Eden achieved. And then the bubble breaks.

Yet all of this—critic and cynic and patriot—is the ordinary discourse of democracy. Democracy is deliberately noisy, so beware the silence. Change and doubt are democracy's currencies. But in an age of terror, these democratic necessities only increase the fear of the fearful and so enlarge terror's voice. So it is that new necessities appear. So-called culture wars are symptomatic as we grow impatient with the First Amendment, insist on moves toward moral purity, demand piety as the price of citizenship. With that, democracy moves toward its inverse. The transformation is blurred. Fearfulness is tamed, normalized.

a) Liberty, Equality, Community . . .

It was only a short time ago that civil rights, civil liberties, due process, and justice for all were taken for granted. To be sure, none of these survived without struggle, without defenders, and without missteps. But in the world of terror, democratic assumptions have a way of vanishing. In an age of terror, the form is sustained even as the substance vanishes. Sadly, for all too many, the form is sufficient promise that nothing really has changed and that the old American verities are still in place. Indeed, were democratic substance restored, we would be uncomfortable with its uncertainties, even repugnant to an anxious people.

b) The Use and Abuse of Government

The US Constitution begins with "we the people" and promises a "more perfect union." Over time, the constitutional promise gained content and meaning, expanded as the world expanded, grew more complicated as the world grew more complicated. But the initiating genius remains. At its center is a notion of limited and responsive governance that, while limited, is nevertheless the chief reliance against tyranny. In short, the achievement of democratic government is the climactic event of democratic politics. Thereby, the public good and the public interest are served and defended.

And if government forgets its mission, it was deliberately set up so that it is forced to limit itself, criticize itself, amend itself. Hence the so-called separation of powers, judicial review, congressional control of budgets and taxes—all the comforts of the high school civics lesson. But, thinking to answer to the needs of a global politics and a global economics, we have instead achieved the "imperial presidency"—the most powerful office in the world, as people say. True, for a short while it was a constitutional imperialism and amenable to limits and adjustments. Thus Johnson and Nixon discovered constitutionality to their dismay. In an age of terror, however, separation of powers is surrendered to a single center of power. The constitutional limit even of an imperial presidency is effectively dissolved.

Government becomes an object of scorn and suspicion. Ironically, we turn to the presidency as petitioners once turned to the monarch for relief from unjust or ineffective government, even from government itself. And the presidency responds by alienating itself from its own government. Nearly all post-WWII aspirants seeking to become head of government, chief magistrate and commander-in-chief have separated themselves from government, which gives these titles meaning. The candidate is from "outside the beltway," as the jargon has it. Not to know the Capitol and actual governance is the salient political virtue, even a prerequisite for office. And these strange goings on, tolerable, even humorous under other conditions, feed the needs of an anxious people in a time of terror. Above the battle, surrounded by both the reality and the symbol of power, the presidency now becomes the chief guarantor of survival when survival is threatened or felt to be threatened every day. The democratic state, government in short, is relegated to echo.

c) *Permanent Revolution*

There is some warrant in the founding of the Republic for this escape from government. In a moment of utopian fantasy, Mr. Jefferson urged a "revolution every twenty years," although he was dissuaded from pursing the idea by the more sensible James Madison. Jefferson sensed the dangers of any establishment, even a democratic establishment, and knew the temptations of permanence. A democracy was intended to change, intended to be unstable over time. Above all, a democracy had to respond to its changing constituencies, the march of generations not least among them. But those in possession would not yield power and place willingly. Hence, the need for overturn if new constituencies were not merely to make noises but be listened to. Change, however, is always unsettling and becomes intolerable in an age of terror. Too much is at risk in an already risk-filled world. So it is that incumbents—in the Congress, in the state house—are removed from office by mortality and not by electorates. So it is that few voices are heard challenging with democratic sensibility this democratic scandal. Jefferson's "revolution" has metamorphosed into its opposite.

The reality of imperfection contends with the hope of per-fectibility in democratic polity. That, as Condorcet recognized, was the Enlightenment dialectic whether in science, ethics, or politics. It was the notion behind the First Amendment, a monument to the virtues of doubt, which enshrines the interplay of knowledge, belief, politics and law in the structure of democratic society.

With the confession of imperfection in our constitutive law, reform becomes a permanent part of the democratic diet, alternately resisted and celebrated. The discourse between reform and its oppo-nent is dialectical. No one in the perennial democratic debate admits its imperfection for fear of compromise. In fact, however, everyone is altered in unacknowledged awareness of universal imperfection. Dialectic demands that we admit, even enjoy, our need to change, just as it demands that we admit the possibility of some good and some truth in the other. . . . Anxious people, however, will have none of that, will have nothing to do with imperfection.

IV. BETWEEN HOPE AND DESPAIR

a) We Have Been There before—and Survived

The story of the Republic is a story of renewal. Each moment in its history has had its critics, its cynics, its malcontents. Each moment has had its patriots and opportunists, often in the same person. We have known the trauma of civil war, the scandals of Reconstruction and the KKK, the one-hundred-year struggle for inclusion. We have known depression, the millions homeless and hungry. We have known tyran-nies with massive powers, fascism and Nazism and Stalinism. And with all of that, we have survived. *Why, then, is this moment different, or is it?*

b) We Have Been There before—and Survived

Civil liberty and civil right have never lived easily among us. Always there have been the many who could not tolerate or even fathom the few, the noisy, the troubling, the often noxious few. Even when power and populace were aligned against them, civil liberty and civil right have in the end not only remained but strengthened, their domain enlarged. The list is much too long, but recall by way of instance equality of race and gender or the umbrella of religious freedom that begins with mere Protestant pluralism and enlarges to enclose Mormonism, Roman Catholicism, Eastern Orthodoxy, Islam, Judaism, Buddhism, Hinduism, the vast array of religious experiments like Zen and Black Muslim, the Temple of Venus and the Reverend Moon, a thousand disparate sects, and even Humanism and disbelief. True, there is never an end to the struggle. Yet, even when the lawless have appeared at the very center of the law, civil liberty and civil right remained and strengthened.

Aside—David Cole, "The New McCarthyism: Repeating History in the War on Terrorism," *Harvard Civil Rights—Civil Liberties Review* 38: 1–30, p. 24:

> In addition to the enemy combatant designations, the government has dusted off the Palmer Raids tactics, using its immigration authority to arrest and detain large numbers of persons without any showing that they are connected to terrorism.
>
> Shortly after September 11, Attorney General John Ashcroft announced that he would use every law on the books, including immigration law, to target and detain "suspected terrorists" in order to prevent future acts of terrorism. Pursuant to that plan, the Justice Department reported that 1182 individuals had been detained in the first seven weeks of the post–September 11 investigation. After November 5, facing criticism that it had arrested so many people but had charged none with any terrorist crimes, the Justice Department simply stopped issuing a running tally of its detentions. But as the arrests have continued, even a conservative estimate would number the detentions at approximately two thousand as of November 2002, fourteen months after the campaign began.

Why, then, is this moment different, or is it?

c) We Have Been There before—and Survived

We have known untruth and deceptive leadership. The minimalist Jefferson built a navy and engaged North African piracy, achieved the first moment of empire with the Louisiana Purchase. The enlightened Monroe declared two continents an American dominion—or began to—with his "Monroe doctrine." The great emancipator set habeas corpus aside in the Civil War. The first Mr. Roosevelt's "great white fleet" was an omen of super power to come. Wilson's racism and moralism some how joined in his paradoxical commitment to imposed democracy. And, to be sure, there was FDR's "lend-lease" our self-designed invitation to WWII. The more recent presidency has had its moments too, the hesitations of Eisenhower before the challenge of McCarthy, Kennedy's Bay of Pigs, Johnson's Vietnam, Nixon's Watergate, Reagan's little adventure in Granada, his bigger adventure in Central America and, of course, "Iran-gate."

We have known shameful behavior, too. The "frontier" was conquered but few noticed that it was not a frontier at all for its inhabitants, who, being few in number and untutored in technology, were likely victims of racism, conquest, official thievery and death. Slavery might have ended with Lincoln's proclamation, but racism has not ended yet. The list would be too long to be manageable. *Why, then, is this moment different . . . or is it?*

d) We Have Been There before—and Survived

We learned the politics of corruption early in our history, seizing land from the unwilling, writing treaties we did not intend to honor. With the growth of the great cities we enjoyed the machinations of Tammany Hall and latterly Chicago's Mayor Daley the first, the scandals of the Grant administration, the thievery of Teapot Dome. It was not very long into the story of the Republic, and indeed echoing a lesson learned by land-grabbing colonialists, that we learned the advantages of colonialism. And entering the modern age, we enacted military occupation in Haiti, Nicaragua, Puerto Rico, the Philippines, "dollar diplomacy." "Banana republics" in Latin America confirmed us in our superiority and benefited us in the market place. *Why, then, is this moment different . . . or is it?*

But as they say on Wall Street, past performance does not guarantee future performance. Have we really been there before? Is the democratic situation in an age of terror like the situation of civil war, depression, world war? Have we really been there before?

V. REVISITING DEMOCRACY

There is, I suppose, a tone of despair that may be said to shape our history. Of course, we are the richest, the strongest that ever was.

Aside—*Ozymandias of Egypt*, Percy Bysshe Shelley:

> I met a traveler from an antique land
> Who said: Two vast and trunkless legs of stone
> Stand in the desert. Near them on the sand
> Half sunk, a shattered visage lies, whose frown
> And wrinkled lip and sneer of cold command
> Tell that its sculptor well those passions read
> Which yet survive, stamped on these lifeless things,
> The hand that mocked them and the heart that fed;
> And on the pedestal these words appear:
> "My name is Ozymandias, king of kings:
> Look on my works, ye mighty, and despair!"
> Nothing beside remains. Round the decay
> Of that colossal wreck, homeless and bare,
> The lone and level sands stretch far away.

And for those who measure success by wealth and strength—the modern incarnation of Plato's Thrasymachus—the notion of despair makes no sense at all. Yet wealth as we have learned most dramatically in recent times is easily dissipated in the struggle against terror, which, like the mythical dragon's teeth, refuses to be destroyed. Strength vanishes before the strength of the helpless. Terror, as it were, paralyzes armies firing blindly at the enemy who will not stand still. Wealth and strength are notoriously fragile under any circumstance and become even more so in a time of terror.

In a time of terror the institutions of democracy grow arthritic. They are fixed in legal and political stone as a defense against change, which is in itself frightening. The genius of democracy, its value as life and life-way is thus subverted by its own institutional evolution in a time of terror. Democracy's reliance on challenge and change simply adds to fearfulness in a time of terror. In defense, the form of democracy builds a fortress against the reality of democracy. As it were, the strategy of terror forces us to destroy ourselves. Wealth and strength are hollow shells. Against terror's strategy, then, anxious people can hardly muster effective defense, which requires them to dispel the shadows of their own creation.

Democratic values—integrity of persons, trustfulness between persons, hopefulness from persons—endure beyond wealth and strength. It is these values that together make democracy not merely a political arrangement but a mode of living. And it is to these values that we need turn as a counter-strategy to terror. But, final irony, it is precisely these values that are most elusive in a time of terror. Anxiety, among other things, isolates us from the other, interprets the other as threat, shrinks from association. It is to the overturn of these social symptoms of our response to terror that we need turn. And it will not be easy as guns and shouts and boasts of virtue are easy.

VI. WHERE, THEN, SHALL WE TURN?— A FINAL SET OF QUESTIONS

a) Where are the reformers; who are the reformers; what shall reform look like? From time to time there are political moments when reform seems again on the horizon. It is the frustration of a time of terror that these moments are brief and often useless. Consider the mobilization before the invasion of Iraq—the numbers, the proud words, the protests—and consider its near evanescence. Patriotism trumps all, but is it patriotism or paralysis? And, after all, who is a patriot in a time of terror?

b) Where are the leaders? Democracy needs its leadership, but who and what and where are the leaders? On all sides, the political game and the money game are played. Even those who genuinely seek democratic leadership are trapped by democratic institution. Poll-taking replaces intelligence, and wealth replaces ability. Perhaps, with the founding fathers, we need look for models in a classical world, look for our Pericles, our Cicero. But where shall we look for their incarnation?

c) Where are the critics, the prophets who call community back to its moral source and reconstruct its moral mission? Of course, we do not want to listen and perhaps without moral therapy cannot listen. But then, who said the task of prophet and critic was easy?

d) Where are the institutions? "Ideas need legs," and the democratic idea needs legs. In a time of terror, public acts are better left undone not for fear of terror but for fear of those who would defend against terror. Thus it is that the public life surrenders to the private life, the pulpit retreats to the faith, and the academy to the library.

In a time of terror, we rapidly grow tired, are easily dismayed, become hopeless and cynical. It is just in such a time and against the habits and practices of fear and defense that the few are needed to reconstitute once again in history a prophetic moment. Thus, the humanist agenda in a time of terror, a second Enlightenment.

12.

Is America a
Post-Democratic Society?

Paul Kurtz

I.

At the conclusion of the Constitutional Convention in Philadelphia in September 1787, a citizen approached Benjamin Franklin and asked what sort of government the assembled statesmen had given them. "A Republic, if you can keep it," Franklin is reputed to have replied. "Can we keep it?" is an urgent question that needs to be asked anew today, more than two centuries after the inauguration of the American Republic. The Roman Republic lasted for two centuries until it was supplanted by emperors. Has the American democratic Republic become so fragile that its survival is in doubt?

This is a gnawing question that is being raised again, as we face ominous terrorist threats, and demands of security pre-empt concerns for civil liberties. America has faced awesome challenges in its past. Slavery engulfed the young Republic in discord, for it contradicted the very premise of the new democracy—that each person was equal in dignity and value. Only the Civil War could resolve that conflict. The Great Depression of the 1930s, and the cold war in post–World War II, also presented great challenges. Similarly the exclusion of women, blacks, gays, and other minorities from full participation in American democracy has aroused great controversy.

There are ominous threats to our democratic Republic today, and I wish to examine some of these trends, which have been building up for decades—before the confrontation with the Islamic jihad. Has American democracy been so eroded that we are already a post-democratic society?

II.

I wish to point out that both liberal and humanist philosophers have provided a theoretical basis for democracy. Beginning in the seventeenth and eighteenth centuries John Locke, the French *philosophes* of the Enlightenment, and the founders of the American Republic (especially Jefferson and Madison) paved the way for the Right of Revolution, the declaration of the Rights of Man, and the American constitutional system (influenced of course by Montesquieu). Democracy was not based upon divine fiat, but upon the rights of the people to secure life, liberty, the pursuit of happiness, and to limit the power of the monarchy. John Stuart Mill in the nineteenth century eloquently defended liberty, the free market of ideas, and the rights of minorities against the tyranny of the majority.

In the twentieth century, John Dewey presented a new defense of liberal democracy. The "method of pooled intelligence," he said, was the best way of solving social problems and achieving necessary reforms. This presupposed an important role for education. The best guarantee of democratic freedom would be an informed citizenry capable of making wise judgments. Humanist philosopher Sidney Hook argued that the democratic philosophy presupposed certain ethical principles: the centrality of human freedom, which a democratic society sought to enlarge and enhance, and the principle of equality, each person in society was guaranteed equality before the law and entitled to an equality of concern, the poor person no less than the rich. Hook's defense of democracy is unique; it did not draw upon a metaphysical doctrine of inherent human rights (though the rights of citizens need to be recognized and defended); rather, democracy was to be justified empirically by its pragmatic consequences. Democratic societies tended to have less cruelty, duplicity, and fear than undemocratic ones, and they tended to contribute to a more peaceful, freer, and more prosperous society with greater opportunities for cultural enrichment than non-democratic authoritarian or totalitarian societies. Hook was indefatigable in his battle against fascism in the 1930s and '40s, and against communist totalitarianism from the 1930s to the '80s. Karl Popper, in his influential book *The Open Society*, argued that the open pluralistic society was essential for a functioning democracy, in contradistinction to closed totalitarian societies.

Political democracy was a precondition for a just democratic society. A political democracy is one in which the basic policies of a nation and the key officials of government to carry them out depends upon the freely given consent of a majority of the adult citizen population voting in free elections. Representative democracy presupposes (a) the legal right of opposition, (b) civil liberties, (c) the right to petition the government for redress of grievances, (d) widespread participation of citizens at all levels of decision making, (e) the rule of law (a just legal system with open trials), and (f) a strong civil society.

For democracy to function fully, not merely formally but actually, it was essential that there be at least four other basic preconditions fulfilled.

First, economic democracy, (a) a large middle class with rising expectations of improved standards of living; (b) this entailed some measure of equality of opportunity for the sons and daughters of disadvantaged persons, the ability to rise to the top, a meritocracy not a plutocracy based on wealth or conditions of birth; (c) some fairness in the distribution of income for the fruits of one's labor; and (d) the ability of ordinary people to accumulate savings and own property.

Second, social democracy, this means (a) non-discrimination based on class, race, religion, ethnic origin, gender, or age; (b) the non-exclusion of anyone in a democracy from public facilities and amenities; (c) the opportunity for the education of all children and adults and for cultural enrichment in the arts and sciences; (d) the right to leisure, rest, and relaxation; and (e) a peaceful and harmonious society, without excessive fear, intimidation, or coercion.

The American experiment in democracy was unique in adding two further preconditions: Third, that there would be no establishment of religion, and there would be the free exercise of religion and the separation of church and state. Freedom of conscience was thus guaranteed by the First Amendment. Fourth, especially in recent decades, the right of privacy of each person to fulfill his or her own moral values and goals as long as these did not prevent others from fulfilling theirs.

These theoretical principles are no doubt familiar to advocates of the democratic philosophy, and the American system has functioned remarkably well as the land of liberty, equality, and opportunity. It has afforded wave after wave of new immigrants "to make it in America." In one sense it is the universal culture, for every racial, religious, and ethnic group is represented here, and individuals have been able to pursue their diverse careers and lives in relative freedom. Formerly repressed groups are being gradually emancipated—blacks and women, gays, handicapped people, and other minorities—and they have taken their rightful place in American society.

There are many serious threats to this democratic framework. Because of a lack of space, I will touch on only four especially dangerous trends.

III. PLUTOCRACY

The first danger is the growth of plutocracy, which I define as "government of, for, and by the wealthy class in society." There have been other periods in our past history when the moneyed classes held great power: the Founding Fathers were well-established men of wealth and influence; the wealthy plantation owners of the South held inordinate power (they were defeated by the Civil War); during the "Gilded Age" at the turn of the nineteenth century when there were no income or estate taxes and vast fortunes were amassed; the roaring 1920s stock market boom (followed by the crash); and the Reagan-Clinton go-go years of the 1980s and 1990s. It is this latter phenomenon that should bother us. The legacy of the "New Deal" and the "Great Society" enabled the average worker after World War II to make great strides. These gains now seem to have been curtailed, even reversed, especially since Reagan's reforms. We have been deluged by the libertarian mantra, that government is evil, and that regulations and taxation have stifled the free market, that welfare is abused and needs to be drastically reduced, and that the amassing of wealth is the basic American virtue. A form of plutomania has overcome us, as during the speculative stock market bubble of the 1990s. Many have considered this to be sanctified by God. I have called the reigning sacred cow "Evangelical Capitalism." Marxism has been virtually defeated in the last two decades, and there have been all too few critics of the excesses of capitalist greed or defenders of social justice.

Our entire political system has been polluted by corruption, that is, by lobbyists running amuck at all levels of government—from the Congress and the White House to State Legislatures and local governments. Pork barrel perks are doled out to favorites with abandon. A key part of this corruption is the fact that campaign contributions inordinately influence elections, and this applies to both major political parties, as Ralph Nader and Noam Chomsky have pointed out. Both the Democratic and Republican parties drink deeply at the well of corporate largesse, and both parties have wealthy men and women in positions of leadership. Why are members of the Congress and State Legislature predominantly businessmen or lawyers? Why are there so few teachers, professors, nurses, computer specialists, housewives, scientists, philosophers, and labor union people represented in our legislative body? It costs money to run for office, and this prevents ordinary persons from serving.

Undoubtedly the Democrats are far more amenable to social-welfare policies than are the Republicans, who are far more callous. However, 40 million Americans are without health insurance; retirement coverage has been cut; an adequate minimum wage has not been enacted; and American workers work more hours than their European counterparts (an estimated 350 hours more per year); they enjoy shorter vacation time; the USA has the highest ratio of two-income households including women with children who need to work (64%). There are all too few radical reforms enacted by our legislative system because the plutocrats control it and they assiduously protect their interests—with all too few notable exceptions. In one sense, the heated debates between candidates serve as a facade, for the basic interests of those who control the country are never in contention.

Kevin Phillips, in the remarkable book *Wealth and Democracy*, points out that the US now has the highest degree of inequality of income and wealth of any of the major affluent democracies, that an entrenched plutocratic class has emerged and that its power is growing. Phillips presents statistics showing that "between 1979 and 1989 the portion of wealth held by the top 1% nearly doubled, sky-rocketing from 22% to 39%" (*Wealth and Democracy*, p. 92). At the same time average Americans were falling behind, even during the Clinton years. He shows that in 1999 "the average real after-tax income of the middle 60% of the population was lower than in 1977" (ibid., p. 111). The stock market boom of the 1990s perhaps inflated these figures. But ever since the presidency of George W. Bush, these trends have exacerbated, and the disparities continue to widen.

One can read "Forbes 400" every year to see who the billionaires are. But there are also multi-millionaires who are part of the top 1 percent; there are new billionaires who enter the list every year—technology companies have replaced real estate, oil, or heavy industry of the past. Phillips shows that the plutocratic classes pass on their wealth to their families in the form of trusts (such as the Rockefellers and Duponts), which provide income for future generations; and that these fortunes continue to grow, even into the fourth and fifth generations. He estimates that at least 100,000 families ($\frac{1}{10}$ of 1% of the population) doubled or quadrupled their wealth between 1982 and 1999. The top 1 percent share of household wealth had grown from 19.9 percent in 1972 to 40.1 percent in 1997. This inequality is greater than in France, England, and other class-ridden societies.

Indeed, we are today in danger of developing a hereditary aristocracy of absentee rentier landlords and shareholders. And this trend will dramatically solidify if the current taxation-reduction policies of the Bush II Administration are not repealed. I am referring here to (1) estate taxes ("death taxes" falsely labeled by the Republicans), which are being reduced annually and will disappear entirely in a few years (if allowed to stand, huge fortunes will compound untouched), and (2) the reduction of higher tax brackets for the wealthy, including the reduction of capital gains and dividend tax rates (15%).

This latter tax-reduction plan, supported by a significant number of Democrats and virtually all Republicans, was enacted in order to bolster the faltering stock market and to increase the "wealth factor." Three caveats are in order: First, the bulk of these tax perks went to the wealthy. Second, why is unearned income taxed at a lower rate than income earned by labor or services? The entire Socialist critique of Capitalism was based on the "labor theory of value." Marx argued that the laboring worker (industrial, technological, or service) is unable to buy the goods and services he produces in the form of wages. It is unfair to tax profits, dividends, and capital gains (often based on purely speculative growth) at a lower rate than that earned by labor. This is particularly true for those who inherit their wealth, for paying reduced taxes on dividends and capital gains into the second third or fourth generations would seem to lack any rationale. Third, the gradual undermining of the principle of progressive taxation in my view can be deplored on moral grounds.

A functioning democracy presupposes a strong middle class. Unfortunately, we are today dismayed by the exportation of jobs overseas (outsourcing) and the increased "Wal-Marting" of the workforce in America, with lower-paying jobs and benefits doled out at home.

MEGA-CORPORATIONS

This brings to the fore a second danger to the democratic state: the emergence of corporations as the dominant players in the market place. This economic reality has been developing for well over a century and a half. There are two implications that flow from it: First, the classical Adam Smith doctrine of a free market presupposed small firms and independent entrepreneurs, consumers, and working people. To focus on supply and demand referred to a free market unrestrained by powerful and entrenched interests. In many industries today, only two or three major corporations (oligopolies) dominate production and distribution. And these companies are incestuously intertwined with politicians, legislatures, and the courts. Being so large in scale, industrial unions responded in the earlier part of the twentieth century by bargaining collectively. The labor movement since then has declined in percentage of the laboring force, and many of its members are government workers. In earlier days the role of government was to act as a countervailing force between labor and management; today it's more like the handmaiden of business interests.

Thus the regulative role for government has been drastically curtailed because of the powerful inducement of corporations to reduce costs and hence to threaten to move out of a community or country, if it does not do its bidding. The same bargaining chip is used by management against labor to reduce workers' benefits and hold the line on wage increases. The key new factor is that corporations have become global, and many of them are larger in financial power and clout than most of the countries of the world. These are transnational mega-corporations, such as General Electric, General Motors, SONY, Esso-Mobil, Lever Bros., and Citicorp. In the United States, municipalities and states compete with each other in order to have companies stay in their area or relocate from another region or state. All sorts of incentives are offered—lower real estate, utility, or tax rates; investment in the infrastructure for the company by local and state governments; and other inducements.

For many conservative thinkers, the business of government is business and this takes precedence over all other considerations or values such as: preservation of the environment, the reduction of global warming, strengthening of the health care system, building viable transit systems, or providing affordable housing to the inner cities. Democratic legislatures can enact whatever they want, but not if it means that industrial and technological firms will depart for lower tax havens. In the last analysis, all too often economic forces outtrump political considerations.

This is especially the case if one examines what has been happening to corporate tax rates in the USA in the past two decades. From 1996 to 2000, 63 percent of US corporations paid no taxes at all, while 94 percent paid taxes equal to less than 5 percent of their net income. Moreover, the CEOs of corporations paid themselves huge salaries, bonuses, and stock options, even if their corporations had no increase in profits; this is at a time when millions of jobs were lost to the labor force by outsourcing and wage increases were kept low.

What is the upshot of my argument? That classical democratic theory is unable to accommodate huge transnational mega-corporations and conglomerates that compete with state power; these make decisions that governments, executives, or legislatures are unable to control or circumvent. Is America already in a post-democracy stage of development in the sense that political leaders and the public at-large are impotent in controlling corporate power?

Theodore Roosevelt introduced legislation to break up huge trusts and monopolies at the beginning of the twentieth century, and various presidents, such as Wilson and FDR, tried to restrain their power. Today it is difficult to regulate their activities, though the European common market attempts to do so, as do the castrated FCC and FTC within the United States. Transnational in scope, many of them have no single national homeland; they are beyond the power of any one country to restrain; this constitutes a major problem for national democratic governments.

I wish to conclude this section with one further observation, and that is the warning of President Dwight Eisenhower that Americans should be cautious of the growth of the military-industrial complex and its great influence on public policy. I wish to reiterate this warning, but add the technology sector to the complex. America's behemoth power status in the world is made possible because of its military-industrial-technological capacities, and American foreign policy is intimately related to its economic power and its global military capability. This enormous power has led to American triumphalism and imperialism. We are afforded great opportunities to spread our democratic ideals worldwide, but there are also great dangers inherent in the military adventures that we embark upon and the fact that we are now over-extended beyond our means.

MEDIA-OCRACY

This brings us to a third threat, which some consider to be virtually a "clear and present danger" signal today. I am here touching on the central principle upon which liberal democratic society rests; i.e., its dependence on a free market of ideas. John Stuart Mill argued that a democratic society encourages the free exchange of ideas. John Dewey held that the method of pooled intelligence enables the public to make reflective judgments. Karl Popper extolled the open society.

This had some meaning at a time when individual citizens could speak out on a soapbox at Hyde Park or Union Square, distribute pamphlets and leaflets on street corners, when many voices could be heard in the town hall, and every major city published several newspapers.

Today the public square has been inundated by the mass media of communications, which all too often drowns out dissenting viewpoints. Secularists and humanists opposed totalitarian societies because the ministries of propaganda spewed forth the official party line and squelched opposing viewpoints. We are surely not at that point today, but a kind of iron curtain is closing American society, and a quasi-official propaganda line is too often the only one heard. For example: it is widely held that capital punishment is the only way to deal with murderers, that violence is the most effective response to evil, that long prison sentences are necessary for drug dealers and heavy users; that government is wasteful; that the free market is the only way to get anything done, that we need to privatize everything and judge all services by the bottom line; that we should consider those who possess great wealth to be role models (e.g., Donald Trump); and that self-righteous chauvinistic nationalistic patriotism, which venerates the flag and sings "God bless America," is the only posture to assume, ad nauseum!

But seriously and forebodingly: the trend toward mega-corporate domination of our media is ongoing. Today there are fewer and fewer large players: General Electric (NBC, CNBC, MSNBC), Time Warner (CNN), News Corp (Murdoch's FOX network), Disney (ABC), Viacom (CBS). Mega-corporations dominate TV, and they own most of the cable networks and movie production studios.

But they also gobble up the print media, book and magazine publishers. I am familiar with book publishing, where I have seen the acquisitions of most independent publishers in the thirty-five years since I founded Prometheus Books. Similarly for book chains, distributors, and wholesalers. Five companies now control 75 percent of the US book market. These companies are transnational: Bertelsmann, a German mega-corporation, publishes 30 percent of the trade books published in the United States; and Pearson, a British company, dominates 30 percent of the American textbook market. The phenomenon is true in other capitalist countries: For example, in Italy Silvio Berlusconi dominates the TV mass media, and media moguls in Germany, France, the UK, and other countries do the same, though these countries have alternative public TV and radio networks.

The point is that mega media corporations are interested first and foremost in profits; hence they produce media programs in terms of their marketability; the criterion is what will sell, not what is true. Entertainment out-matches information and education. Regrettably, diversity in ideas and values are drying up, and as such, the parameters of the open, free, and democratic society are limited. I am not overlooking the role of the Internet, which we all use, though I suspect that a limited number of main players will come to dominate this medium as well. In my view we need to apply the Sherman anti-trust laws to media conglomerates, bring back the Fairness Doctrine (killed off during the Reagan years) and establish at least one other independent public radio and TV network.

THEOCRACY

The fourth major danger to our democratic Republic is the frightening possibility that the United States is becoming a theocracy, or at the very least a quasi-theocracy. Major assaults are being made on the First Amendment, and the widespread public support that the principle of the separation of church and state enjoyed only two decades ago is now being rapidly eroded.

Major assaults have been advanced by the Religious Right. Should this powerful force ally itself with religious conservatives, we are in for a fundamental challenge to our view that the United States is a secular democracy, that it should be neutral about religion, and that it should not favor religion over nonreligion. The First Amendment states that "Congress shall make no law respecting an establishment of religion, or prohibiting the free exercise thereof." This is being reinterpreted by Justices Rehnquist, Scalia, and Thomas to mean that Congress shall not favor—or establish—any one sect or denomination of religion over any other, but this does not mean, they said, that the government cannot favor religion over non-religion. There seems to be strong public support for monotheism (even among many liberals), that is, for those religions that emanate from the Book of Abraham (Christianity, Judaism, and Islam), or at the very least, some form of ceremonial Deism is being established. Inasmuch as there are millions of Hindus, Buddhists, Sikhs, atheists, agnostics, and secular humanists in the United States, it is difficult to see what legal argument any future conservative court may introduce to deny them equal protection under the First Amendment. The effort by the Bush administration to support faith-based charities, vouchers, and provide public monies for religious organizations is an ongoing battle. This of course draws on the free exercise clause of the First Amendment.

A second assault on the First Amendment by the Right Wing has not been taken sufficiently seriously in my judgment by the Humanist movement in the United States. First introduced in the late 1970s and early 1980s, the Religious Right maintained that "secular humanism is a religion," and as such, it needs to be extirpated from the public schools and universities, the courts, and all other governmentally supported institutions. The legal argument for this is rather convoluted. If secular humanism is a religion, they say, it violates the establishment clause of the First Amendment. The Council for Secular Humanism has denied that secular humanism is a religion, though other humanist organizations maintain that it is.

This challenge took two forms in the early 1980s. First, in Mobile, Alabama, Federal District Court Judge Brevard Hand banned forty-five books from the public schools (from John Dewey and A. H. Maslow to Richard Hofstadter), for espousing "the religion of secular humanism." I was asked by the ACLU and People for the American Way to represent the view that it was not a religion. I maintained that this smacked of a New Inquisition. Fortunately, the ruling by Judge Hand was overturned in the Appeals Court. It was never taken to the Supreme Court.

A second series of legal challenges sought to have "creation science" taught in the public schools alongside evolutionary theory, which the Religious Right again argued represented "the religion of secular humanism." None of these challenges were successful; and by the 1990s most liberals and humanists thought that these legal arguments had been defeated—at least until the year 2000.

For concurrent with the election of George W. Bush, new outcries were again being heard. These challenges were ignited by Tim LaHaye (author of the *Left Behind* series of books, the most popular ever published) and David Nobel, head of Summit Ministries. The gauntlet was laid down in *Mind Siege*. This book even hit the *New*

York Times best-seller list. The same litany of charges have resurfaced, namely, that secular humanism is a religion and that millions of Evangelical foot soldiers need to root it out from all walks of life, including the public schools, but especially the colleges and universities. A campaign is now underway in tens of thousands of churches. Hundreds of thousands of books have been distributed free on college and university campuses to help route secular humanism.

Should this challenge be taken seriously, or should it be dismissed as nonsense? Regrettably, Tim LaHaye and his cohorts have had strong influence on the Bush administration, and *New York Times* columnists Paul Krugman and Nicolas Kristof, CBS's *60 Minutes*, and others have pointed out their powerful influence on the corridors of power.

The ferocious Creationist challenge has also resurfaced, but this time in sheep's clothing as "intelligent design," with new allies. Evolution is being challenged in state after state to provide equal time for "intelligent design." Should Bush be re-elected and should he be able to appoint conservative judges, these challenges most likely will be waged in the courts anew. Given the shift in the public square in favor of pious religiosity, we have no guarantee that the Religious Right will not prevail. Even if Mr. Bush fails in his bid for a second term, I am afraid that this battle will not go away and that the challenge to defend secularism—even the integrity of freedom of inquiry and science—will be ongoing.

IV. CONCLUSION

It is time to draw some conclusions from my analysis. I submit that American democracy is endangered because (1) of the growth of an entrenched plutocracy with enormous wealth and power; (2) the emergence of global mega-corporations allied with the military-industrial-technological complex; (3) the virtual domination of the media of communication by mega media corporations (a media-ocracy); and (4) the danger that we are becoming a quasi-theocracy: one nation under God with unbelief considered un-American. We need to ask: are we already in a post-democracy stage? Is it still possible to stem the tide and restore American democracy? In my optimistic mood, my response in the short and mid-run is yes we can, but we face enormous political battles. In the long run, we need to embark upon a New Enlightenment, defending reason, science, free inquiry, and non-religious ethical alternatives—if there is still time to do so.

In my pessimistic mood, democratic institutions are endangered for still another reason. It is virtually impossible for any one nation-state (democratic or non-democratic) to solve its economic, cultural, social, and environmental problems alone. Neither France, nor Germany, nor China, nor Brazil, nor Britain, nor the United States is capable of dealing with these problems in isolation from the impact on others in the world. For the problems we face are planetary in scope. The Europeans have discovered this truism, and they are working hard to create new European institutions, a European Common Market, and a European Parliament, and a new constitution.

Only the present leadership of America stands in haughty isolation, refusing to acknowledge the legitimacy of the World Court or to abide by treaties; only the United States has abandoned the principle of Collective Security and the United Nations; only the United States assumes for itself the role of policeman to the world. Possessing a preponderance of weapons of mass destruction, it seeks to impose its will on others. Incredibly, only the United States among the major powers is fixated on a pre-modern theological worldview.

This provides a great opportunity for liberal humanists to lead the way—in recognizing and working for a global democratic world. Our foreign policy had been a beacon in the past—from Presidents Wilson, Roosevelt, Eisenhower, Kennedy, Johnson, Nixon, Carter, and others in working for democracy and human rights on the planetary scale. And this battle seems to auger a great opening for planetary humanism. We need to intensify our efforts in favor of new transnational democratic institutions: a democratic World Parliament, the World Court, collective security, an environmental monitoring agency, a world income tax to stimulate development in the underdeveloped portions of the globe, and some global institutions to regulate megacorporations.

The key ethical principle enunciated in Humanist Manifesto 2000 is that every person on the planet should be considered to have equal dignity and value. Thus we should do what we can to defend and extend democracy to every country and region of the world, on a decentralized basis. But also need uniquely to build new viable democratic institutions on the planetary level. In my view this is the daring new frontier for democracy in the twenty-first century.

Thus the battleground is not simply to restore democracy in the United States, but more importantly to expand democratic institutions on the global scale. If this noble goal is to be achieved, we need to overcome intolerant xenophobic, racist, ethnic, nationalistic, and religious prejudices. We need to define and defend planetary ethics, to strive to build a new democratic humanistic civilization based on shared human rights and human values.

Contributors

VERN L. BULLOUGH. Distinguished Professor Emeritus of History, Former Dean at SUNY College, Buffalo; Former Outstanding Professor, California State University, Northridge; former professor, USC; fellow in the Medieval and Renaissance Center at UCLA; former Co-President, International Humanist & Ethical Union.

JOSEPH CHUMAN. Leader of the Ethical Culture Society of Bergen County, New Jersey; Visiting Professor of Religion and Human Rights at Columbia University; GSAS United Nations University for Peace, Costa Rica.

CARMELA EPRIGHT. Assistant Professor of Philosophy, Furman University; Clinical bioethicist and ethics consultant for several medical and psychiatric institutions in Greenville, S.C.

KURT JOHNSON. National Service Conference of AEU and InterSpiritual Dialogue at United Nations; Research Scientist, Florida State Collection of Arthropods' McGuire Center for Tropical Biology.

PAUL KURTZ. Professor Emeritus of Philosophy, State University of New York, Buffalo; Founder and Chair of the Council for Secular Humanism.

SARAH OELBERG. Former minister of Nora Church Unitarian Universalist in Hanska, Minnesota; Former teacher at Yeshiva University, NYU, and Buena Vista College, Iowa; Vice President, HUUmanists.

HOWARD RADEST. Former Director, Ethical Culture & Fieldston Schools, New York; Leader, American Ethical Union; Adjunct Professor of Philosophy, University of South Carolina, Beaufort.

PHILIP REGAL. Professor of Ecology, Evolution and Behavior, University of Minnesota, Minneapolis.

ANDREAS ROSENBERG. Professor (emeritus) of Laboratory Medicine, Pathology, Biochemistry, and Biophysics, University of Minnesota, Minneapolis.

HARVEY SARLES. Professor of Cultural Studies and Comparative Literature, University of Minnesota, Minneapolis.

ROBERT B. TAPP. Professor (emeritus) of Humanities, Religious Studies, and South Asian Studies, University of Minnesota, Minneapolis; Dean, The Humanist Institute, New York City.

MICHAEL WERNER. Sales and marketing, high-tech adhesives; Former President, American Humanist Association.